OECD Development Pathways

Multi-dimensional Review of Thailand

VOLUME 1. INITIAL ASSESSMENT

OECD

dev
DEVELOPMENT CENTRE

Please cite this publication as:
OECD (2018), *Multi-dimensional Review of Thailand: Volume 1. Initial Assessment*, OECD Development Pathways, OECD Publishing, Paris.
http://dx.doi.org/10.1787/9789264293311-en

ISBN 978-92-64-29327-4 (print)
ISBN 978-92-64-29331-1 (PDF)
ISBN 978-92-64-29338-0 (ePub)

Series: OECD Development Pathways
ISSN 2308-734X (print)
ISSN 2308-7358 (online)

Photo credits: Cover © design by the OECD Development Centre.

Corrigenda to OECD publications may be found on line at: *www.oecd.org/about/publishing/corrigenda.htm*

Foreword

Economic growth matters, but is just one facet of development. Policy makers are required to reconcile economic, social and environmental objectives to ensure that their country's development path is sustainable and that the lives of its citizens improve.

OECD Multidimensional Country Reviews (MDCR) help governments identify the main constraints to more equitable and sustainable growth. Governments aiming for economic, social and environmental objectives need comprehensive and well sequenced strategies for reform that factor in the complementarities and trade-offs across policies. The MDCR methodology builds on the Sustainable Development Goals (SDGs) and takes a crosscutting, rather than a sectoral perspective, which allows for the discussion of policy interactions.

The MDCRs are composed of three distinct phases: Initial Assessment, In-depth Analysis and Recommendations, and From Analysis to Action. *This approach allows for progressive learning and co-creation of reforms that fully respond to the country's specific challenges and opportunities and come with guidance on implementation. The process conjugates expert policy analysis with participatory approaches including Foresight and Governmental Learning that involve actors from the private and public sectors, civil society, and academia. Analytical work is based on all available statistics on Thailand, including well-being, macro- and microeconomic data, at national, sectoral, household and firm levels, using both domestic and international sources. The analysis is also based on forecasts and indicators constructed in-house.*

Benchmarking and comparison of results and experiences with other countries is a key element of the OECD method. For each MDCR a set of comparator countries is identified that includes regional peers, countries from other regions with similar structural characteristics, OECD members, and aspirational peers. Throughout the report, whenever relevant and subject to data availability, Thailand is thus compared with a set of benchmark countries in Asia (China, Indonesia, Korea, Malaysia, the Philippines, Singapore and Viet Nam) and beyond (Colombia, Mexico, Poland, South Africa and Turkey).

The MDCR of Thailand – Volume 1 "Initial Assessment" builds on the SDGs' structure of People, Prosperity, Partnerships, Planet and Peace. It identifies the main barriers to further inclusive development and provides a first set of high-level policy recommendations. The report highlights that tackling informality and inequality, boosting productivity, improving management of natural resources and reforming institutions should be at the core of Thailand's development strategies.

This MDCR is designed to help Thailand formulate these development strategies, and identify and support the policy reforms needed to achieve further sustainable and inclusive development. This first volume presents a broad diagnosis of a range of constraints to development and a first set of high level recommendations. Forthcoming volumes will present a more in-depth analysis of the main constraints, with more specific recommendations for reform and suggestions for action. These analyses support Thailand's own development agenda towards achieving a brighter future for its citizens.

Acknowledgements

Multi-dimensional Country Reviews are the result of a collaborative effort of the OECD and the country under review. Work on the first phase of the MDCR of Thailand was carried out jointly by the OECD Development Centre, the OECD Economics Department and the OECD Statistics Directorate, with excellent support from the National Economic and Social Development Board in Thailand. The review was initiated with an OECD mission to Bangkok in July 2017.

The review was produced under the guidance of Alvaro Pereira – Acting OECD Chief Economist and Director of the Country Studies Branch at the Economics Department, Mario Pezzini – Director of the OECD Development Centre, Martine Durand – OECD Chief Statistician. The review was led and coordinated by Vincent Koen, Head of Division at the OECD Economics Department, and Jan Rieländer, Head of the MDCR Unit at the Development Centre. It was drafted by Hidekatsu Asada, Adam Bogiatzis, Abu Zeid Mohd Arif, Mohamed Rizwan Habeeb Rahuman (OECD Economics Department), Martha Baxter and Andrea Colombo (OECD Development Centre), Lara Fleischer and Koffi Zougbédé (OECD Statistics Directorate). Deirdre Culley (OECD Development Centre) managed the Foresight work stream, including the workshop "Thailand: Vision and Challenges" held in Bangkok on 18 July 2017 and provided significant inputs to the report. Vararat Atisophon and Catriona Marshall (OECD Development Centre) provided excellent project management and statistical support. The review also benefited from the contributions made by Kazuki Hao and Carine Viac (OECD Development Centre). Secretarial assistance was provided by Myriam Andrieux (OECD Development Centre), Mercedes Burgos and Sisse Nielsen (OECD Economics Department).

The team is grateful for insightful contributions and comments provided by Christine Lewis, Haruki Seitani, Margit Molnar and Patrice Ollivaud (OECD Economics Department), Céline Colin,Juan De Laiglesia, Nejma Bouchama, Lea Fuiret, Alessandra Heinemann, Caroline Tassot and Riku Elovainio (OECD Development Centre), Elizabeth Fordham (OECD Education and Skills Directorate), Bert Brys (OECD Centre for Tax Policy and Administration), Ruben Maximiano (OECD Directorate for Financial and Enterprise Affairs), Filippo Cavassini, Jeroen Michels, Julio Bacio Terracino, Yukihiko Hamada and Winona Rei Bolislis (OECD Public Governance and Territorial Development Directorate), Inese Rozensteine, Janos Ferencz, Kaveri Bopiah and Shingo Kimura (OECD Trade and Agriculture Directorate), Katherine Scrivens (OECD Statistics Directorate) and participants of the workshop "Thailand: Vision and Challenges" held in Bangkok in July 2017, which brought together actors from a variety of sectors to discuss the diagnostic phase of the report as well as the main development challenges Thailand faces.

On the side of the Thai government, the review has benefited from the support of Porametee Vimolsiri, Secretary General of the Office of the National Economic and Social Development Board (NESDB) of the Kingdom of Thailand, and his staff. Pattama Teanravisitsagool (Deputy Secretary General of the NESDB), Marayart Samootsakorn (Senior Advisor in Policy and Plan) and their respective teams have been a valuable counterpart throughout the process, both technically and analytically. Athipong Hiranraengchok and Nisawan Pitchdumrong played a key role in the continuous interaction between the OECD team, the NESDB and other representatives from the Government of Thailand. The Multi-dimensional Country Review team met and is grateful to the Office of the Prime Minister (especially the Office of the Council of State, Office of the Civil Service Commission, Office of SMEs Promotion), the Office of the Public Sector Development Commission, the Bank of Thailand, the Ministry of Finance (in particular the Public Debt and Management Office and the Revenue Department), the Ministry of Agriculture and Cooperatives, the Ministry of Commerce, the Ministry of Digital Economy and Society (especially the Office of the Permanent Secretary and the National Statistical Office), the Ministry of Education, the Ministry of Energy (and its Energy Policy and Planning Office), the Ministry of Industry (especially the Office of the Permanent Secretary), the Ministry of Interior (and its Department of Local Administration and Department of Disaster Prevention and Mitigation), the Ministry of Justice, the Ministry of Labour (in particular, the Department of Skill Development and the Thai's Social Security Office), the Ministry of National Resources and Environment, the Ministry of Public Health, the Ministry of Social Development and Human Security (especially the Department of Social Development and Welfare and the Department of Women Affairs and Family Development), the Ministry of Transport, the National Health Security Office, the National Science Technology and Innovation Policy Office, the Office of the National Anti-Corruption Commission, and the Office of the Law Reform Commission of Thailand. The report benefited from insights by the Federation of Thai Industries, the Friends of Women Foundation, the Thailand Development Research Institute, the Faculty of Archaeology of Silpakorn University, the Faculty of Economics of Thammasat University, the Institute of Human Rights and Peace Studies of Mahidol University and the School of Social Innovation of Mae Fah Luang University. The team is also grateful for inputs received from Tatchalerm Sudhipongpracha (Office of the Prime Minister of Thailand) and all the other interlocutors of the Policy Mission held in Bangkok in December 2017 who reviewed the initial draft of this report.

Finally, the team acknowledges David McDonald for editing the manuscript. Aida Buendia, Delphine Grandrieux and Elizabeth Nash from the OECD Development Centre's Communications and Publications Unit edited, laid out and produced the report.

The draft report was discussed at a meeting of the OECD Economic and Development Review Committee on 19 February 2018, and at a meeting of the OECD Development Centre's Mutual Learning Group on 20 February 2018, with the participation of representatives of Thailand's authorities. The draft was then revised in the light of the discussions.

The editorial cut-off date for this report is 7 March 2018.

Support from the governments of Japan, Australia and Malaysia is gratefully acknowledged.

Table of contents

Tables

Figures

Boxes

Acronyms and abbreviations

12th Plan	Twelfth National Economic and Social Development Plan
ADB	Asian Development Bank
AEC	ASEAN Economic Community
ASEAN	Association of Southeast Asian Nations
BEPS	Base erosion and profit shifting
BMR	Bangkok Metropolitan Region
BMA	Bangkok Metropolitan Administration
BOP	Balance of payments
BPM	Balance of Payments Manual
CBD	Convention on Biological Diversity
CEPII	Centre d'Études Prospectives et d'Informations Internationales
CPI	Consumer Price Index
CO2	Carbon dioxide
DGR	Department of Groundwater Resources
DLT	Department of Land Transport
EDC	Electronic data capture
EEC	Eastern Economic Corridor
EFTOPS	Electronic funds transfer at point of sale
EIA	Environmental Impact Assessments
EPA	Environmental Protected Areas
FAO	Food and Agriculture Organization of the United Nations
FDI	Foreign direct investment
FTAs	Free trade agreements
FY	Fiscal year
GDP	Gross domestic product
GFSM	Government Finance Statistics Manual
GVCs	Global Value Chains
HELE	High-efficiency, low-emissions
HIV/AIDS	Human immunodeficiency virus and acquired immune deficiency syndrome
ICT	Information and communication technology
IEA	International Energy Agency

IEE	Initial Environmental Examination
ILO	International Labour Organization
IMF	International Monetary Fund
ISO	International Organization for Standardization
ITU	International Telecommunications Union
JETRO	Japan External Trade Organisation
KPIs	Key performance indicators
LAOs	Local administrative organisations
LGBTI	Lesbian, gay, bisexual, transgender and intersex
LPG	Liquefied petroleum gas
LTC	Long-term care
MICS	Multiple Indicator Cluster Survey
MEDS	Ministry of Digital Economy and Society
MFA Netherlands	Ministry of Foreign Affairs of the Netherlands
MOE	Ministry of Energy
MOI	Ministry of Interior
MOOCS	Massive open online courses
NACC	National Anti-Corruption Commission
NAP	National Adaptation Plan
NBSAP	National Policies, Strategies and Action Plan on the Conservation and Sustainable Use of Biodiversity
NEB	National Environmental Board
NESDB	National Economic and Social Development Board
NESDPs	National Economic and Social Development Plans
NRPA	National Reform Plans and Procedures Act 2017
NSC	National Strategy Committee
NSF	National Savings Fund
NSO	National Statistics Office
NSPA	National Strategy Preparation Act 2017
NSTIPO	National Science Technology and Innovation Policy Office
NWFPC	National Water Resources and Flood Policy Committee
NWRC	National Water Resource Committee
OAE	Office of Agriculture Economics
OECD	Organisation for Economic Co-operation and Development
ONEP	Office of Natural Resources and Environmental Policy and Planning
OPDC	Office of the Public Sector Development Commission
OSCC	One Stop Crisis Centre
PACC	Public Sector Anti-Corruption Commission
PAOs	Provincial Administrative Organisations
PCD	Pollution Control Department

PDP	Power Development Plan
PISA	Programme for International Student Assessment
PPP	Public-Private Partnership
PRD	Government Public Relations Department
QR	Quick response
R&D	Research and development
RBCs	River Basin Committees
RFD	Royal Forest Department
RIA	Regulatory Impact Analysis
RID	Royal Irrigation Department
SAOs	Sub-district Administrative Organisations
SBCGC	Small Business Credit Guarantee Corporation
SDDS	Special Data Dissemination Standard
SDGs	Sustainable Development Goals
SEAs	Strategic Environmental Assessments
SEI	Stockholm Environment Institute Asia
SEZs	Special Economic Zones
SME	Small and medium-sized enterprise
SNA	System of National Accounts
SPI	Social Protection Index
SSF	Social Security Fund
STEM	Science, technology, engineering and mathematics
STRI	Services Trade Restrictiveness Index
TCC	Trade Competition Committee
TFP	Total factor productivity
THB	Thai baht
TSMP	Thailand's Statistical Master Plan
TVET	Technical and vocational education and training
UCS	Universal Coverage Scheme
UNCTAD	United Nations Conference on Trade and Development
UNESCAP	United Nations Economic and Social Commission for Asia and the Pacific
USD	US dollar
VAT	Value-added tax
V-ETS	Voluntary Emissions Trading Scheme
VNR Taskforce	Voluntary National Review Taskforce of Thailand
VOCs	Volatile organic compounds
WEF	World Economic Forum
WFMC	Water Flood Management Commission
WTO	World Trade Organization

Editorial

Thailand has made impressive progress over the past several decades, both in economic and social terms. Sustained strong growth and a rapidly modernising economy have turned Thailand into an upper-middle income country with Bangkok as a strong urban centre. Economic success has brought impressive social advancement. Based on national definitions, poverty has plummeted from 60% in 1990 to 7% today, while education and health services have considerably expanded and improved.

These achievements have brought a new set of challenges. Rising prosperity has not been shared equally across the country and economic transformation needs a boost. More than half of the working population is in precarious jobs. The creation of new activities replacing low-productivity ones has slowed in recent years, and rural migrants and urban poor lack the skills required for modern jobs. While Bangkok's success as a metropolis has been key to Thailand's transformation, thriving secondary cities are needed to develop new sources of growth and make progress on the Sustainable Development Goals.

Today, Thailand strives to achieve a sustainable development path that could benefit all, reinvigorate economic transformation and reduce multifaceted inequalities. The "National Strategy 2036" and "Thailand 4.0" attest to these ambitions. In doing so, Thailand will need to adapt to an ageing society, while developing new engines for further economic transformation and new approaches to overcome regional inequalities and ensure well-being for all. Environmental disasters, particularly those related to water, will continue to challenge Thailand's ability to manage prevention and effective service delivery.

Experience shows that development is not about getting everything right, but about getting right what matters most. This Initial Assessment of the Multi-dimensional Country Review (MDCR) endeavours to identify the challenges and key constraints that Thailand must overcome to succeed, and offers a number of high-level policy recommendations. To move ahead, Thailand will need to tackle informality, boost productivity across all regions and improve the management of natural resources, particularly water. Progress on all of these fronts requires a more effective government, which today is held back by an overly complex organisation and is insufficiently adapted to delivering quality services in all regions. The next volumes of the MDCR will provide further suggestions for action to address these challenges.

This report represents a truly multidisciplinary effort involving several OECD directorates and committees and combining economic, social, statistical, environmental and institutional expertise. It comes as a precursor to a broad Country Programme between Thailand and the OECD that will span three years and involve a wide range of reviews and OECD instruments.

Mario Pezzini
Director of the OECD Development Centre and Special Advisor to the OECD Secretary-General on Development

Martine Durand
OECD Chief Statistician
Director of the Statistics Directorate

Alvaro Pereira
Acting OECD Chief Economist and Director of Country Studies in the Economics Department

Facts and figures of Thailand

(2016 unless noted otherwise, numbers in parentheses refer to the OECD average or total OECD)

People: Towards better lives for all

Population (millions)	68.8	(1 289.9)	Life expectancy (years)	75.1*	(80.3)*
Under 15 (%)	17.7	(18.1)	Men	71.4*	(77.7)*
Over 65 (%)	10.9	(16.3)	Women	78.9*	(82.9)*
Urban population (% of total)	51.5	(80.5)	Health care expenditure, public and private (% of GDP)	4.1**	(12.3)**
Income inequality (Gini coefficient)[1]	43.1***	(31.8)***	Education outcomes: PISA 2015 score average of reading, math and science	415	(492)
Poorest / richest region GDP per capita	5.8*	(2.8)	Education expenditure, public (% of GDP)	4.1***	(5.3)**
Unemployment rate (% of total labour force, national estimates)	1.0	(6.3)	Labour force participation rate (% of total population ages 15-64, national estimates)	75.5*	(71.3)*
Youth unemployment rate (% of total labour force, ages 15-24, national estimate)	4.9	(13.9)	Men	83.5*	(79.8)*
Informal employment (% of total labour force)[2]	55.6	-	Women	67.9*	(63.1)*
Firms with female top manager (% of firms)	64.8	(15.8)	Share of women in parliament (% of seats in national parliaments)	6.1	(28.2)

Prosperity: Boosting productivity

GDP in current billion USD	406.8	(47 394)	Share of GDP: Agriculture (%)	8.3	(1.5)*
GDP growth (annual %)	3.3	(1.7)	Industry (%)	35.8	(24.3)*
GDP per capita, PPP (constant 2011 international $)	15 682	(38 725)	Services (%)	55.8	(74.2)*
GDP per capita growth (annual %)	2.9	(1.1)	Gross domestic expenditure on R&D (% of GDP)	0.6*	(2.4)*
Exchange rate (THB per USD, annual average)	35.3	-	Fixed broadband subscriptions (per 100 people)	10.7	(29.9)
Exports of goods and services (% of GDP)	68.5	(27.8)	Current account balance (% of GDP)	11.7	(0.1)*
Imports of goods and services (% of GDP)	53.7	(27.2)	Travel services revenue (% GDP)	11.9	(1.6)
Gross FDI inflows (% of GDP)	0.4	(2.3)	Tertiary educational attainment 25-64 year-olds (%)	16.0	(35.5)

Partnerships: Sustainably financing development

General government revenue (% of GDP)	21.9	(42.2)*	General government total expenditure (% of GDP)	21.3	(43.8)*
General government tax revenues (% GDP)[3]	18.2	(34.3)	Domestic credit to private sector (% of GDP)	147	(147)
Public debt, total (% of GDP)[4]	41.7	(85.6)*	Total foreign exchange reserves (% of total external debt)	141	-

Planet: Conserving nature

Land area (thousand sq. km)	511	(344 044)	Agricultural land (% of land area)	43.2*	(34.2)*
Forest area (% of land area)	32.1*	(31.3)*	Arable land (% of land area)	32.9*	(11.2)*
Total primary energy supply (TPES) per capita (toe)	1.9*	(4.1)	CO_2 emissions from fuel combustion per capita (tonnes)	3.6**	(9.4)**
Renewables (% of TPES)	19.2*	(9.7)	Fine particulate matter concentration (PM2.5, µg/m3)	26.4*	(15.2)*
Annual freshwater withdrawals, total (% of internal resources)	26**	(10.1)**			

Peace: Strengthening governance

Share of public sector employees in total employment[5]	8.9*	(17.7)*	Corruption perceptions index[6]	35	(69.2)
Intentional homicides (per 100 000 population)	3.5*	(3.6)*	% of population who feel safe walking alone at night	68	(71.4)

1. Gini coefficient for household disposable income as in Solt (2016). 2. Comparable OECD data not available. 3. Includes social security contributions. 4. Includes general government and state-owned enterprises debt. 5. Public sector employees include all government sector employment plus employees of publicly-owned resident enterprises and companies, operating at central, state (or regional) and local levels of government. 6. Index ranges from 0 (highly corrupt) to 100 (very clean).

Note: Last year available when other than 2016 or not explicitly mentioned is marked with: * for 2015, ** for 2014, *** for 2013. The average OECD poorest-richest region GDP per capita ratio based on 2012 and 2013 values. The average OECD tertiary education attainment ratio is based on 2015 and 2016 values.

Source: Calculations based on data extracted from the databases of the following organisations: OECD, Gallup World Poll, International Energy Agency, Transparency International, World Bank, International Monetary Fund, World Values Surveys, and various national sources

Multi-dimensional Review of Thailand
Volume 1. Initial Assessment

Executive summary

- Structural change is needed to create more quality jobs and overcome regional imbalances
- Better provision and funding of social protection is key given ageing and pervasive informality
- Environmental conservation and disaster risk management should be prioritised

Structural change is needed to create more quality jobs and overcome regional imbalances

GDP per capita in per cent of OECD average, computed at 2016 PPP USD

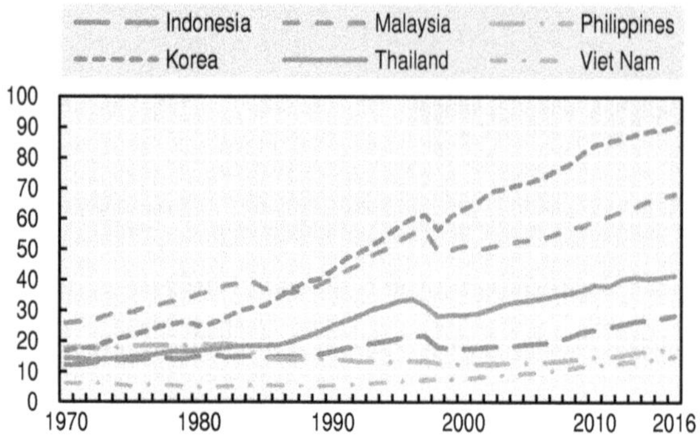

Source: Conference Board and OECD calculations.

StatLink http://dx.doi.org/10.1787/888933691192

Since 1970, Thailand's GDP growth per capita has averaged 4.2% per year in purchasing power parity terms. In 2016, income per head stood at 42% of the OECD average. Nevertheless, faster growth is needed for Thailand to reach its goal of high-income status by 2036. This calls for structural reforms to boost economic potential and inclusiveness, by improving education and skills training in all regions, fostering innovation, facilitating domestic competition, reducing cross-border barriers and accelerating public spending on infrastructure. Overcoming past implementation challenges requires strengthening institutions to ensure the delivery of the critical reforms outlined in the 12th Plan (2017-2021).

Better provision and funding of social protection is key given ageing and pervasive informality

Elderly dependency ratio

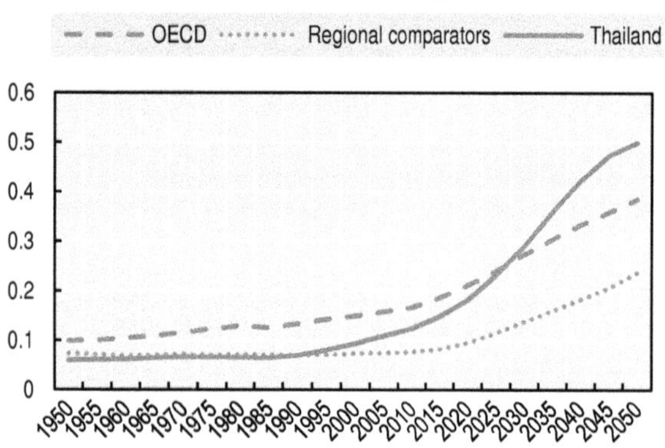

Source: UN Population projections, 2017 revision.

StatLink http://dx.doi.org/10.1787/888933691211

Extreme poverty has largely been eliminated but disparities remain. The fragmented social security system does not adequately protect the large informal and precariously employed labour force, and many elderly are at risk of poverty. Better social security and pension coverage is essential for inclusive growth. While public finances are presently in robust shape, gradual revenue increases will be called for to fund rising pension and healthcare outlays amid a rapidly ageing population and a declining workforce. Inducing greater formal labour market participation will be key to expand social protection and boost tax revenue.

Environmental conservation and disaster risk management should be prioritised

CO_2 emissions per unit of GDP

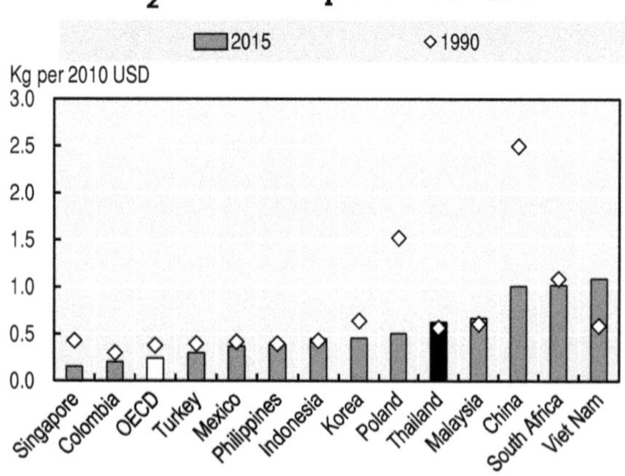

Source: IEA (2017), CO2 *Emissions from Fuel Combustion 2017 Edition.*

StatLink http://dx.doi.org/10.1787/888933691230

Economic development has exerted a heavy environmental toll. Despite recent improvements, notably with reforestation, Thailand has to further enhance the management of its natural resources to safeguard sustainable development. Rapid urbanisation has put pressure on water resources and water quality. Water management needs to become more effective to minimise damage from droughts and floods. Solid waste has grown considerably, most of which is poorly managed. Policies to better mitigate and adapt to climate change are necessary to meet agreed international commitments and minimise economic and social losses.

Key constraints for socio-economic development and policy recommendations

Key constraints and related outcomes	Selected policy recommendations
Chapter 1: People – towards better lives for all	
Informality remains widespread and informal workers are not well covered by the social protection system.	Encourage formalisation through tax and regulatory measures. Harmonise social protection schemes and streamline procedures.
Pension arrangements do not prevent old-age poverty and will become even more inadequate as the population ages.	Index the non-contributory allowance for older people to minimum required living costs.
Basic education outcomes fall short of global benchmarks.	Strengthen teacher capacity, curriculum coherence, student assessment procedures and ICT use in schools.
	Improve access to quality pre-school education.
Tertiary and vocational education does not adequately equip students with the necessary skills required by industry.	Expand co-operation between vocational institutions, the private sector and academia to improve course development and incentivise enrolment in the disciplines most demanded by the labour market.
Chapter 2: Prosperity – boosting productivity	
Slow economic transformation within sectors, notably agriculture, and across the economy holds back productivity growth.	Invest in lifelong learning and skills training.
	Upgrade business skills and foster greater ICT use in agriculture.
Low innovation and research with limited commercialisation potential adversely affect competitiveness and productivity.	Ensure coordination and reduce institutional overlap in the innovation system.
	Boost public R&D spending to no less than 1.5% of GDP by 2021, as planned.
SME access to financing is costly and constrains development.	Create a special lower-cost bourse in the Thai stock exchange.
	Ensure effective co-ordination across existing agencies responsible for SMEs development and promotion in the delivery of financial and other support.
Some cross-border barriers to services trade and investment remain significant, notwithstanding ongoing liberalisation in the context of ASEAN.	Review regulations on foreign business operations including restrictions on foreign firms' entry and movement of people.
Chapter 3: Partnerships – sustainably financing development	
Despite a sound fiscal position, current revenue will not suffice to fund commitments over the medium term. Further improvements to the tax mix are needed to foster growth and competitiveness.	Continue fiscal prudence and increase revenue to fund impending commitments by boosting tax efficiency, increasing compliance and relying more heavily on less distortive tax bases.
Inefficient infrastructure financing increases costs, while public-private partnership (PPP) policies are not boosting private investment.	Make greater use of alternative financing sources such as infrastructure bonds priced in Thai baht.
	Align PPP policies with the OECD's Principles for Public Governance of PPPs.
The public cost of healthcare and pension systems will grow and become increasingly unaffordable.	Invest in preventive and primary care as well as promote healthy lifestyles. Reduce exemptions to healthcare co-payments.
	Increase the pensionable age in line with improving life expectancy.
Chapter 4: Planet – conserving nature	
Highly fragmented water management is leading to overlapping responsibilities, conflicting interests and a lack of co-ordination.	Ensure effective co-ordination across existing agencies, at all levels of governance.
The repeated pattern of floods and droughts causes loss of life and economic disruption.	Improve disaster prevention and response capacity at the local level.
Environmental quality of life is undermined by insufficient progress on air and water pollution, and waste generation.	Make polluters pay more directly, for example via wastewater tariffs based on water usage.
Current power sector plans may lock Thailand into a more carbon-intensive path.	Step up investment in renewables and consider increasing environmental taxation.
The governance framework does not sufficiently integrate environmental concerns into public plans and policies.	Carry out Strategic Environmental Assessments more frequently and effectively.
Chapter 5: Peace – strengthening governance	
Institutional capacity to implement reform falls short, including with respect to co-ordination across ministries and agencies.	Review the size, role and responsibilities of ministries. Clarify public service delivery responsibilities across levels of government.
Imbalance between central and local governments hinders policy reform.	Pursue decentralisation by empowering local administrations to effectively provide services.
Competition legislation has not been adequately enforced.	Strengthen the capacity of the Trade Competition Commission and ensure its membership reflects various stakeholder interests.
Continuing government efforts to reduce corruption are needed.	Further strengthen existing integrity measures and streamline the anti-corruption mandates of various institutions.

Overview

Thailand has made remarkable socio-economic progress over the past several decades. Sustained strong growth has turned it into an upper-middle income country, brought down poverty and delivered advances in a number of well-being dimensions. Even so, rising prosperity has not been shared equally across the country. Today, Thailand strives to pursue a development path to benefit all, seeking to reinvigorate economic transformation and reduce multifaceted inequalities in the face of a rapidly ageing population and technological change. This overview presents Thailand's development from a comparative and historical perspective and assesses performance across a range of well-being outcomes. On the basis of the analysis in the subsequent chapters, which cover the five critical areas of the Sustainable Development Goals – people, prosperity, partnerships, planet and peace – the overview identifies the key constraints facing policy makers in their pursuit of inclusive development.

Thailand is striving to realise an ambitious long-term development vision. Strong growth since the 1970s enabled the country to join the group of upper-middle-income economies in the early 2010s and has seen Thailand perform well in many areas. Poverty has plummeted and well-being has improved considerably, notably with respect to health and education. At the same time, economic development has taken a toll on the environment and the benefits of prosperity have not been shared evenly nationwide. Moreover, a very large share of the labour force remains in informal work. Moving forward, Thailand needs to achieve faster but also more inclusive economic growth, while contending with demographic and other challenging structural transitions.

The Multi-dimensional Country Review (MDCR) is being undertaken to support Thailand in achieving its development objectives. It consists of three phases and reports. This first volume builds on the 2030 Agenda for Sustainable Development and its Sustainable Development Goals (SDGs) to identify the main constraints to achieving inclusive sustainable development. The second review phase will consist of an in-depth analysis of those constraints to formulate more detailed policy recommendations that can be integrated into Thailand's development planning processes. The third and final phase of the MDCR will focus on moving from analysis to action.

This overview describes Thailand's performance across well-being dimensions and brings together the results of the thematic chapters to identify the key constraints to development. First, it outlines the history and context of Thailand's development and describes the country's vision for the future. Second, it presents performance across a range of well-being indicators. The overview then draws lessons from the subsequent five thematic chapters, which follow the five Ps of the 2030 Agenda: People, Prosperity, Partnerships, Planet and Peace. The final section reviews the key transitions needed for Thailand to achieve its development ambitions. Whenever relevant and subject to data availability, Thailand is compared with a set of benchmark countries in Asia (China, Indonesia, Korea, Malaysia, the Philippines, Singapore and Viet Nam) and beyond (Colombia, Mexico, Poland, South Africa and Turkey).

A brief history of Thailand's development

Thailand has developed from a feudal trading hub connecting South with East Asia in the 18th and 19th centuries into a rapidly modernising urban economy. Remarkable progress has been made since the introduction of constitutional rule in 1932, but several challenges remain.

The second half of the 20th century saw rapid economic expansion and transformation towards an urban economy dominated by manufacturing and services. Building on reforms promoting openness and investment in the 1960s, the composition of Thai exports shifted from mainly agricultural base materials to electronics and textiles. Tourism has boomed since the 1970s, resulting in revenues of USD 9 billion or some 5% of GDP as of 1995. This transformation was driven largely by Thailand's urban centres, which offered jobs and higher living standards. By the mid-1990s, 18 million citizens (30%) resided in urban areas, up from 7 million in 1970. Productivity rose fast and continued to propel the economy as urban jobs replaced rural ones.

The Asian financial crisis of the late 1990s hit Thailand hard (Figure 1) and highlighted shortcomings, but became an opportunity to improve economic management and governance. Capital account liberalisation in the 1980s and early 1990s facilitated inward foreign investment, but limited regulatory capacity constrained the government's ability to rein in risky investments and corporate cronyism. At the same time, human capital emerged as a weakness, as real wages increased faster than educational attainment. This caused many Thai and foreign firms to relocate to countries with cheaper and often better educated labour. As foreign exchange reserves dwindled and business sentiment turned sour, the baht collapsed in mid-1997 amid substantial capital flight, causing a deep recession. This cycle was soon repeated elsewhere in key emerging Asian economies, an event now known as the Asian financial crisis of 1997-98. The lessons learnt from the crisis have guided Thai economic policy in subsequent years, leading to substantial structural reforms.

Figure 1. **Per capita incomes have soared, but the share of formal employment has progressed less**

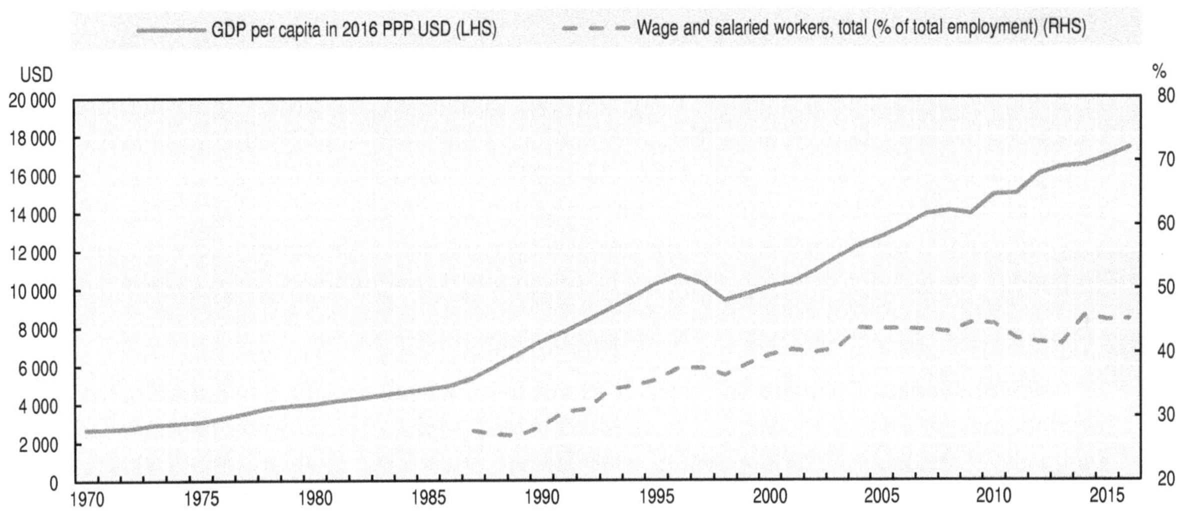

Source: World Bank (2017a), World Development Indicators database; Conference Board (2017), Total Economy Database, May.

StatLink http://dx.doi.org/10.1787/888933691249

With an enhanced policy framework in place, robust growth resumed, and the economy was better prepared to weather the global financial crisis in 2008 and periodic natural disasters. Post-Asian financial crisis reforms included strengthening public finances, establishing a more prudent financial system by restructuring banks, restoring business confidence through debt forbearance, rebuilding foreign exchange reserves, introducing inflation targeting and diversifying the economy by developing the services sector. By the mid-2000s, Thailand had regained pre-crisis levels of GDP per capita. Exports continued to pull the economy forward, reaching 70% of GDP by 2008. The share of high-tech products – including automobiles, electronics and electrical appliances – and that of processed agricultural products has increased. However, exports slowed down in the context of the global financial crisis in 2008 and the devastating floods in 2011. Even so, the economy continued to grow, albeit more slowly in recent years. Thailand has become an integral part of global value chains (GVCs) for automobile and electronics, which account for some 30% and 20% of total manufacturing output respectively, up from about 10% for both sectors in 1996.

Economic success has brought impressive social progress. Poverty has plummeted from 60% in 1990 to 7% today measured against the national poverty line, while social services in education and health have expanded considerably and improved. The introduction of the Universal Health Coverage Scheme in 2002 represented a major step towards basic social protection for all, including those living in informal circumstances, and was complemented by the introduction of a universal monthly old-age allowance for the elderly in 2009.

However, as transformation slowed, social and regional imbalances came to the fore. The share of those in precarious employment stagnated at around half of the working population following the mid-2000s, after falling from 70% in the late 1980s, when records started. This reflects the high share of poor agricultural workers in rural areas and significant urban informality. The creation of new activities replacing low-productivity employment has slowed down and the skills required for modern urban jobs exceed those of rural migrants and the urban poor. Today, only 11% of Thai citizens say that they can live comfortably with their current income (Gallup, 2017). While Bangkok's success as a metropolis has been key to Thailand's transformation, the country suffers from a lack of booming secondary cities. Such cities could provide more urban opportunities and help overcome the territorial disparities in household income and consumption that remain, with sizeable pockets of poverty in the Northeast, North, and South regions.

Over the past several decades, Thailand has seen frequent political changes. Since Thailand became a constitutional monarchy in 1932, it has had 20 different constitutions, oscillating between democratic participation and elite rule, while slowly adding elements of regional decision-making to a traditionally highly centralised state. The slower pace of economic transformation, quality job creation and reduction of regional inequalities in the new millennium has put pressure on the political system, and on the ability of the state to respond to the growing need for better public services and environmental management.

Future challenges and Thailand's development ambitions

Moving forward, Thailand will need to adapt to an ageing society, while developing new engines for further economic transformation and approaches to overcome regional inequality. The share of the population over the age of 65 is set to double from 15% to 30% between now and 2030. With around half of Thailand's workforce still in precarious employment, public finances will be under growing pressure and many elderly people at risk of poverty.

Environmental disasters, particularly those related to water, will continue to challenge Thailand's ability to manage prevention and effective service delivery. The cost of floods averaged over THB 6 billion (nearly USD 190 million) per year between 1989 and 2013, and is likely to increase given climate change.

Meanwhile, continuing regional integration provides significant opportunities, while the broader international environment presents challenges. Southeast Asia will remain among the world's most dynamic economic regions for the foreseeable future and ASEAN integration will open up new opportunities for Thailand. However, regional integration will also create challenges through intensified foreign direct investment (FDI) and trade competition with regional peers, notably the Philippines and Viet Nam. Uncertainties about global economic prospects point to the need for resilience in the event of another financial crisis or slowdown, or geopolitical shocks.

Three frameworks outline Thailand's official strategic development ambitions in response to these challenges and reflect citizens' aspirations. Strategy Thailand 2036 sets out a vision of a fast-growing economy, with a targeted growth rate of 5-6% per year, and full achievement of the 2030 SDGs. Building on a long tradition of development planning, the 12th National Economic and Social Development Plan (2017-2021) (12th Plan) translates this broad vision into more concrete goals and reforms (NESDB, 2016a). Thailand 4.0 presents a desired future economic model for a more innovative, inclusive and sustainable economy and encapsulates the key objectives of the Strategy and the Plan. The aspirations of a small sample of citizens have been collected as part of this review and reflect similar hopes (Box 1).

Box 1. **Thailand 2036 and citizens' vision for the future**

To increase policy continuity from one administration to the next, the government has recently ratified the National Strategy Preparation Act 2017. The National Strategy spans 2017 to 2036, and aims to make Thailand a high-income economy enjoying "security, prosperity and sustainability" based on the sufficiency-economy philosophy. The National Strategy sets out the agenda for economic, social and administrative development. It rests on six key pillars: national security, creation of equal opportunity and society, building competitiveness, human capacity building, improving quality of life and the environment, and balance and development in public administration. Beyond these pillars, the strategy sets out five broad objectives:

1. Economic prosperity – to create a strong and competitive economy driven by innovation, technology and creativity. The strategy aims to boost research and development expenditure to 4% of GDP, raise the economic growth rate to 5-6% over the next 20 years, and reach the threshold of a high-income country.
2. Social well-being – to create an inclusive society that moves forward without leaving anyone behind through the realisation of the full potential of all members of society. The goals are to reduce income disparity as measured by the Gini coefficient from 0.47 in 2013 to below 0.36 by 2036, to ensure fair access to job opportunities and public services for every Thai and to turn at least 20 000 households into "smart farmers" within five years.
3. Human resource development and empowerment – to transform Thai citizens into "competent human beings in the 21st century" and "Thais 4.0 in the first world". The objective is to raise Thailand's human development index from 0.722 to 0.8 or to place the nation in the top 50 countries within 10 years, and to ensure at least five Thai universities rank among the world's top 100 within 20 years.
4. Environmental protection – to become a liveable, low-carbon society with an economic system capable of adjusting to climate change. The main targets are to develop at least ten cities into the world's most liveable cities and to reduce the risk of terrorism.
5. Public sector governance – to improve public sector administration and reduce corruption. The main targets are to achieve second best ranking among ASEAN countries in the IMD Global Competitiveness Report for public governance, and to improve Thailand's score on the Transparency International's Corruption Perceptions Index to above 50.

To capture a society's aspirations beyond official documents, MDCRs include a stakeholder exercise which brings together representatives of society (government agencies and representatives of the private sector, public sector, civil society and academia, etc.) in order to develop ideas for the country's future. In Thailand, this exercise assembled a number of participants in Bangkok in July 2017 and gave them the task of describing citizens' lives in 2030.

Aspirations for the future lives of citizens in Thailand focused strongly on the world of work, raising questions about how global trends will shape opportunities and lifestyles. Participants described a future transformed by technology, which would offer new socio-economic opportunities, as well as improvements in well-being. Online opportunities related to the provision of services or trading in goods on the global

Box 1. **Thailand 2036 and citizens' vision for the future** *(cont.)*

market would radically change professions and working patterns. Urban citizens would be independent innovative entrepreneurs with multiple jobs and income sources, and have greater agency to decide on their working hours, place of work and type of economic activity. Rural citizens' lives would also be transformed by technology, enabling greater sustainability of farming practices and improved productivity through the "Internet of Things".

Participants also discussed idiosyncratic Thai behaviour and values, and how these might affect development prospects and relate to the SDGs. They drew attention to the Thai concept "น้ำใจ" (*nam-jai*), which is related to kindness, and the Sufficiency Economy Philosophy, as two elements driving social cohesion and consensus towards national development goals. Elitism, patronage and perceptions of a lack of meritocracy were discussed as obstacles to social cohesion and realising national economic aspirations. The participants also noted that the skills and characteristics required to realise the national development plan included entrepreneurship, independence, risk-taking and being a self-starter.

Source: Vimolsiri (2017); OECD/NESDB Workshop: "Thailand 2030: vision and challenges", held on 18 July 2017 in Bangkok.

Assessment and key constraints to development in Thailand

Progress with respect to the above frameworks can be assessed from various perspectives. One perspective is to evaluate citizens' well-being, which can be thought of as an ultimate policy objective. Another complementary perspective is to examine Thailand's progression on each of the SDGs.

How's life in Thailand? Through the OECD well-being lens

In order to assess Thailand's overall performance with respect to the well-being of its citizens, it is useful to compare progress across various dimensions using the OECD's "How's Life?" toolbox. Well-being encompasses material conditions (e.g. income, jobs and housing), but also the broader quality of people's lives including their health, education, environment, social connections and subjective well-being. Recognising the importance of how people themselves evaluate their lives, the OECD Framework for Measuring Well-Being and Progress uses a mix of objective and subjective indicators (Boarini et al., 2014; OECD, 2011).

Compared to countries at a similar level of development, Thailand performs relatively well in most well-being dimensions (Figure 2). Performance is especially strong with respect to life evaluation, social connections, security, and housing and infrastructure. The picture is more mixed when it comes to other dimensions, such as the environment, education and skills, or work. For instance, while levels of unemployment are very low, working conditions are worse than might be expected given Thailand's level of development.

Moving ahead on the SDGs

The SDGs consist of 17 goals and 169 targets with the ultimate objective of ending poverty, protecting the planet and ensuring prosperity and peace for all. They came into effect in January 2016 and provide guidelines for all countries up to 2030. Thailand has committed to achieving these goals and has embedded them into its national vision.

Thailand generally performs well across the SDGs, but further progress towards a more inclusive and sustainable economy is needed (Figure 3). Overall, benchmarking past performance against SDG targets attests to Thailand's impressive performance, particularly on outcomes related to people and prosperity. Progress in poverty reduction and boosts to innovation and electricity infrastructure are especially notable. At the same time, the underlying structure of the labour market has hardly changed and about half of the working population continues to work informally with limited access to protection and services. Major environmental challenges remain as well, notably with respect to emissions and pollution.

Figure 2. **Current and expected well-being outcomes for Thailand: worldwide comparison**

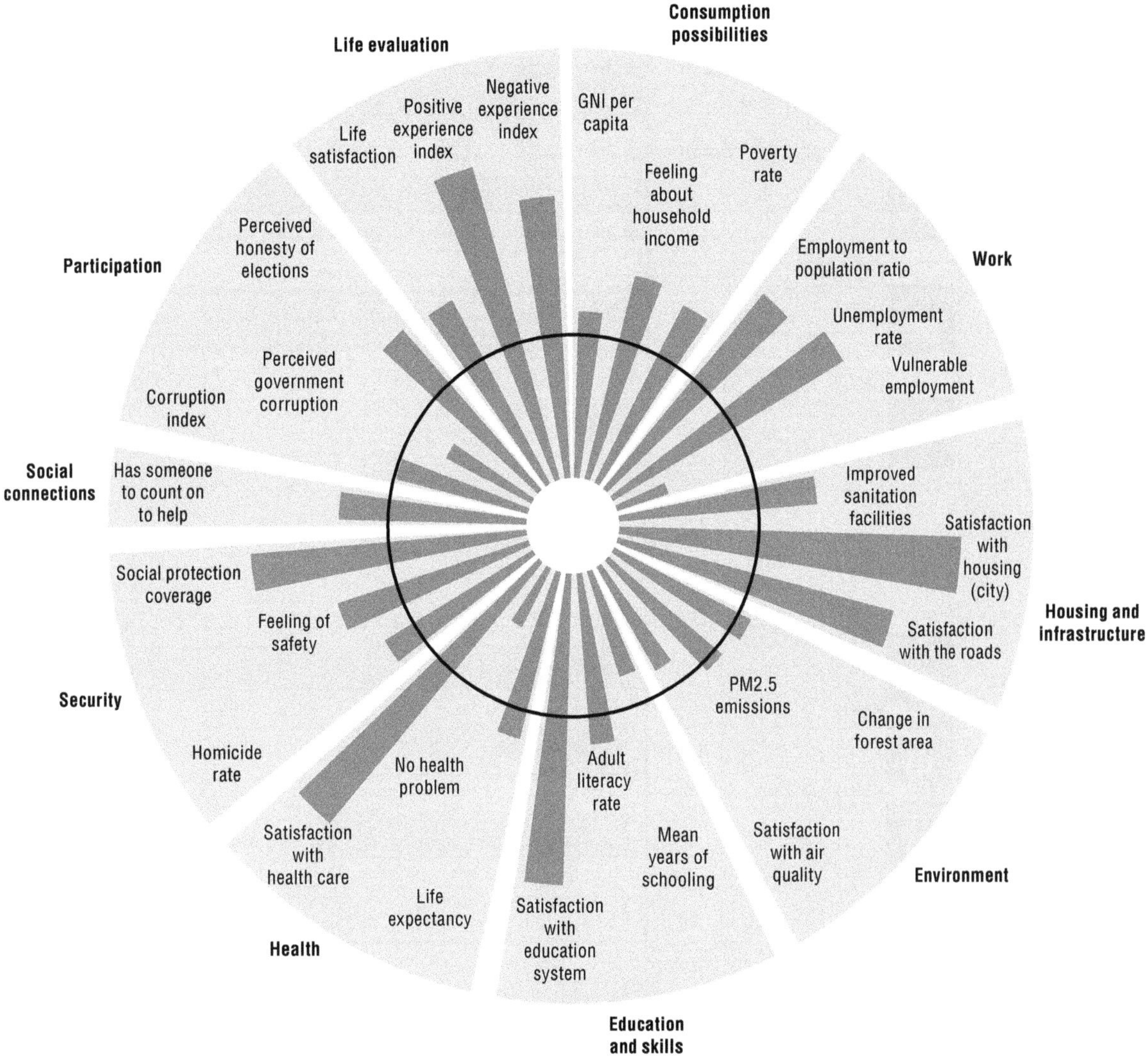

Note: The bars represent the observed well-being values for Thailand and the black circle shows the expected values based on Thailand's level of GDP per capita. The latter stem from a set of bivariate regressions with GDP as the predictor and the various well-being outcomes as dependent variables from a cross-country dataset of around 150 countries with a population over a million. All indicators are normalised in terms of standard deviations across the panel. The observed values falling inside the black circle indicate areas where Thailand performs poorly in terms of what might be expected from a country with a similar level of GDP per capita. As this figure only shows outcomes at the national level, disparities between regions might be masked.

Source: OECD (2015), PISA Database, *www.oecd.org/pisa/data/2015database*; Transparency International (2016), 2016 Corruption Perceptions Index, *www.transparency.org/cpi2016*; Gallup (2017), Gallup World Poll, *www.gallup.com/services/170945/world-poll.aspx*; and World Bank (2017a), World Development *Indicators* (database), *https://data.worldbank.org/data-catalog/world-development-indicators*.

Figure 3. **Progress towards the Sustainable Development Goals (SDGs)**

2000 | 2016 (or latest available)

People: Towards better lives for all

Indicator	SDG	2000	2016 (or latest available)	2030
Poverty headcount ratio at national poverty lines (% of population)	1 No poverty	42	8.6	5
Prevalence of undernourishment (% of population)	2 Zero hunger	19	10 (2015)	0
Life expectancy at birth, total (years)[1]	3 Good health and well-being	71	75 (2015)	81[a]
Adult literacy rate, population 15+ years, both sexes (%)	4 Quality education	93	93 (2015)	100
Proportion of seats held by women in national parliaments (%)	5 Gender equality	5	6	50

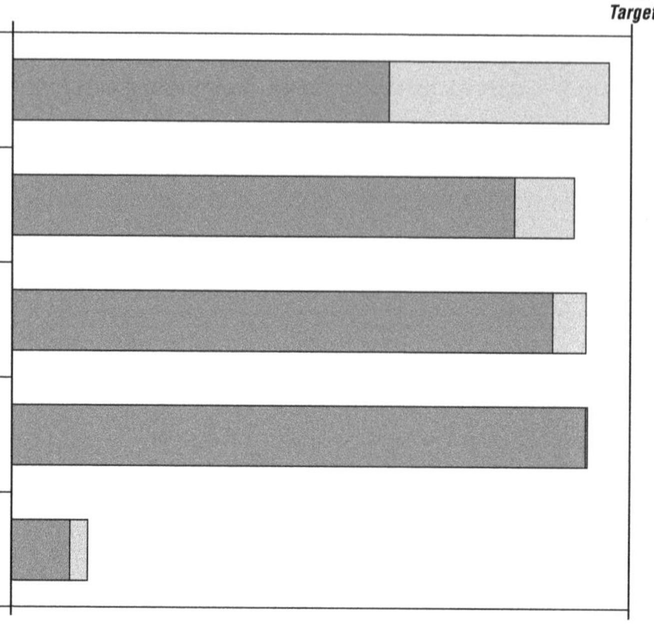

Prosperity: Boosting productivity

Indicator	SDG	2000	2016 (or latest available)	2030
Access to electricity (% of population)	7 Affordable and clean energy	82	99.9	100
Agriculture value added per worker (constant 2010 USD)	8 Decent work and economic growth	1 446	2 041 (2015)	4 082
Wage and salaried workers, total (% of total employment)[1]	8 Decent work and economic growth	40	45	84[a]
Account at a financial institution (% age 15+)	8 Decent work and economic growth	-	78 (2014)	90[a]
Researchers in R&D (per million people)	9 Industry, innovation and infrastructure	-	874 (2015)	3 961[a]
Individuals using the Internet (% of population)	9 Industry, innovation and infrastructure	4	48	79[a]
% of population satisfied with roads and highways[1]	9 Industry, innovation and infrastructure	-	73	100
Income share held by bottom 40%	10 Reduced inequalities	16	14.3 (2015)	20[a]
Population living in slums, (% of urban population)	11 Sustainable cities and communities	-	25 (2014)	0

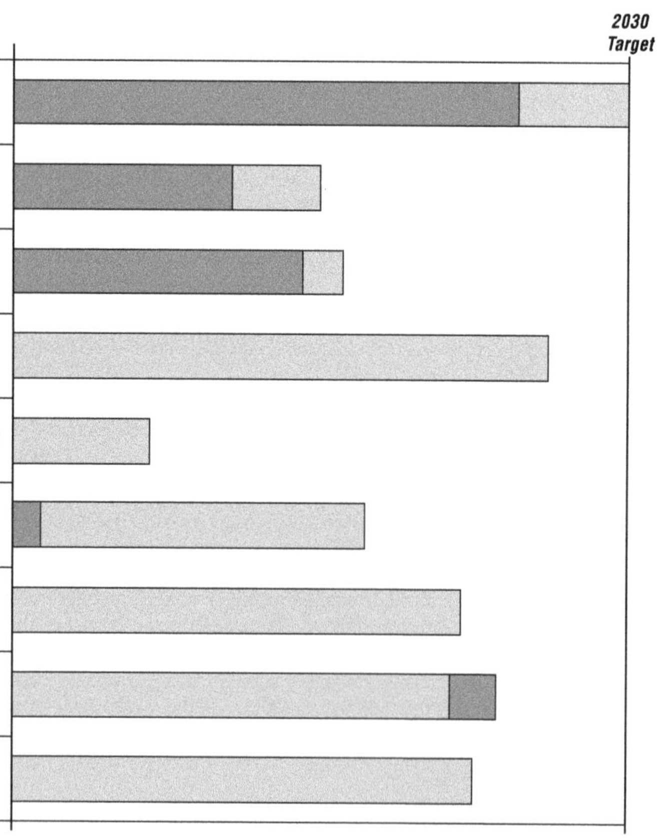

Figure 3. **Progress towards the Sustainable Development Goals (SDGs)** *(cont.)*

Partnerships: Sustainably financing development

	SDG	2005	2016	2030
General government tax revenues (% GDP)	17 Partnerships for the goals	13	16	19[a]
Total debt service (% of exports and primary income)	17 Partnerships for the goals	16	5	3[a]

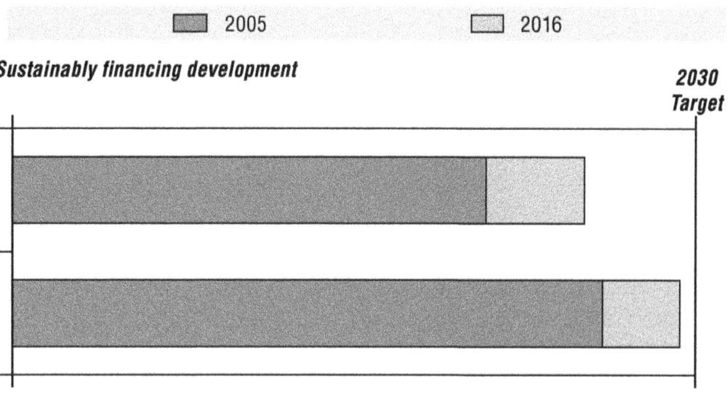

Planet: Conserving nature

	SDG	2000	2016 (or latest available)	2030
Improved water source (% of population with access)	6 Clean water and sanitation	91	93 (2015)	100
Renewable energy consumption (% of total final energy consumption)	7 Affordable and clean energy	22	24 (2014)	47[a]
PM2.5 air pollution, mean annual exposure (micrograms per cubic meter)	11 Sustainable cities and communities; 12 Responsible consumption and production	24	26 (2015)	10[a]
CO2 emissions (kg per 2010 USD of GDP)[1]	13 Climate action	0.83	0.83 (2014)	0.26[a]
Marine protected areas (% of territorial waters)	14 Life below water	4	2	17[a]
Terrestrial protected areas (% of total land area)	15 Life on land	17	19	22[a]

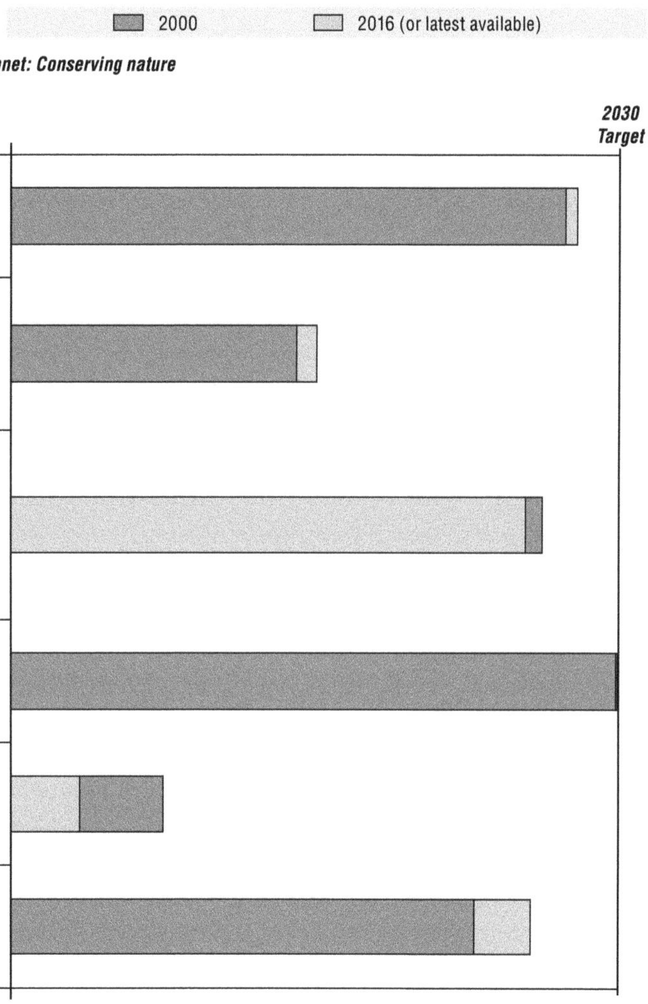

Figure 3. **Progress towards the Sustainable Development Goals (SDGs)** *(cont.)*

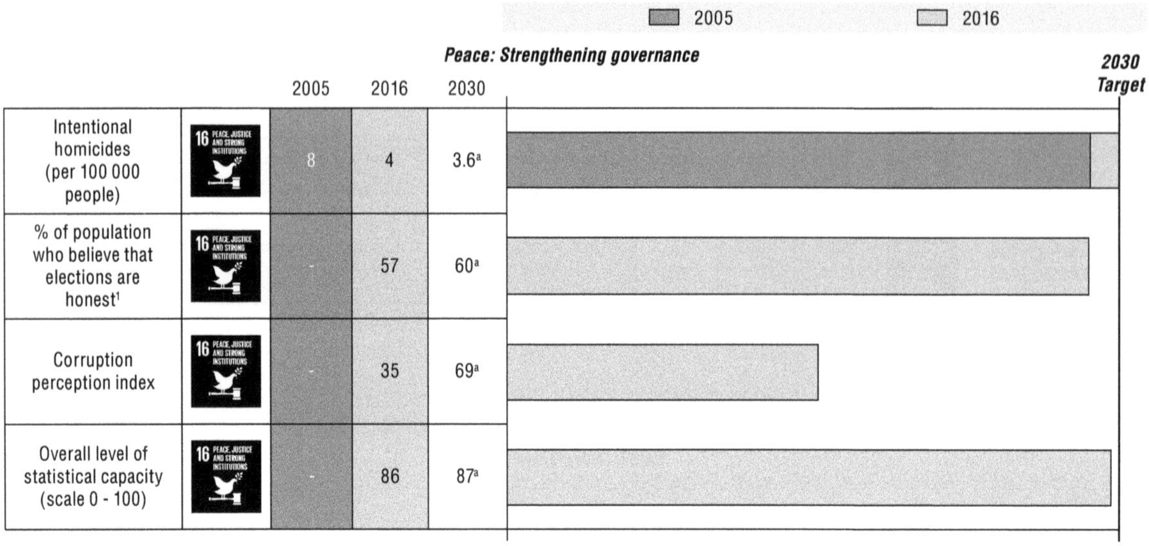

Note: The bars measure Thailand's performance in 2000 and 2016 (or latest year – as indicated accordingly) for a selection of 26 indicators across the 17 Sustainable Development Goals (SDGs). The 2030 aspirational target values refer to the pre-defined UN target (established by the UN IAEG and available at: *https://unstats.un.org/sdgs/iaeg-sdgs/metadata-compilation/*). Targets are all normalised to 100 for representation and comparison purposes.

a. When UN 2030 targets were not quantifiable, targets were calibrated to the average performance of OECD countries, in accordance with the methodology outlined in a recent OECD study on measuring distance to the SDGs targets (OECD, 2017g). However, the target for "Total debt service" was calibrated to the average value of the top 3 performers in the ASEAN region, due to data unavailability in OECD countries.

1. Indicators were chosen in line with the UN global indicator framework. When they were not measurable, indicators were selected that approximate the respective SDGs and at the same time ensure international comparability.

Source: World Bank (2017a), World Development Indicators, *https://data.worldbank.org/data-catalog/world-development-indicators;* National Statistical Office of Thailand (NSO) and NESDB calculations; Inter-Parliamentary Union (IPU), United Nations Educational, Scientific, and Cultural Organization (UNESCO) Institute for Statistics; OECD International Energy Agency; International Monetary Fund; Gallup World Poll, *www.gallup.com/services/170945/world-poll.aspx*; and Bertelsmann Stiftung's Transformation Index (BTI).

Progress and challenges on the five Ps

The thematic chapters that follow delve in greater detail into each of the above five critical areas, and identify a number of bottlenecks that appear to constrain policy makers as they design and implement policies to reach the SDGs.

People: Towards better lives for all

Poverty has fallen impressively and inequality is on a downwards trend, but more efforts are needed to reduce persistent, substantial regional inequalities and further improve living standards, especially for the large informal workforce. To achieve these objectives, the government needs to: (i) boost the participation rates of informal workers in social protection schemes; (ii) expand adequate social safety nets for poor households and the elderly; (iii) prepare the healthcare system for an ageing and modernising society; and (iv) improve educational outcomes, particularly in rural areas. Gaps also remain in ensuring women's political participation and reducing gender-based violence and discrimination.

Future growth needs to be inclusive

During the first half of the 2010s, living standards improved less rapidly than in most comparator countries. Despite Thailand's impressive track record of poverty reduction, 6.7 million people or close to 10% of the population live at most 20% above the national poverty line, and are thus vulnerable to falling back into poverty. The majority live in rural areas and work in agriculture.

Inequality in Thailand has a strong regional dimension. Inhabitants of the poorer North, Northeast and Southern regions lag behind the more prosperous Bangkok and Central regions, both in terms of income and other dimensions of well-being such as employment conditions, education attainment, health outcomes, and transport and communication infrastructure (Figure 4). Mainstreaming equality considerations into the policy formulation process and directing efforts towards narrowing Thailand's regional gaps, as recognised in the 12th Plan, is likely to improve social cohesion.

Figure 4. **The Bangkok metropolitan region outperforms others in most dimensions of well-being**

Achievement scores from 0 (worst) to 1 (best), 2017

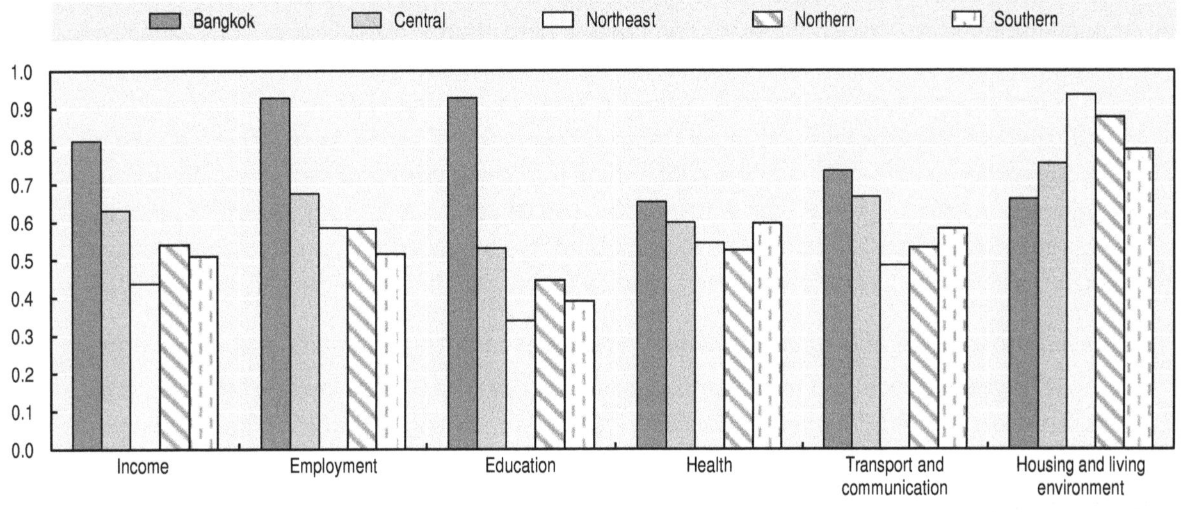

Note: The Human Achievement Index is a composite index that compares regional performance with achievement scores that use the worst and best performance observed in the provinces. These scores are calculated for a range of indicators for relevant sub-indices (e.g. for employees covered by social security, occupational injuries, unemployment and underemployment rates in the case of the employment sub-index). For the purpose of this report, only the scores for the sub-indices of income, employment, education, health, transport and communication, and housing and living conditions are shown, since their underlying indicators come closest to the SDGs. The Central region as shown here excludes the Bangkok Metropolitan Area.

Source: NESDB (2017a), Thailand Human Achievement Index 2017, *www.nesdb.go.th/nesdb_en/download/article/social2-2560-eng.pdf.*

StatLink http://dx.doi.org/10.1787/888933691268

Informality is very prevalent

Although the official unemployment rate is exceptionally low, the majority of workers remain in informal occupations and are more likely to be exposed to unstable contractual situations, long hours and hazardous working conditions. Thailand's relatively strict labour protections, particularly individual dismissal and temporary employment regulations, may contribute to informal employment. However, informality has many other drivers, including tax and social security (dis)incentives to formalise labour, rigid wage structures, low worker productivity and the overall structure of the economy.

Thailand relies heavily on migrant workers primarily from neighbouring ASEAN countries. There are an estimated 3.5 million migrants workers, making up 9% of the labour force. Many industries, such as agriculture, fishing, construction, domestic service, manufacturing and retail, depend on low-skilled migrant labour. Furthermore, immigrant workers are relatively young and thus represent a fresh labour supply in the face of an ageing native-born population.

Compliance with the minimum wage and, more generally, the enforcement of labour protection measures need to improve for both Thai and migrant workers. One-third of private sector workers and over half of young and low-skilled workers received wages below the minimum rate in 2013, unemployment insurance is only available to employees in the formal sector, and unionisation rates are low in international comparison.

Women's participation in politics should be increased, and gender-based violence remains a problem

Women's labour participation and wages are lower than men's, but the gap is smaller than the average for OECD countries. Moreover, Thailand outperforms comparator countries in terms of senior private sector management roles occupied by women. In contrast, a major gender gap exists in terms of political empowerment, with women holding only 6% of seats in the national parliament.

Women face continued incidences of domestic violence. Although the Act on the Prevention and Resolution of Domestic Violence criminalises perpetrators, overall convictions have been low due to the emphasis on mediation and family reunification, rather than encouraging victims of violence to speak up. Human trafficking and forced labour, especially in the commercial sex industry and domestic work sector, represent another form of gender-based violence. Despite strong government commitments to fight human trafficking, greater efforts are needed in legal enforcement and to reduce official complicity. The OECD Guiding Principles on Combatting Corruption related to Trafficking in Persons underline the fundamental role that corruption plays in the trafficking process and stress the importance of tackling both issues together (OECD, 2016).

Social protection needs to be broadened, notably for informal workers and the elderly

The gradual evolution of Thailand's social security schemes has resulted in a relatively comprehensive but fragmented system, calling for simplification and harmonisation of programmes. Benefit eligibility is largely tied to employment status, with different programmes for civil servants, people holding formal jobs and informal workers.

Social protection coverage needs to expand further, notably for informal workers who mostly access benefits through voluntary schemes. Easier registration procedures, including flexibility on the required documents, the opportunity to register and claim in different localities, the development of an online registration system, and the use of behavioural nudges would help improve low participation rates. A universal old-age allowance supports informal workers without pension coverage, but the adequacy of benefits can be improved to prevent old-age poverty. The recent addition of means-tested benefits that target people below a certain income threshold, such as a child grant and a welfare card for low-income earners, is an encouraging step towards reducing inequality.

Thailand established universal healthcare in 2002, and both subjective and objective health outcomes confirm the solid performance of the Thai health system. As in many developing and middle-income countries, disease profiles have evolved alongside changing lifestyle patterns and non-communicable chronic diseases and associated curative costs are on the rise. To fight obesity, which is of particular concern, the government is taking steps to encourage healthier diets and more active lifestyles. Such efforts should be expanded.

Moving forward, the healthcare system needs to adapt to an ageing society by developing a long-term care (LTC) system. While the 12th Plan recognises the need for such a system, current services are still embryonic and there is limited evidence that proposed policies aiming to integrate family and community care into the LTC system are feasible. More efficient primary care, more funding for prevention and health promotion, and increased use of information and communication technology (ICT) are needed to improve quality and ensure the fiscal sustainability of the healthcare system.

Improving basic education quality and performance will be essential

At around 4% of GDP, Thailand's public expenditure on education is among the highest in the region. Access is near universal for primary and secondary education, but improvements are required to boost enrolment in pre-primary education with as many as one-quarter of three to five year olds not enrolled. Improvements to the quality of education are also needed as basic education performance falls short of global benchmarks. Inefficient and inequitable allocation of resources has undermined investment effectiveness and ultimately hampered learning outcomes. The 2015 results of the OECD Programme for International Student Assessment (PISA) show that the performance of Thai students trails most comparator countries and is far below the OECD average. Moreover, compared with PISA 2012, Thailand's scores declined significantly in science and reading. Reading performance is particularly worrisome, with only around half of Thailand's 15 year-olds demonstrating reading skills that would classify them as functionally literate. Inequalities in educational outcomes are high, and students from poorer, often rural, backgrounds are less likely to have access to quality schools with adequately-trained teachers. On one estimate, around one-fifth of Thai schools do not meet minimum quality standards, the majority of which are in rural areas (OECD, 2014a).

The government recognises the shortcomings of the education system and has put into place various strategic plans. A recent policy review by the OECD and UNESCO offered recommendations to support the development of a high-quality education system in Thailand, centred on four priority areas: curriculum reform, improved testing procedures, investment in teacher quality, and enhancing digital learning and ICT use, particularly in rural schools (OECD and UNESCO, 2016).

Higher education and lifelong learning outcomes remain wanting

Upgrading human capital is crucial for the success of Thailand 4.0 and managing the transition to an ageing society. Thailand's higher education and vocational educational institutions are not fully equipping individuals with the skills required by industry. In tertiary education, enrolment is comparatively high, but graduate numbers in the science, technology, engineering and mathematics fields are lower than industry requires. Moreover, the quality and relevance of university programmes needs to be raised. In this regard, the government is pursuing a reform strategy that grants universities more autonomy to develop courses in line with industry and student demands.

Technical and vocational education do not attract enough students, even though skills shortages are more acute for graduates with vocational training. In 2015, only 34% of upper secondary school students were enrolled in vocational programmes – down from 36% in 2011 and well below the government's 45-55% target (MOE, 2017). Moreover, the quality of training programmes needs improvement to better equip graduates with the skills needed by industry. Under the aegis of the 12th Education Development Plan, the government is seeking to increase the quality and attractiveness of vocational programmes by expanding industry input into the design of courses and providing financial incentives to students and medium-sized workplaces to participate in the Dual Vocational Training Programme.

Lifelong skills training will also be important to ensure Thailand's labour force can readily adapt to evolving industry requirements and prepare them for a digital economy. To this end, the 2002 Skills Development Promotion Act requires enterprises with more than 100 staff to provide training to at least half of employees once a year. Nevertheless, additional efforts are needed, as over 90% of employees are not interested in further developing their skills (NSO, 2016).

Prosperity: Boosting productivity

Over the past decade, limited structural reform and capital investment have held back productivity growth and improvements in well-being, and Thailand has lost ground vis-à-vis regional comparators. More recently, however, economic growth has started to regain momentum, helped by a pick-up in global trade which has supported exports, and by a substantial public infrastructure investment programme. Moving forward, Thailand will need to boost productive capacity in the face of intensified competition with regional peers and rapid demographic ageing, and productivity gains will be increasingly necessary to drive growth. This will require improving human resource development, encouraging technology diffusion via cluster development policy, promoting innovation and digitalisation, improving the SME policy framework and expanding regional integration, as emphasised in the 12th Plan and Thailand 4.0.

Growth has recently picked up

While Thailand's growth remained sub-par in recent years (Figure 5A), lately it has regained momentum, propelled by higher electronics exports, buoyant tourist arrivals and public investment. Growth is projected to increase to 4.0% in 2018 and 4.1% in 2019 (Table 1), with support from a cyclical uptick in global demand. Headline inflation is below target. On the external side, Thailand has sizeable buffers with the current account surplus close to 11% of GDP in 2017. Overall, the financial sector is sound, notwithstanding the risks posed by high household debt, rising non-performing loans and possible vulnerabilities in the expanding shadow banking sector.

For trend GDP growth to approach the 5-6% targeted rate, a revival in investment is needed (Figure 5B). The government's extensive public investment programme, particularly in infrastructure, may help lift the anaemic private investment rate. Although it is important that Thailand remain fiscally prudent, undertaking targeted public investment in productivity-enhancing infrastructure is necessary to increase economic potential. Even with a timely implementation of the government's investment programme, in the near-term the fiscal outlook remains sound. Subsidies have been reduced substantially, in line with the government's commitment to rationalise non-productive subsidy programmes, via fuel subsidy reform and the replacement of the rice pledging scheme. Moreover, ongoing tax reforms to boost collection efficiency and introduce new inheritance and land and building taxes will help raise revenue.

Figure 5. **Growth has been picking up, but investment has been lacklustre**

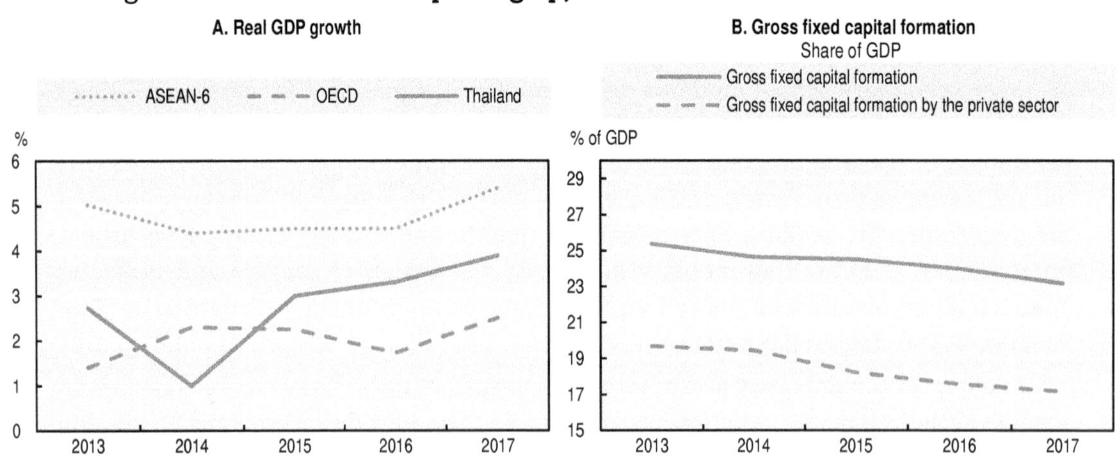

Note: ASEAN-6 is the weighted average growth rates of Indonesia, Malaysia, Philippines, Thailand, Singapore and Viet Nam.

Source: OECD (2017d), National Accounts database; Datastream and Bank of Thailand.

StatLink http://dx.doi.org/10.1787/888933691287

Boosting productivity and creating higher value-added industries

To attain high-income country status, Thailand's economic growth needs to be driven by productivity gains, rather than by the sheer accumulation of capital and labour inputs. Accordingly, Thailand's 12th Plan and Thailand 4.0 are pursuing an economic transformation where productivity improvements resulting from increases in innovation, human capital development, regulatory reform and infrastructure development drive growth.

Table 1. **Macroeconomic indicators and projections**

Annual percentage changes unless specified

	2013	2014	2015	2016	2017	2018	2019
						Projection	
Real GDP	2.7	1.0	3.0	3.3	3.9	4.0	4.1
Private consumption	0.9	0.8	2.3	3.0	3.2	3.2	3.4
Public consumption	1.5	2.8	2.5	2.2	0.5	3.5	2.5
Gross fixed capital formation	-1.0	-2.2	4.3	2.8	0.9	4.2	4.7
- Private	*-1.5*	*-0.9*	*-2.1*	*0.5*	*1.7*	*2.2*	*2.5*
- Public	*0.8*	*-6.6*	*28.4*	*9.5*	*-1.2*	*9.8*	*10.4*
Exports (goods and services)	2.7	0.3	1.6	2.8	5.5	5.3	5.9
Imports (goods and services)	1.7	-5.3	0.0	-1.0	6.8	6.6	6.8
Consumer prices	2.2	1.9	-0.9	0.2	0.7	1.2	1.5
Current account balance (% of GDP)	-1.2	3.7	8.1	11.7	10.8	8.5	8.0
General government fiscal balance (% of GDP, fiscal year)	0.5	-0.8	0.1	0.6	-1.7[1]	-1.8	-1.8
Public debt (% of GDP, fiscal year)[2]	42.2	43.4	42.5	41.8	41.9	41.2	40.6

1. This figure is a projection. Final outcome was unavailable at the time of publication.
2. As of the end of the fiscal year. Includes general government and state-owned enterprises debt.
Source: CEIC; NESDB; Bank of Thailand; and Public Debt Management Office.

Traditionally, labour reallocation from the agricultural sector in rural areas to more advanced sectors in urban areas supports productivity improvements and is a key feature of catch-up growth and structural transformation. However, over the past 30 years, the contribution of labour reallocation to overall labour productivity growth has declined in Thailand (Figure 6). To remedy this, the government should encourage such reallocation by narrowing skills mismatches through lifelong learning and skills training. In addition, productivity gains can be achieved by more effectively promoting innovation, and by upgrading management skills and encouraging greater ICT use in agriculture.

To foster the development of more productive and higher value-added industries, the government aims to improve industrial value chains by strengthening linkages among firms, researchers and academic institutions, and public organisations within a geographical area. In particular, the government is targeting a set of priority sectors selected from those that have recorded strong export performance. The sectors are comprised of "First S-Curve" industries where the industrial base of pre-existing sectors would be upgraded (e.g. next-generation automotive, smart electronics, agriculture and biotechnology, and affluent, medical and wellness tourism), and "New S-Curve" industries that can be developed through increased technological sophistication (e.g. robotics, aviation and logistics, biofuels and biochemicals, and digital and medical hubs). To this end, the government has launched a range of investment promotion measures and incentives in designated Special Economic Zones, which include the flagship Eastern Economic Corridor project.

Figure 6. **Labour reallocation has not boosted productivity substantially in Thailand**

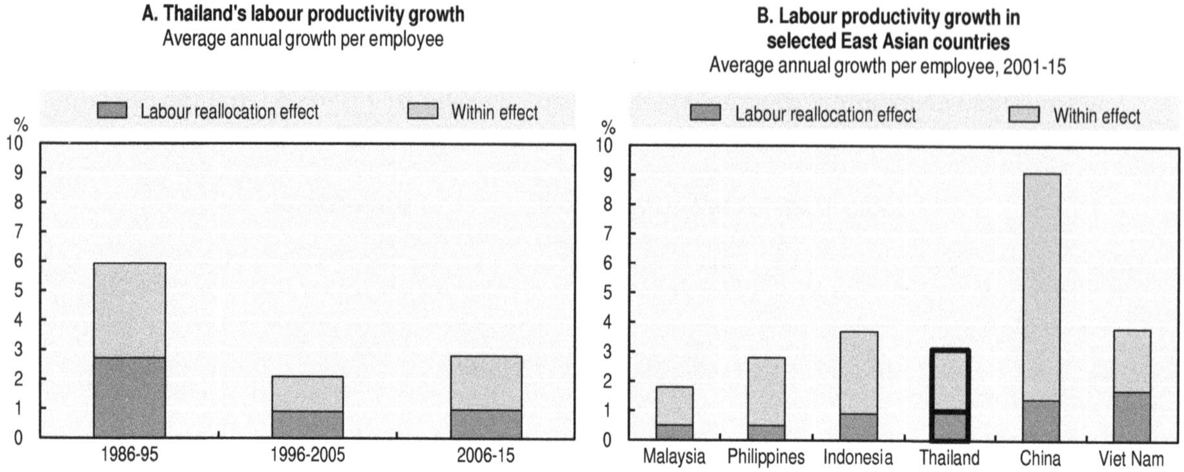

Note: The "within effect" refers to the contribution to total labour productivity growth from productivity growth within sectors. The "labour reallocation effect" refers to the contribution of the movement of labour from lower to higher-productivity sectors, where sectors are disaggregated into nine categories: (i) primary; (ii) mining; (iii) manufacturing; (iv) construction; (v) electricity, gas and water supply; (vi) wholesale and retail trade, and hotels and restaurants; (vii) transport and communications; (viii) financial intermediation, real estate and business activities; and (ix) community, social and personal services.

Source: OECD calculations based on Asia Productivity Organization (2017), Productivity database 2017 Version 1, *www.apo-tokyo.org/wedo/measurement*.

StatLink http://dx.doi.org/10.1787/888933691306

Toward innovation-led and digitalisation-driven productivity gains

Improving innovation in existing sectors is critical to boosting competitiveness and productivity, and to producing higher value-added products. However, Thailand's innovation performance has either fallen behind or lost ground vis-à-vis some comparator East Asian countries. Governance issues including poor co-ordination and lack of clarity around institutional roles and responsibilities have hindered innovation. To address these issues, the government established the National Research and Innovation Policy Council in late 2016 as a single body to set the direction for research and innovation policy.

Access to talent is also a major barrier to innovation. Weak collaboration between academia and industry limits the flow of researchers between the two sectors. To help foster mobility, the government has established a Talent Mobility Programme, which enables industry and/or the government to reimburse universities for access to talent. It also launched the Eastern Economic Corridor of Innovation project to create a regional innovation hub that attracts international talent and fosters R&D in the public sector, the private sector, academia and local communities.

Digitalisation can boost productivity and efficiency, as well as broader socio-economic development. It allows for better governance arrangements and a more inclusive society through improved access to and quality of key services such as health, education and banking. It aids innovation and helps countries move up value chains (OECD, 2017a). Promoting digitalisation also goes hand in hand with Thailand 4.0 (Box 2).

Box 2. **Digitalising Thailand**

Digital technologies can play an important role in promoting inclusive economic growth. They are also disruptive and are changing familiar structures and expectations of government, business and broader society. Thailand has developed a 20-year Digital Master Plan and is pursuing a bold digital transformation strategy as part of Thailand 4.0. However, a number of challenges must be addressed to ensure Thailand is ready to embrace the digital revolution and all Thai citizens are well placed to participate in the digital economy.

Thailand has made progress in the provision of reliable and affordable networks, but has room to improve. According to the 2016 Network Readiness Index, Thailand's ICT infrastructure is in the middle of the pack vis-à-vis comparator countries (Figure 7), while the number of internet users is on the low side. Regarding skills, further efforts are needed to increase ICT literacy across the economy including through school education and established Digital Community Centres. Finally, Thailand needs to boost cyber-security to nurture confidence and encourage greater ICT use.

Figure 7. **Thailand has room to improve in digital infrastructure and skills readiness**

Index, scale 1-7 from lowest to highest level of readiness, 2016

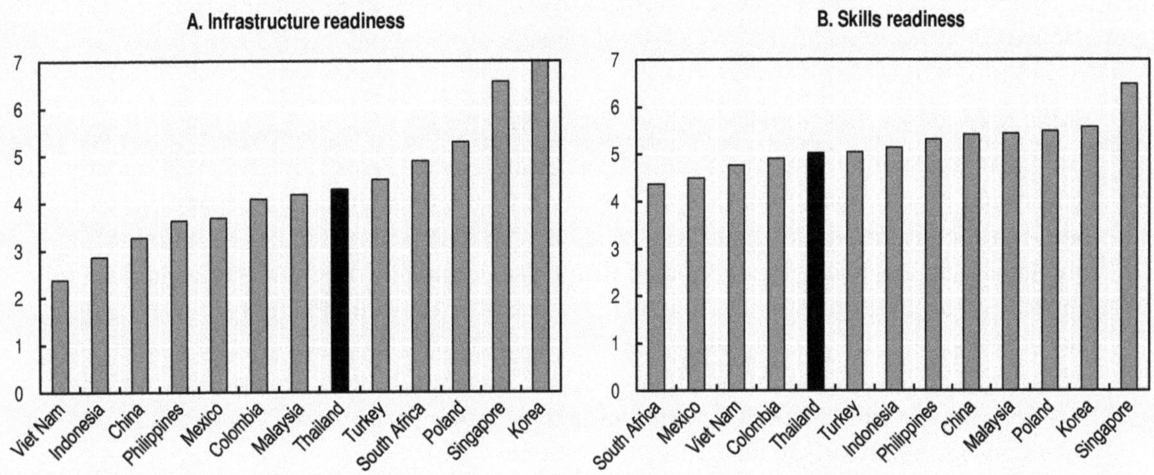

Source: World Economic Forum (2016), Network Readiness Index, *http://reports.weforum.org/global-information-technology-report-2016/networked-readiness-index*.

StatLink http://dx.doi.org/10.1787/888933691325

Under the 20-year Master Plan, Thailand aims to maximise the use of digital technology across all socio-economic activities. It seeks to leverage off digital technologies to increase capacity and competitiveness in all economic sectors with a strong focus on SMEs, reduce inequality by providing better access to health and education services, and improve the provision of government services. Indeed, a number of initiatives are already underway.

Thailand is facilitating e-commerce to help people run their businesses online, with a National e-Commerce Master Plan (2017-21) that includes measures to improve ICT access and promote an SME e-payment service for cheaper and easier transactions. In addition, the Bank of Thailand has eliminated charges on electronic transfers of less than THB 5 000 (about USD 150) to encourage uptake. The government is helping to address the shortfall in ICT literacy by providing coaching to SMEs on online trading. It is also establishing a digital park to support the development of digital businesses, offering a range of tax and non-tax incentives (e.g. simplified visa and work permit procedures). In the agricultural sector, digital technologies are being used to increase efficiencies and value-added. For instance, a digital "Agri Map" has been developed to help farmers identify which crops are most suitable for their farmland.

Box 2. **Digitalising Thailand** *(cont.)*

In healthcare, Thailand plans to consolidate its ICT infrastructure to promote better management, performance and increased savings on operational expenditure (Estospace, 2016). A number of pilot projects are underway to monitor the health of the elderly using smart devices and sensors in residential accommodation. Looking ahead, Thailand should build on its broadband investment programme and promote digital primary care consultation, in order to boost affordable access and improve the efficiency of the healthcare system.

In education, Thailand aims to provide broadband access to all schools and free Wi-Fi access to non-formal and informal schools. The government should further increase access to distant learning and open education resources, as a means to address teacher shortages and improve access to quality education for remote students.

Thailand is also boosting the uptake of digital technologies in the public sector, which to date has been slow. The Digital Government Development Plan (2017-21) foresees greater access to government data, more transparency and civic participation, and integration of back-office infrastructure. The government is developing a mobile government communication system (G-Chat), introducing digital laws to build confidence in online transactions, rolling out a shared ICT platform for government agencies and building a one-stop portal to access government services. It is also piloting a 'GovLab' programme to experiment with new technical solutions to public service delivery challenges.

SMEs need to be better financed and properly incentivised

Small and medium enterprises (SMEs) generate about 42% of Thailand's GDP, mostly in services. Promoting SMEs is crucial for economy-wide growth and reducing inequality between regions and individuals (Lee et al. 2017). SMEs face a number of interrelated problems including inadequate financing, insufficient upgrading of capital stock and slower adoption of technology, as well as inadequate regional integration (Charoenrat and Harvie, 2017). The government has developed an SME Promotion Masterplan (2017-21) with the objective of increasing the SME share in GDP to at least 50% by 2021. Its priorities include streamlining licensing procedures, promoting skills training with an emphasis on ICT, and providing entrepreneurship education and finance.

Better access to financing is key, as Thai SMEs often struggle in this area. Even though collateral requirements for SME loans are much stricter, the share of non-performing loans has been rising for SMEs. The bulk of SME loans are disbursed through specialised financial institutions, which may affect the degree of credit access between sectors and regions. To address this issue, Thailand could broaden the appeal of the Small Business Credit Guarantee Corporation by boosting its funding and offering more targeted guarantee-related products. Additionally, reliance on bank financing could be reduced by allowing SMEs to access the capital market via the creation of a special lower-cost bourse in the Thai Stock Exchange. Financial measures, however, need to be complemented by non-financial measures for SME development and promotion.

Furthering global value chain participation and regional integration

Trade and foreign investment have long been major drivers of Thailand's industrialisation. Foreign trade amounted to 123% of GDP in 2017, more than double the OECD average, reflecting active participation in GVCs. Making the best of opportunities brought about by participation in GVCs calls for efficient and cheap access to imported intermediate and capital goods. In this regard, Thailand has made substantial progress, almost halving the weighted applied mean tariff rate for manufacturing goods over the past decade. During the same period, a series of free trade agreements (FTAs) were concluded, either bilaterally or regionally through ASEAN, with major trade partners such as Australia, China, India, Japan, Korea and New Zealand. Trade costs can also be reduced by streamlining trade-related procedures and enhancing the quality of related infrastructure and services.

Trade liberalisation and facilitation has lagged somewhat in the services sector, which accounts for close to 60% of GDP in Thailand, but is key for productivity and competitiveness. Open and well-regulated services markets are the gateway to GVCs, ensuring access to information, skills and technology, reducing costs and improving service quality (OECD, 2017b). This is true in particular for digital, logistics and professional services used in high value-added activities. However, a pilot project to compute the OECD Services Trade Restrictiveness Index for Thailand shows that the country's regulatory framework creates international trade impediments in both the construction and architecture service sectors. These impediments result from both economy-wide and sector-specific regulations. The former include residency requirements for boards of directors, foreign land acquisition restrictions and a 49% cap on foreign ownership for companies without a foreign business license. In public procurement markets, preference is given to local suppliers. Sector-specific restrictions are present in both sectors, notably in the form of requirements with respect to the recognition of foreign qualifications.

FDI has played an essential role in Thailand's industrialisation and export growth through the provision of capital, technology and managerial skills, contributing substantially to productivity gains. In recent years, Thailand has become a major source of FDI to other Southeast Asian countries, notably Cambodia, Lao PDR and Myanmar, thereby contributing to regional integration. Nevertheless, the rules governing inward FDI remain comparatively restrictive in Thailand (Figure 8).

Figure 8. **FDI is still subject to substantial restrictions**

As of 2016; index ranges from 0 (open) to 1 (closed)

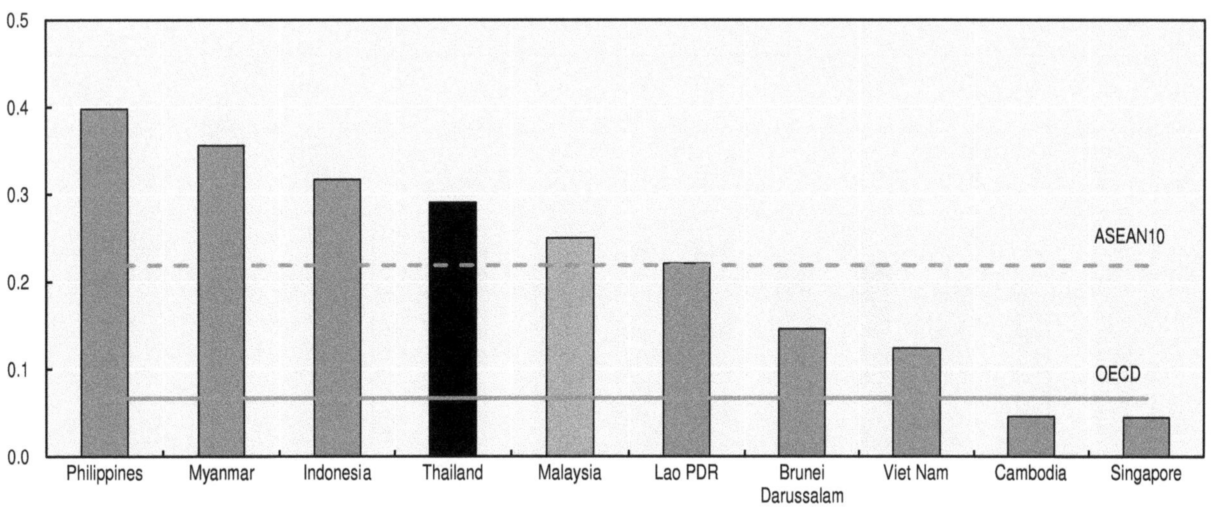

Note: The OECD FDI Regulatory Restrictiveness Index covers only statutory measures discriminating against foreign investors (e.g. foreign equity limits, screening and approval procedures, restrictions on key foreign personnel and other operational measures). Other important aspects of the investment climate (e.g. the implementation of regulations and state monopolies) are not considered. Data for Brunei Darussalam, Thailand and Singapore are preliminary.

ASEAN 10 comprises Brunei Darussalam, Cambodia, Indonesia, Lao PDR, Malaysia, Myanmar, Philippines, Singapore, Thailand and Viet Nam.

Source: OECD (2017i), FDI Regulatory Restrictiveness Index database, *www.oecd.org/investment/fdiindex.htm*.

StatLink http://dx.doi.org/10.1787/888933691344

The furthering of regional integration is helping to promote trade and investment liberalisation, as well as reform in areas related to trade and investment facilitation, such as more efficient customs procedures, streamlining and digitalisation of formalities, and regulatory reform on entry into the services sector. In addition to the ASEAN Economic Community and FTAs with major trade partners in Asia, further progress could be achieved by concluding FTAs with the European Union and the United States.

Partnerships: Sustainably financing development

Over the past ten years, Thailand's public debt has averaged 40% of GDP and the general fiscal balance has averaged a surplus of 0.1% of GDP. Moving forward, Thailand is seeking to strengthen fiscal discipline through a Fiscal Responsibility Bill. The Bill imposes a requirement on future governments to prepare medium-term economic forecasts of up to five years, as well as projections for public debt, revenue, expenditure and contingent liabilities. Despite Thailand's strong fiscal position, its rapidly ageing population and shrinking workforce will exert pressure on public finances over the medium term. To meet future social, environmental and infrastructure requirements Thailand will therefore need to reform the tax system to boost both revenue and competitiveness, reduce costs in the provision of infrastructure through greater private sector participation, and increase the efficiency and effectiveness of the healthcare and pension systems.

Increasing tax revenues to fund foreseeable expenditure pressures

Over the past five years, Thailand's total public revenues and tax collections averaged 21.7% and 17.7% of GDP, respectively. This is broadly in line with regional comparators, but much lower than the OECD average (Figure 9). Recognising the need to boost revenues, the government has set a target of raising total tax collection to 20% of GDP by 2020.

Figure 9. **General government revenue is broadly in line with regional comparators**
In % of GDP, average over 2011-15

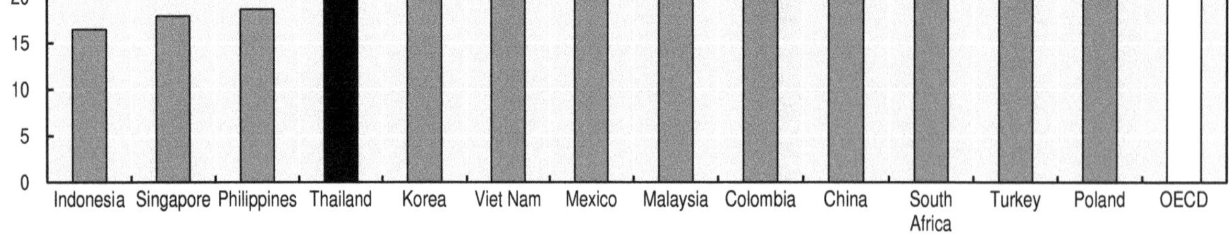

Source: Datastream; OECD Revenue Statistics (2017).

StatLink http://dx.doi.org/10.1787/888933691363

Direct taxes, which account for 41% of total tax collections, have undergone reform in recent years. The corporate tax rate was cut by a third to 20% pushing it to the lower end of the range and leading to a fall in corporate tax collection. Thailand also adjusted personal income tax settings, with the top rate cut from 37% to 35% and thresholds and deductibles raised. Given the higher thresholds and high rates of labour force informality (56% in 2016), only one-fifth of the working age population (15-64) pay income tax. Gradually reducing informality is key not only to improving revenue collection, but also to ensuring people enjoy better social protection.

Indirect taxes are an important source of revenue for Thailand, with the value-added tax (VAT) accounting for a third of indirect taxes. The statutory VAT rate is 10%, but it has been set at 7% since 1999 making it one of the lowest rates in the world. Moreover, high rates of exemptions and non-compliance undermine collections with an estimated VAT revenue ratio of 38%, below the OECD average of 56%. Thailand should consider gradually broadening the VAT scope and raising its rate, using additional revenues to fund targeted increases in social protection.

Improving tax efficiency and compliance also offers opportunities to increase revenue. In this regard, the government is pursuing a multipronged approach that includes easing compliance through technological innovation, providing incentives to discourage tax avoidance and informality, and strengthening enforcement on tax evasion.

Identifying potential efficiencies in the provision of public infrastructure will also be important to reduce the public expenditure burden. Thailand could consider additional infrastructure financing sources to reduce costs of investment and optimise risk allocation. In particular, infrastructure bonds priced in Thai baht can be less costly than bank financing and better match the long-term nature of such investments. Another way forward is to reinvigorate private sector involvement through improved public-private partnership (PPP) processes. In this regard, the government has sought to reduce red tape and improve bureaucratic efficiency, reforming PPP legislation in 2013 with the introduction of time limits and standardised contracts. Furthermore, Thailand has set up a Future Fund to provide additional instruments to finance major transportation infrastructure.

Improving the sustainability of the healthcare and pension system

With a rapidly ageing population, the burden on public finances to provide healthcare and social security for the elderly will continue to grow. In 2014, government health expenditure accounted for 3.2% of GDP. Though manageable, costs are bound to rise. In 2015, public expenditure on pensions accounted for 2.2% of GDP. While this is below regional comparators, future liabilities will likely grow faster, particularly if the government seeks to improve the very low replacement ratios for social pension recipients. Although some cost escalation is inevitable, improving the design of both the health and pension system can deliver efficiency gains and cost containment.

In healthcare, Thailand should avoid near-term regressive and often ineffective blanket cuts to the health budget and instead implement targeted structural reforms that will be beneficial over the longer run. For example, to prevent overburdening of hospitals, Thailand could increase health provision through preventive and primary care by boosting the number of family physicians and general practitioners, particularly in rural areas. Healthcare financing could be reformed by reducing the exemptions on co-payments and allowing greater private contributions from those able to afford it.

In relation to pensions, Thailand's shrinking labour force and longer retirements mean there are fewer work years available to support the burgeoning number of retirees. Thailand's private pension scheme has a pensionable age of 55, while the public sector scheme and the social pension both have a pensionable age of 60. OECD research suggests that postponing retirement is an efficient way to both boost retirement income and improve the financial sustainability of the system (OECD, 2013). Thailand could align the pensionable age of the private pension scheme with the public sector and social pension scheme, and progressively increase the official retirement age in line with life expectancy. Moreover, the government could slowly increase the private sector contribution rate, which is currently below most comparator countries and the OECD average.

Planet: Conserving nature

Thailand's natural environment is a vital asset and underpins key economic sectors and millions of livelihoods. As in many emerging economies, rapid economic growth has been achieved through intense use of natural resources, which has exerted a heavy environmental toll. Greater attention to environmental issues began in the 1990s, and resulted in the adoption of a framework law that established the Ministry of Natural Resources and the Environment, and introduced instruments such as Environmental Impact Assessments.

Today, renewed commitment to environmental concerns is warranted, as progress on this front has slowed or even reversed in some cases. Thailand's sustainable development rests on wise management of its natural resources, minimisation of pollution to protect the health of people and ecosystems, and a transition to a low-carbon, climate-resilient future.

The new environment bill, which is under discussion, represents an opportunity to modernise the policy mix and ensure a path towards sustainable development. The introduction of Strategic Environmental Assessments would further enhance environmental protection by integrating environmental concerns into government plans, policies and programmes.

Thailand can improve its management of natural resources

Thailand is exposed to cycles of flooding and drought that cause loss of life and economic disruption. While natural climatic variables are important drivers of these phenomena, other policy-amenable factors are also at play. Poorly planned urban expansion, the intensification of agriculture, and the deterioration or loss of watershed forests have led to the decline of flood-retention areas and flood plains, while water consumption behaviours, agricultural and industrial land development, urbanisation and population growth have contributed to droughts.

A lack of integrated water management hinders an effective response to these challenges. Water management in Thailand is characterised by a highly fragmented institutional framework leading to overlapping responsibilities, conflicting interests and a lack of co-ordination. The government has also tended to focus on hard infrastructure, supply-side solutions, while demand-side measures have received less attention. Thailand would benefit from a more holistic approach to water management and flood defence, complemented by a disaster risk management approach that is sufficiently funded and ensures that local levels have the capacity to prepare and respond to natural disasters.

Compared to other middle-income countries, Thailand performs poorly on several indicators of biodiversity, such as the number of threatened species (Figure 10). Deforestation also remains a problem in the North and Northeast regions, notwithstanding progress at the national level over the past decade.

Figure 10. **Thailand performs poorly on several indicators of biodiversity**

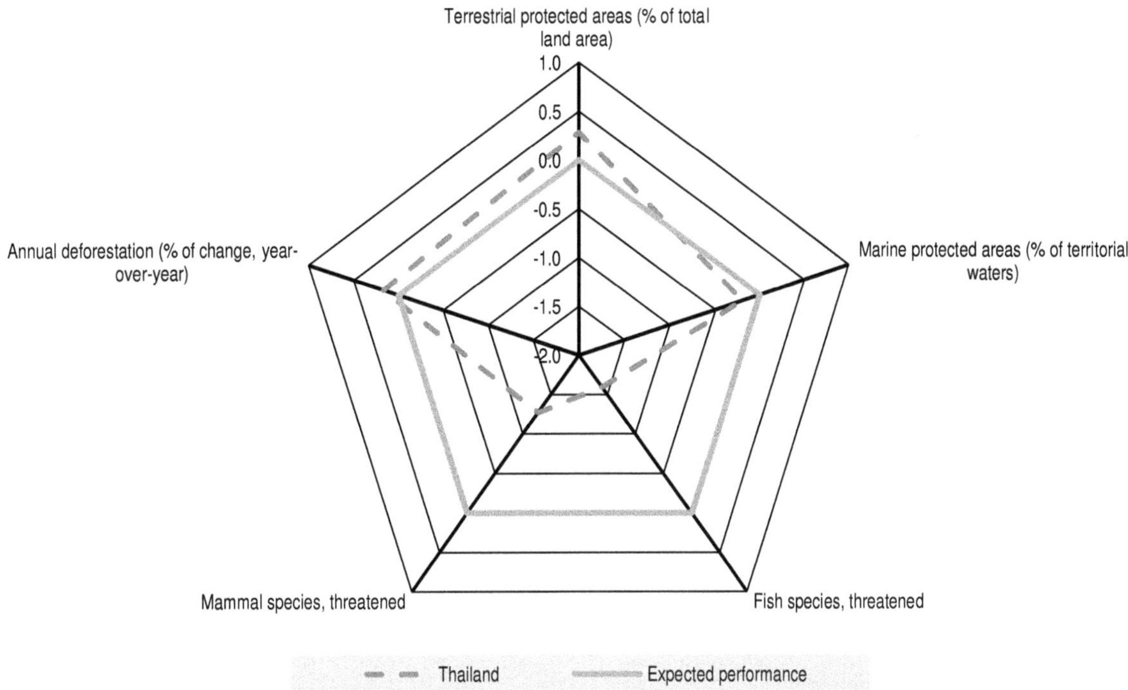

Note: The blue line represents Thailand's performance when benchmarked against other middle-income countries. The grey line represents expected performance given the country's level of income per capita. Places where the blue line lies inside the grey line represent poorer than expected performance on a given indicator.

Source: Authors' calculations based on World Bank (2017a), *World Development Indicators* (database); and World Bank (2017b), *Deforestation and Biodiversity*.

StatLink http://dx.doi.org/10.1787/888933691382

Policy responses will need to address the diverse sources of pressure on biodiversity. Irrigation, farmland encroachment and the invasion of alien species threaten wetlands. Illegal logging, the development of resorts for tourism, and the expansion of agricultural land due to the promotion of cash crops (e.g. rubber and oil palm) lead to deforestation. Pollution affects freshwater systems, and illegal fishing, ocean acidification, tourism and industrial activity impact marine and coral reef ecosystems.

Challenges remain in securing environmental quality of life

Levels of some air pollutants, such as PM2.5 particles, have been creeping up since 2010, after modest improvement since 1990. The problem is particularly acute in pollution hotspots such as the country's major industrial zones, where air pollution frequently exceeds safe limits. Water quality has been improving incrementally, but 23% of surface water is still assessed as poor quality. Greater progress is being held back by a lack of wastewater treatment facilities (only 15% of municipal wastewater is treated), poor compliance with existing regulations and the absence of financial disincentives to pollute.

Finally, solid waste generation is a growing problem, like in many countries in the region. The quantity of solid waste has increased by 80% since 2000, and 43% of waste is disposed of inappropriately through open burning or illegal dumping. The composition of waste, however, shows a high potential for reuse: up to 60% could be composted, recycled or used for energy generation. Appropriate pricing mechanisms are also needed to provide incentives to reduce the absolute quantity of waste generated.

Addressing climate change requires both mitigation and adaptation

Thailand has set ambitious greenhouse gas reduction targets – intending to cut emissions by 20-25% from the projected business-as-usual level by 2030 – and has identified energy and transport as key sectors for mitigation efforts. Some features of current energy plans, however, may be inconsistent with international commitments that are set to become increasingly stringent. In particular, the planned increase in the share of coal in the energy mix will raise the absolute level of carbon emissions. On a positive note, the share of renewables is also slated to rise under current plans. Thailand could be even more ambitious in its adoption of renewables by exploiting untapped potential in the solar photovoltaic sector. It could also consider higher environmental taxation.

As one of the countries most exposed to the impacts of climate change, mitigation efforts need to be complemented by adaptation. The 12th Plan and the National Climate Change Master Plan 2015-2050 aim to enhance Thailand's ability to adapt to climate change – a welcome move as adaptation is largely neglected in current sectoral plans. The true test will be whether these high-level plans translate into awareness, mainstreaming and implementation of adaptation measures across all sectors from national to local levels. Implementation will require effective central co-ordination that involves all relevant stakeholders, a strong evidence base (e.g. for climate projections), capacity building (especially at local levels), sufficient financing, and mechanisms for monitoring, evaluating and adjusting approaches.

Peace: Strengthening governance

Reforming the public sector has long been an important government priority, but involves a number of challenges. The gap between planning and implementation of policy objectives remains large; insufficient public participation in policy making is undermining the efficient allocation of resources toward public needs and development goals; under-development of evidence-based regulations hampers the creation of a business-friendly environment essential to high value-added activities; and high levels of perceived corruption weaken business confidence and public trust in the government.

The gap between policy planning and implementation needs to be narrowed

In Thailand, the existence of several ministries and agencies competing in similar policy spaces, across central government bodies and local administrations, often leads to conflicting policy agendas and impedes implementation. Indeed, Thailand does not compare favourably with respect to the implementation of reforms (Figure 11). Co-ordination issues among ministries and agencies, as well as institutional inflexibility in adapting policies to evolving economic and social conditions, also represent a challenge. Such inefficiencies, together with poorly allocated government spending, can undermine competitiveness.

Thailand is moving towards greater stakeholder engagement for better policy making

Governments need to balance expectations for faster and continuous adaptation with calls for more inclusive policy making, offering information and broader access to stakeholders at earlier stages of decision making (OECD, 2017c). In this regard, Thailand needs to improve stakeholder engagement during policy formulation and the overall coherence of public policies. To help address these issues, Thailand has released Public Consultation Guidelines designed to help government officials carry out public consultations with relevant stakeholders. These take into consideration the OECD *Guiding Principles for Public Consultation* (NESDB, 2016b). Ensuring the guidelines are actively followed across ministries and agencies will be key to progress in this area.

Figure 11. **Thailand's capacity to implement reforms lags behind most comparator countries**

Reform capacity and long-term strategy score (0-4), 2016

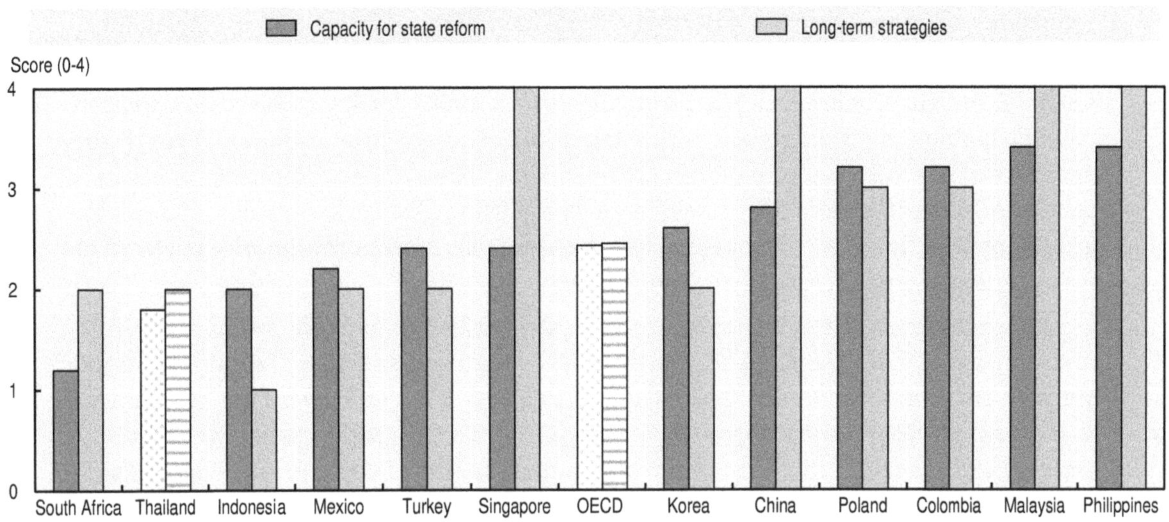

Notes: Capacity for State reform measures the "authorities' ability to decide and actually implement reforms" (scores range from 0 for very low capacity to 4 for strong capacity). Long-term strategies indicate whether "the public authorities have a long-term strategic vision" (scores range from 0 for very weak strategic vision to 4 for strong strategic vision).

Source: CEPII (2016), Institutional Profiles Database.

StatLink http://dx.doi.org/10.1787/888933691401

Improving evaluations of policy implementation will lead to better resource allocation

The 12th Plan stresses the importance of monitoring and evaluation of policy programmes to ensure efficient implementation and consistency with socio-economic development goals. In particular, it strengthens the evaluation framework for key performance indicators (KPIs), which often include indicators developed for international benchmarking (Table 2). With respect to cross-sectional issues across government, joint KPIs are set to evaluate the country's overall development efforts. Policy evaluations based on KPIs are also carried out at the local government level.

Table 2. **Selected KPIs for the Ministry of Digital Economy and Society, FY 2017**

Strategy/Goal	KPIs
Public access to government information and services through a secure broadband network	Improvement in technological infrastructure as assessed by the IMD World Competitiveness Index Percentage of villages with high-speed internet service
Increased economic value of digital technology in business	Additional digital business operators and an increase in e-commerce sales by SMEs and community enterprises
Government services are easy to use, linked and disclosed to all sectors	Improved ranking in the Global Open Data Index by the Open Knowledge Network Accuracy of public information necessary to the public
Public and private individuals receive meteorological information and disaster alerts quickly and easily	Confidence level of people alerted about weather conditions Increase in the number of stakeholders who receive disaster warnings

Source: Office of the Public Sector Development Commission.

Enhancing competition policy and promoting regulatory reform will foster more efficient markets

With the adoption of the 1999 Trade Competition Act, Thailand became one of the first ASEAN countries to introduce competition policy. The Act covers both anti-competitive practices (agreements, abuse of dominant position and mergers) and some forms of restrictive/unfair trade and commercial practices. However, despite nearly a hundred complaints submitted since its enactment, there have been no findings of infringement.

A revised Trade Competition Act was adopted in 2017, against the backdrop of the ASEAN Economic Community Blueprint 2015, which called for harmonised competition policies. It strengthens alignment with international best practice, including through the introduction of a prior approval merger control regime. It also covers commercial operations of state-owned enterprises to ensure a more level playing field between public and private firms. Moreover, some anti-competitive practices are now subject to administrative rather than criminal penalties, simplifying enforcement.

Efforts have also been deployed to reform the Trade Competition Commission (TCC) to a more independent legal institution, with its own budget and staff separated from the Ministry of Commerce. For the new legal framework to work effectively, the government should endow the TCC with adequate financial and human resources together with sufficient autonomy to use them. This will require substantial training of all staff, including decision makers and case handlers.

Improving regulatory impact analysis will promote good regulatory practice

More generally, good regulatory practice helps effective resource allocation, promotes fair and robust competition and minimises the compliance burden on business. The Recommendation of the OECD Council on Regulatory Policy and Governance recognises that a good regulatory management system requires a whole-of-government approach underpinning how it develops, implements and evaluates regulation (OECD, 2012). Thailand's quality of regulation has not improved significantly over the past decade, in contrast with some of the other regional comparators such as Malaysia.

The government launched a "Regulatory Guillotine" project in 2017 to streamline unnecessary regulations that hinder socio-economic development. The first phase aims to improve Thailand's ranking in the World Bank's Ease of Doing Business Index, with aim of becoming one of the top 20 countries by 2019. The focus here is on access to credit, trading across borders and the insolvency regime. The second phase, from late 2017 onwards, involves a further extensive review of existing regulations and licensing, with a view to creating a more business-friendly environment.

Despite efforts, corruption holds back development

Thailand has long recognised the need to address corruption, which undermines trust and efficiency. Anti-corruption laws have increased and broadened over time, improving the independence and effectiveness of the National Anti-Corruption Commission (NACC). Over the years, several other agencies have been set up that complement and support the efforts of the NACC, including the Constitutional Court, the Administrative Court, the Office of the Auditor-General and the Public Sector Anti-Corruption Commission (PACC). Even so, the perception of corruption remains higher than in the average of OECD and ASEAN countries, and over 40% of surveyed citizens report having to pay bribes, offer a gift or perform a favour for somebody when accessing public services.

To intensify anti-corruption efforts, the third phase of Thailand's National Anti-Corruption Strategy (2017-2021) includes bold strategies to fight corruption and to mitigate corruption risks. In this context, the Thai Government asked the OECD to undertake an Integrity Review of Thailand (OECD, 2018), to provide in-depth analysis with reference to the recently-adopted OECD Recommendation on Public Integrity. The Review shows that Thailand could consider streamlining the anti-corruption mandates of various institutions, particularly the NACC and the PACC, in order to enhance the coherence of integrity and anti-corruption policies. Thailand could also benefit from further elaborating civil servants' ethical obligations and ethics training. Setting high ethical standards would help restore trust in the public sector and the proper use of public funds. In order to strengthen accountability and manage possible conflicts of interest of public officials, the scope of asset disclosure could be expanded to include senior public officials and other at-risk officials, while also strengthening the online auditing capacity of the NACC. In addition, Thailand could develop a dedicated whistle-blower protection law to clearly define the scope of whistleblowing, wrongdoings and retaliation, and offer protection to whistle-blowers. This would foster an open public organisational culture where integrity concerns can be discussed, leading to effective detection of ethical violations.

Key constraints on development and necessary transitions for Thailand

In summary, the multidimensional analysis in this report identifies numerous constraints on development that span the economy, society, government and the environment in Thailand (Figure 12).

Figure 12. **Key constraints on sustainable development**

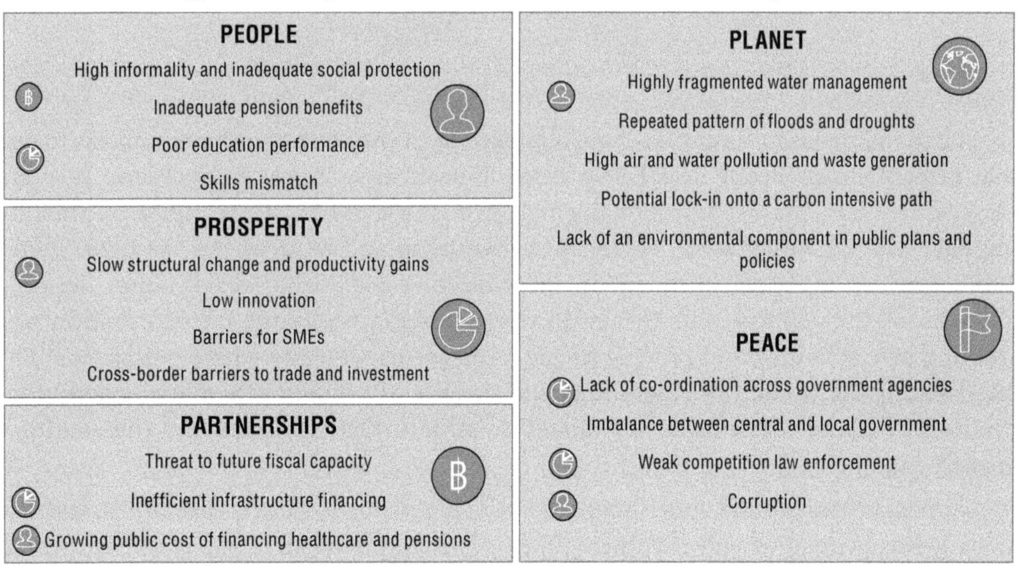

Mapping these constraints across all areas points to four cross-cutting development challenges (Figure 13): high structural inequalities, resource-intensive growth with costly natural disasters, a fragmented social protection system in the context of informality and an ageing population, and fragmented management and delivery of public services.

Figure 13. **Thailand faces four transversal development challenges**

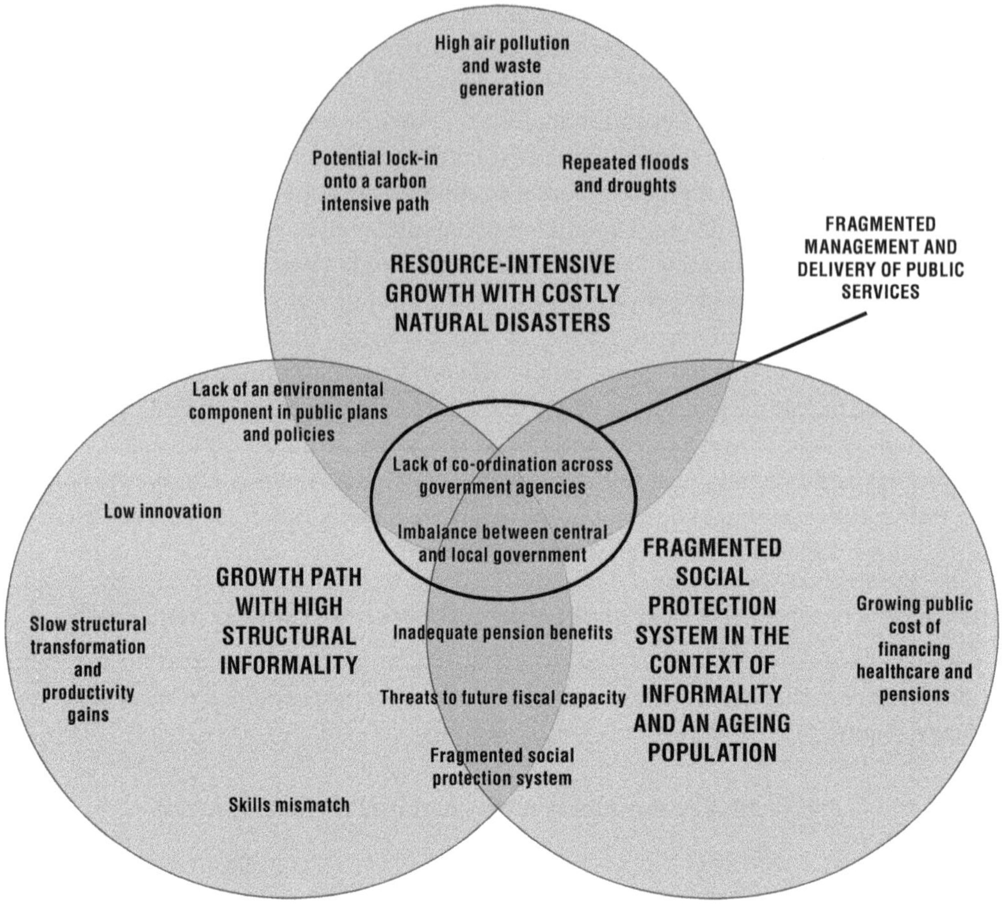

Thailand needs to transition from a growth path with structural inequalities to one that provides quality jobs for all. The share of basic agricultural and precarious urban employment remains disproportionally high given the level of GDP per capita. Informality impedes productivity growth, entrenches inequality and reduces the tax base. Better public services, especially in education, infrastructure and business facilitation, reaching all parts of the country, will be key to reinvigorating economic transformation and creating new activities that provide income and security for the whole population. The forthcoming OECD Country Programme will include a number of thematic reviews that can help Thailand tackle obstacles related to structural inequalities and the country's growth path.

A more accessible and better financed social protection system is essential in the face of an ageing population and continuing high informality. Thailand's age profile is more in line with high-income countries such as Korea and Singapore than regional comparators like Malaysia or Viet Nam. Accordingly, the country has struggled to ensure universal social protection coverage, notwithstanding successes in healthcare. A rapidly ageing population makes it harder to strengthen social protection while maintaining long-term fiscal sustainability. Thailand will need to widen social protection and implement skills upgrading to enable productivity growth to compensate for declining labour input.

Thailand needs to transition from resource-intensive growth against a backdrop of costly natural disasters to more sustainable development with better-managed natural resources, enhanced disaster risk management and reduced pollution. Rapid urbanisation, industrialisation and intensive agriculture have put pressure on water resources and water quality. The government therefore needs to strengthen water resources management and limit the negative effects of natural disasters. Attention also needs to be paid to improving air quality and reducing waste generation.

Finally, the organisation of government and public service delivery lie at the intersection of the previous three development challenges. Levels of government in Thailand need to overcome co-ordination issues and integrate more effectively. Under the current system, the complex organisation and uneven distribution of power and resources across central government bodies and local administrations contribute to co-ordination problems and poor institutional capacity. Political participation and accountability should therefore be coupled with reforms that aim to fiscally empower local municipalities, such as building local capacity to raise revenue and determine expenditure, and guaranteeing transparent and fair access to intergovernmental grants.

References

Asia Productivity Organization (2017), "Productivity database 2017 Version 1" (database), *www.apo-tokyo.org/wedo/measurement*.

Boarini, R., A. Kolev and A. McGregor (2014), "Measuring well-being and progress in countries at different stages of development: Towards a more universal conceptual framework", *OECD Development Centre Working Papers*, No. 325, OECD Publishing, Paris, *http://dx.doi.org/10.1787/5jxss4hv2d8n-en*.

CEPII (2016), *Institutional Profiles Database 2016*, Centre d'Études Prospectives et d'Informations Internationales, AFD and Directorate General of the Treasury (DG Trésor) of the Ministry of Finance, Paris, *www.cepii.fr/institutions/en/ipd.asp*.

Charoenrat, T. and C. Harvie (2017), "Thailand's SME participation in ASEAN and East Asian regional economic integration", *Journal of Southeast Asian Economies*, Vol. 34/1, pp. 148-174, *http://dx.doi.org/10.1355/ae34-1f*.

Conference Board (2017), "Total Economy Database" (database), May 2017, *www.conference-board.org/data/economydatabase*.

Estospace, E. (5 September 2016), "Thailand's Public Health Ministry beefs up eHealth strategy", *Enterprise Innovation*, *www.enterpriseinnovation.net/article/thailands-public-health-ministry-beefs-ehealth-strategy-1541740486*.

Gallup (2017), "Gallup World Poll", *www.gallup.com/services/170945/world-poll.aspx*.

Lee, C., D. Narjoko and S. Oum (2017), "Southeast Asian SMEs and regional economic integration", *Journal of Southeast Asian Economies*, Vol. 34/1, pp. 148-174.

MOE (2017), *Education Development Plan 2017-2021* (in Thai), Ministry of Education, Bangkok, *http://waa.inter.nstda.or.th/stks/pub/2017/20170313-Education-Development-Plan-12.pdf*.

NESDB (2017), *Thailand Human Achievement Index 2017*, Office of the National Economic and Social Development Board, Bangkok, *www.nesdb.go.th/nesdb_en/download/article/social2-2560-eng.pdf*.

NESDB (2016a), *The Twelfth National Economic and Social Development Plan* Office of the National Economic and Social Development Board, the Office of the Prime Minister, Bangkok, *www.nesdb.go.th/nesdb_en/download/article/Social%20Press_Eng_Q4-2559.pdf*.

NESDB (2016b), *Public Consultation Guidelines*, Office of National Economic and Social Development Board, Bangkok, *www.nesdb.go.th/download/RIA/publicConsultationEN.pdf*.

NSO (2016), *The Skills Development Survey*, National Statistical Office of Thailand, Bangkok, *http://web.nso.go.th/en/survey/desire/data/Full_Report2016.pdf*.

OECD (2018), *OECD Integrity Review of Thailand: Towards Coherent and Effective Integrity Policies*, OECD Publishing, Paris, *http://dx.doi.org/10.1787/9789264291928-en*.

OECD (2017a), *Opportunities and Policy Challenges of Digitalisation in Southeast Asia*, OECD Publishing, Paris, *www.oecd.org/southeast-asia/events/regional/forum/Forum_Note_Digital_Transformation_STI.pdf.*

OECD (2017b), *Services Trade Policies and the Global Economy*, OECD Publishing, Paris, *http://dx.doi.org/10.1787/9789264275232-en.*

OECD (2017c), *OECD Guidelines on Measuring Trust*, OECD Publishing, Paris, *http://dx.doi.org/10.1787/9789264278219-en.*

OECD (2017d), "National Accounts" (database), *http://dx.doi.org/10.1787/na-data-en.*

OECD (2017e), "Revenue Statistics" (database), *http://dx.doi.org/10.1787/19963726.*

OECD (2017f), "FDI Regulatory Restrictiveness Index" (database), *www.oecd.org/investment/fdiindex.htm.*

OECD (2017g), "Measuring Distance to the SDGs Targets. An assessment of where OECD countries stand", *http://www.oecd.org/sdd/OECD-Measuring-Distance-to-SDG-Targets.pdf.*

OECD (2016), *Trafficking in Persons and Corruption: Breaking the Chain*, OECD Publishing, Paris. *http://dx.doi.org/10.1787/9789264253728-en.*

OECD (2015), "PISA Database" (database), *www.oecd.org/pisa/data/2015database.*

OECD (2014), *Southeast Asian Economic Outlook 2013 – with Perspectives on China and India*, OECD Publishing, Paris, *http://dx.doi.org/10.1787/saeo-2013-en.*

OECD (2013), *Design and Delivery of Defined Contribution (DC) Pension Schemes. Policy challenges and recommendations*, Cass Business School, London, *www.oecd.org/daf/fin/private-pensions/DCPensionDesignHighlights.pdf.*

OECD (2012), *The Recommendation of the OECD Council on Regulatory Policy and Governance*, OECD Publishing, Paris, *www.oecd.org/governance/regulatory-policy/49990817.pdf.*

OECD (2011), *How's Life? Measuring Well-being*, OECD Publishing, Paris, *http://dx.doi.org/10.1787/9789264121164-en.*

OECD and UNESCO (2016), *Education in Thailand: An OECD-UNESCO Perspective*, Review of National Policies for Education, OECD Publishing, Paris, *http://dx.doi.org/10.1787/9789264259119-en.*

Transparency International (2016), *2016 Corruption Perceptions Index*, Transparency International, Berlin, *www.transparency.org/cpi2016.*

Vimolsiri, P. (2017), "Thailand 20 Year National Strategic Plan and reforms", Presentation at the Thailand Focus 2017 Conference, Stock Exchange of Thailand, Bangkok, *www.set.or.th/thailandfocus/files/20170829_Dr_Porametee.pdf.*

World Bank (2017a), "World Development Indicators" (database), Washington, DC, *https://data.worldbank.org/data-catalog/world-development-indicators.*

World Bank (2017b), "Deforestation and biodiversity", *World Development Indicators*, *http://wdi.worldbank.org/table/3.4#.*

World Economic Forum (2016), "Network Readiness Index" (database), *http://reports.weforum.org/network-readiness-index.*

Multi-dimensional Review of Thailand
Volume 1. Initial Assessment

Chapter 1

People: Towards better lives for all

The People pillar of the 2030 Agenda for Sustainable Development focuses on quality of life in all its dimensions, and emphasises the international community's commitment to ensuring all human beings can fulfil their potential in dignity, equality and good health.

Thailand's path from a low-income to an upper-middle-income country over recent decades is widely hailed as a development success story. Poverty has fallen impressively and inequality is on a downwards trend, but more efforts are needed to reduce still widespread informality and persistent, substantial regional inequalities, and to further improve living standards, especially for those who currently work informally. To achieve these objectives, the government needs to: (i) consider tax and regulatory measures to encourage formalisation; (ii) boost the participation rates of informal workers in social protection schemes; (iii) expand adequate social safety nets for poor households and the elderly; (iv) prepare the healthcare system for an ageing and modernising society; and (v) improve the education system, particularly in rural areas. Gaps also remain in ensuring women's political participation and reducing gender-based violence.

Societal progress is about improvements in well-being beyond the functioning of the economic system, encompassing people's diverse experiences and living conditions. Over recent decades, Thailand's "development miracle" has translated into many well-being improvements for its citizens: poverty and inequality have shrunk dramatically, universal healthcare has been established and a range of Millennium Development Goals – the predecessors of the SDGs – were met ahead of time, including universal primary education, reducing malnutrition and guaranteeing access to clean drinking water and sanitation. Further progress on the People pillar of the SDGs requires policy action to reduce the remaining inequalities between regions, and to continue to improve current and future well-being for all citizens, especially for the country's large informal workforce.

This chapter reviews the evolution of living standards and inequalities in Thailand. It also assesses performance in priority areas to promote inclusive growth, namely the labour market, social protection and the education system. It concludes with a discussion of key aspects of gender equality.

Towards more inclusive growth

Poverty and inequality have declined substantially in Thailand over recent decades and remain a priority in the 12th National Economic and Social Development Plan (2017-2021, hereafter, the 12th Plan) (NESDB, 2017b). Sustained economic growth has translated into rising living standards: since 1990, household spending has risen in line with GDP per capita and more than doubled (Figure 1.1A). Over the same period, the share of the population living below the national poverty line plummeted from 60% to 7% (Figure 1.1B). Extreme poverty has been all but eliminated, with fewer than 1% of the population living on less than USD 3.10 per day (World Bank, 2017a). In contrast with a number of other emerging economies, inequality, as measured by the Gini coefficient for household disposable income, is on a downward trend (Figure 1.1C). Although inequality of household disposable income is lower than in comparator countries such as Indonesia, Colombia, China or South Africa, it remains significantly above the OECD average (Figure 1.1D). Meanwhile wealth inequality is stark with the estimated wealth share of the top 10% households close to 79% in 2017, above all comparator countries for which data was available (Credit Suisse, 2017).

Living standards have improved less rapidly than in most comparator countries

Current overall household consumption in Thailand is comparatively low and during the first half of the 2010s, consumption and GDP lagged behind other fast-growing nations in the region (Figure 1.2). When surveyed on their economic situation, only 11% of Thais say they can live comfortably with their current income (Figure 1.3). Furthermore, despite Thailand's impressive track record in poverty reduction, 6.7 million people or close to 10% of the population live at most 20% above the national poverty line, and are thus vulnerable to falling back into poverty. The majority live in rural areas and work in agriculture. Almost a quarter of Thailand's poor are children, and 15% of people aged over 75 live below the national poverty line (United Nations, 2017; World Bank, 2016a).

Figure 1.1. **Household spending has risen, poverty and inequality have fallen**

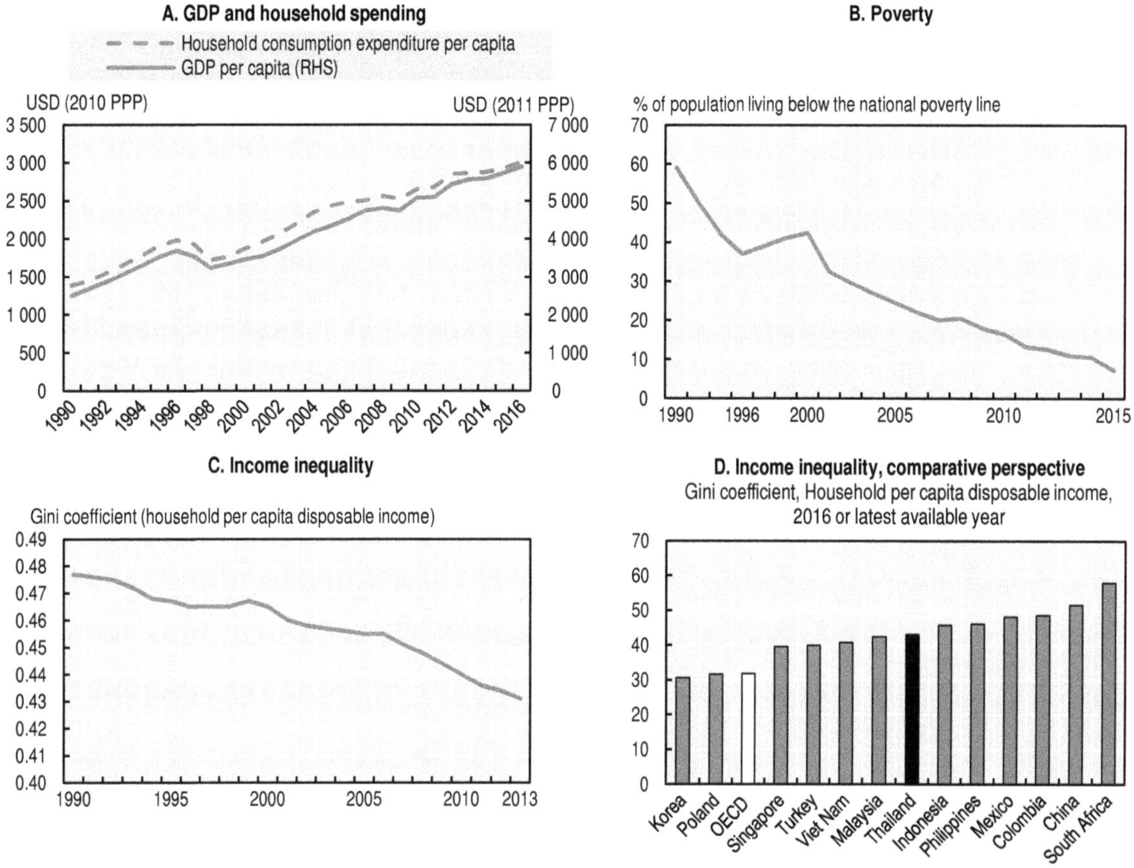

Note: A: Household consumption expenditure per capita is measured in 2010 PPP USD. GDP per capita is measured in 2011 PPP USD. D: Data refers to 2016 for all countries except: China (2014), Indonesia (2015), Malaysia (2014), OECD average (2014), Philippines (2015), Poland (2015), South Africa (2015), Thailand (2013) and Viet Nam (2014).

Source: A and B: World Bank (2017a), *World Development Indicators*, *https://data.worldbank.org/data-catalog/world-development-indicators*; C and D: Solt (2016), "The Standardized World Income Inequality Database", *Social Science Quarterly*, Vol. 97(5), pp. 1267-1281; and OECD (2017a), *Income Distribution Database*, *www.oecd.org/social/income-distribution-database.htm*.

StatLink http://dx.doi.org/10.1787/888933691420

Figure 1.2. **Household consumption in Thailand is lower than in most comparator countries and has grown less in recent years**

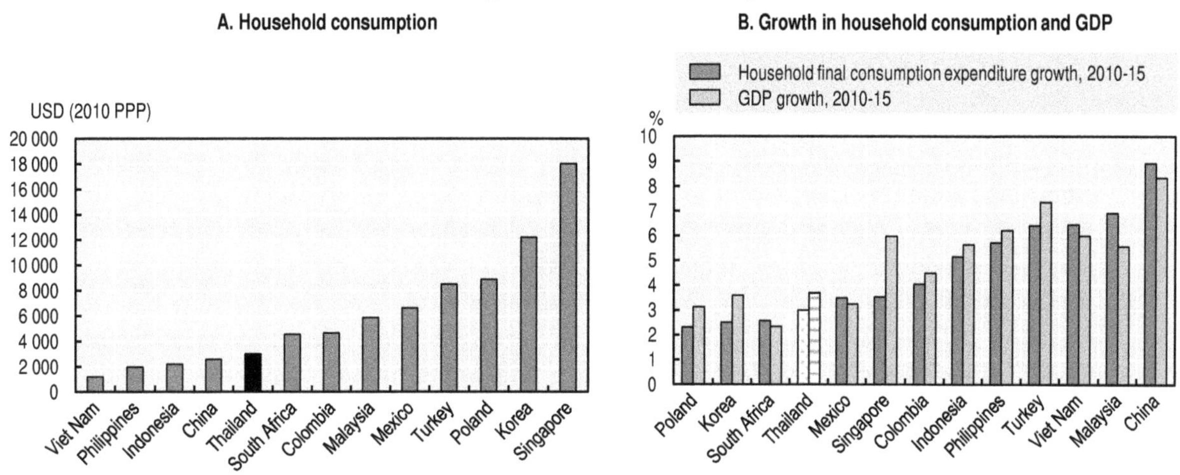

Source: World Bank (2017a), *World Development Indicators*, *https://data.worldbank.org/data-catalog/world-development-indicators*.

StatLink http://dx.doi.org/10.1787/888933691439

Recent and projected increases in economic growth (Chapter 2) will enable Thailand to further reduce poverty and inequality. Prioritising policies that improve job quality and opportunities, social safety nets and educational achievement, especially in disadvantaged regions, will help ensure that growth translates into better well-being outcomes for all citizens.

The North, Northeast and Southern regions are lagging

Income inequality in Thailand has a strong regional dimension, with inhabitants of the North, Northeast and Southern regions lagging behind the more prosperous Bangkok and Central regions. While the gap in GDP per capita between the richest and poorest regions in Thailand has halved over the past two decades, residents in the Bangkok Metropolitan Region (BMR) remain almost six times richer than those in the Northeast (although the gap in living standards may be smaller, insofar as price levels tend to be lower in poorer regions). This gap started to widen again in 2014 as economic growth stalled (Figure 1.4). Poverty rates have also persisted above the national average in the Northeast, the North and the Deep South provinces (World Bank, 2016a).

Figure 1.3. **Thai people are not very satisfied with their current income**

% of respondents living comfortably on their present income, 2016

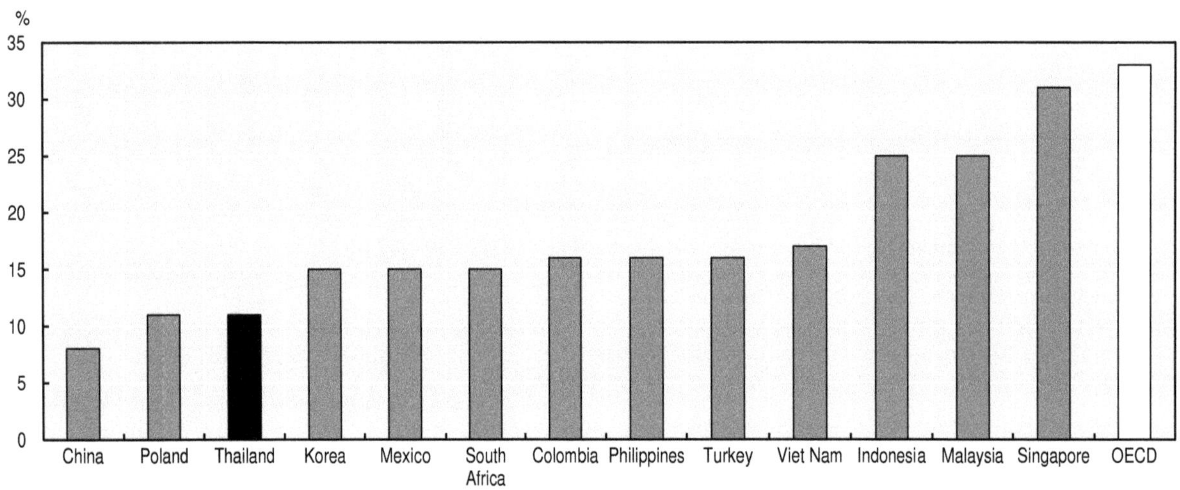

Source: Gallup (2017), *Gallup World Poll*, *www.gallup.com/services/170945/world-poll.aspx*.

StatLink *http://dx.doi.org/10.1787/888933691458*

Regional inequality can also be seen in other dimensions of well-being. According to the 2017 Human Achievement Index, people in the BMR enjoy better employment conditions, educational attainment, health outcomes, and transport and communication infrastructure than in the poorer regions (Figure 1.5). Other regions perform relatively better in terms of housing and living environment, reflecting the higher cost of accommodation and pollution in the megacity. Regional disparity partly reflects differences in access to quality health, education and employment, as well as a Bangkok-centric system of government in terms of both concentration of decision-making power and distribution of budgetary resources (Chapter 3 and 5). Narrowing Thailand's regional gaps, as recognised in the 12th Plan, is likely to improve social cohesion.

Figure 1.4. **Regional inequalities have narrowed but remain pronounced**

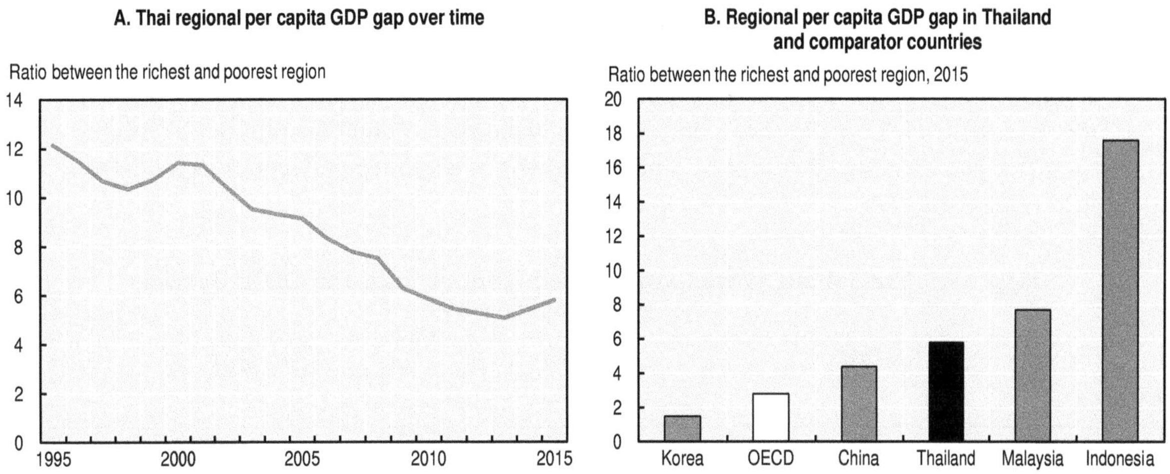

Note: The regional per capita gap refers to the ratio between the richest and poorest region, which are consistently Bangkok and the Northeast region, respectively. The implied regional inequality in living standards may be overstated insofar as price levels tend to be lower in poorer regions. B: Data refers to 2014 for all countries except: Korea (2013), China (2013) and Indonesia (2012).

Source: A: NESDB (2015), *Gross Regional and Provincial Product Chain Volume Measures*, *www.nesdb.go.th/nesdb_th/main.php?filename=gross_regional*; and B: author calculations based on OECD (2013a), *OECD Regional Database*, *http://stats.oecd.org/Index.aspx?DataSetCode=REGION_DEMOGR* and national statistical office data from Indonesia, Malaysia and Thailand.

StatLink http://dx.doi.org/10.1787/888933691477

Figure 1.5. **The Bangkok metropolitan region outperforms others in most dimensions of well-being**

Achievement scores from 0 (worst) to 1 (best), 2017

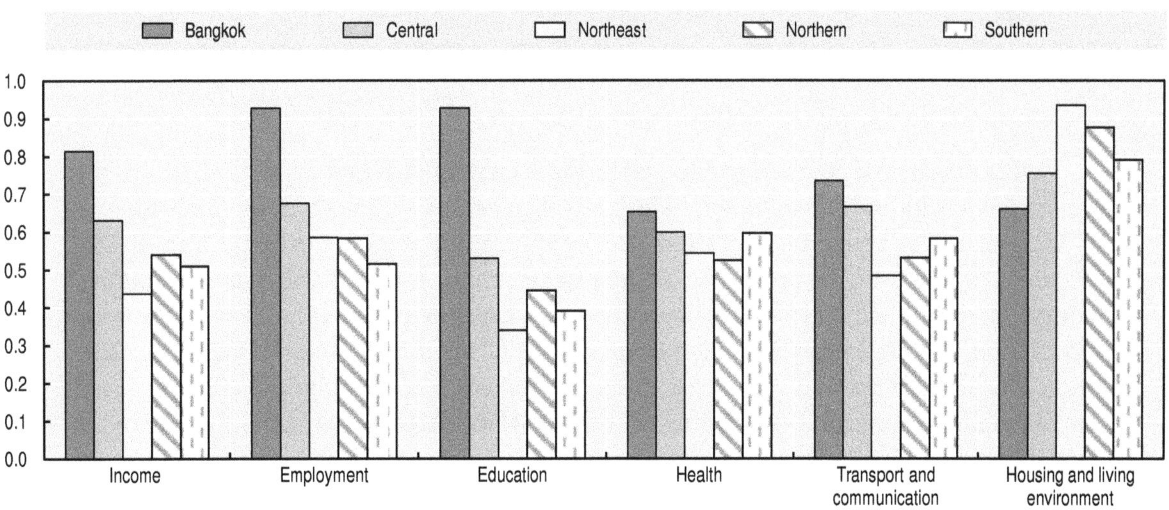

Note: The Human Achievement Index is a composite index that compares regional performance with achievement scores that use the worst and best performance observed in the provinces. These scores are calculated for a range of indicators for relevant sub-indices (e.g. for employees covered by social security, occupational injuries, unemployment and underemployment rates in the case of the employment sub-index). For the purpose of this report, only the scores for the sub-indices of income, employment, education, health, transport and communication, and housing and living conditions are shown, since their underlying indicators come closest to the SDGs. The Central region as shown here excludes the Bangkok Metropolitan Area.

Source: NESDB (2017a), Thailand Human Achievement Index 2017, *www.nesdb.go.th/nesdb_en/download/article/social2-2560-eng.pdf*.

StatLink http://dx.doi.org/10.1787/888933691496

Prioritising quality jobs

Labour market arrangements strongly influence how economic growth improves well-being and reduces poverty. Since 1990, the size of Thailand's labour force has increased from 32 million to almost 39 million people, while unemployment remained low, even in the aftermath of the Asian financial crisis. The labour participation rate is now higher than the OECD average (Figure 1.6). Unemployment is low, but many people work in the informal sector.

Figure 1.6. **The labour participation rate is higher than the OECD average**

Labour participation rate by age, 2016

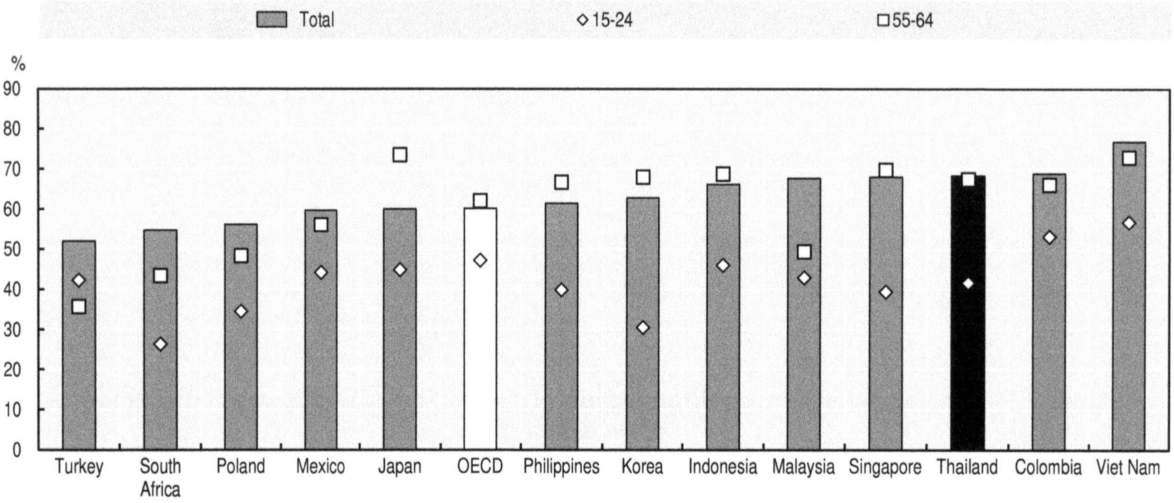

Source: ILO (2017a), *Key Indicators of the Labour Market*, *www.ilo.org/global/statistics-and-databases/research-and-databases/kilm/lang--en/index.htm*; and OECD (2017b), *OECD Labour Force Statistics*, *www.oecd.org/std/labour-stats*.

StatLink http://dx.doi.org/10.1787/888933691515

While measured unemployment rates are exceptionally low at around 1% of the labour force, informal employment – which largely overlaps with precarious employment – is widespread: although its share has declined in recent years, it remains high at 56% (Figure 1.7). Moreover, the prevalence of informal employment is also high in international comparison (Figure 1.8). These workers and their dependents make up 76% of the total population, but are largely excluded from the social security system (ILO, 2017b). Aside from unstable contractual situations, informal workers report being frequently exposed to long hours and hazardous working conditions (NSO, 2016a). Informality in Thailand is not only a rural phenomenon. Next to agriculture and fishing, which together account for 55% of informal employment, one third of informal workers are also working in the service sector (especially wholesale and retail trade, and hotel, restaurant and other community occupations). A large share of migrants from neighbouring ASEAN countries are also employed informally (Box 1.1).

Figure 1.7. **Informality remains high and is concentrated in agriculture and services**

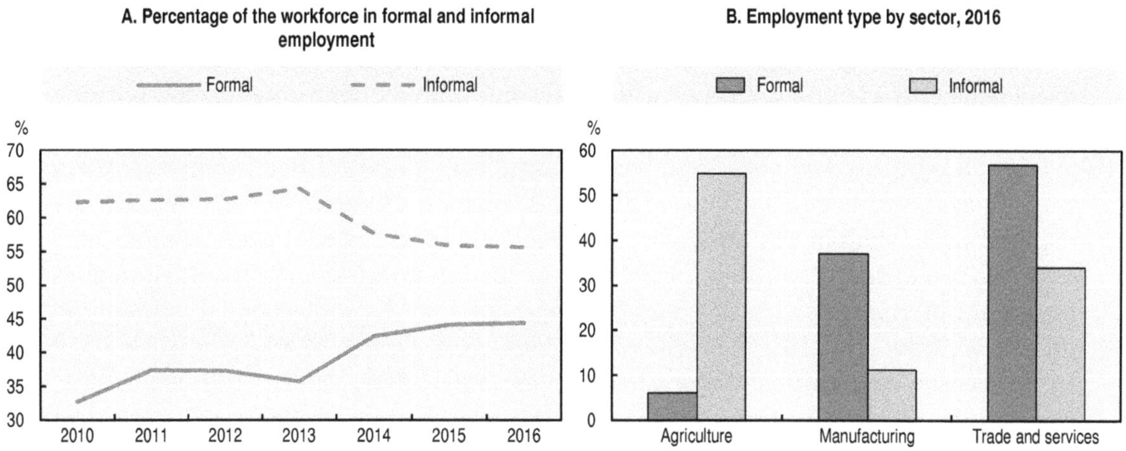

Note: Workers who are not protected by work-related social security schemes are classified as engaging in informal employment.
Source: NSO (2016a), *Informal Employment Survey 2016*, *http://web.nso.go.th/en/survey/lfs/imp/imp09.htm*.
StatLink http://dx.doi.org/10.1787/888933691534

Figure 1.8. **Informality is high by international standards**

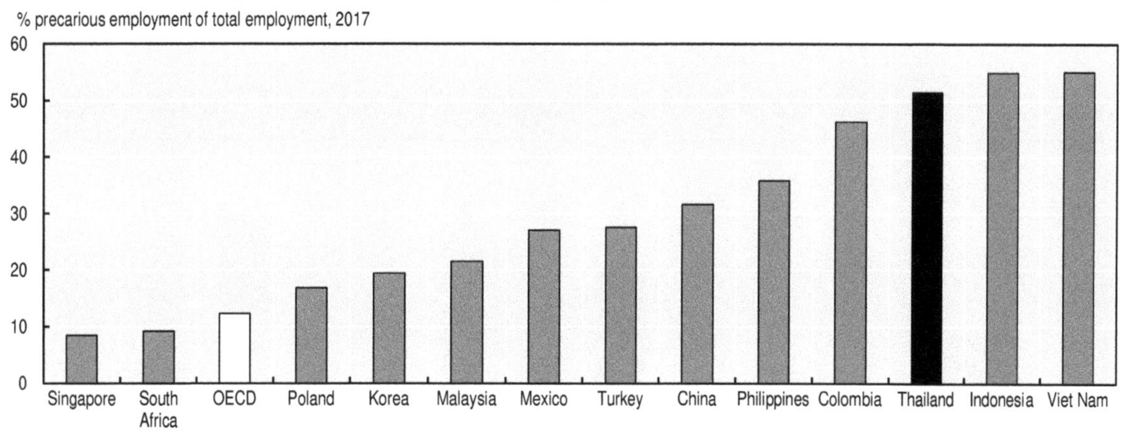

Note: Contributing family workers and own-account workers are classified as engaging in precarious employment.
Source: World Bank (2017a), *World Development Indicators*, *https://data.worldbank.org/data-catalog/world-development-indicators*.
StatLink http://dx.doi.org/10.1787/888933691553

Box 1.1. **Migrant labour in Thailand**

Thailand is a major destination for migrant workers from ASEAN countries, notably Cambodia, Lao PDR and Myanmar. It is estimated that at least 3.5 million migrants were working (mostly informally) in Thailand in 2016, making up 9% of the country's labour force. Many industries, such as agriculture, fishing, construction, domestic service, manufacturing and retail depend on their low-skilled labour. Furthermore, immigrant workers are relatively young and thus represent a fresh labour supply in the face of an ageing native-born population. Importantly, a recent OECD report on the contribution of immigrants to Thailand's economy established that the presence of foreign-born workers has no adverse impact on national native-born employment levels.

About one-third of migrants live below the national poverty line and more than half of Thailand's migrants are undocumented, leaving them vulnerable to human trafficking. Governance of labour migration has so far been ad hoc without an effective enforcement system to regularise migration to Thailand, protect these workers' rights and foster their integration. After a recent executive decree specifying harsh punishments for hiring illegal migrant workers, tens of thousands of undocumented workers, mostly from Myanmar, have reportedly left the country.

Source: ILO (2016a), IOM (2017), OECD (2017c), UNDP (2014) and World Bank (2016a).

Reducing informality requires a package of targeted reforms

Informality has many drivers, including tax and social security (dis)incentives to formalise labour, rigid wage scales, low worker productivity and the overall structure of the economy. In addition, countries with a large informal economy tend to have strict de facto employment regulations (OECD, 2004). Indeed, Thailand's employment protection legislation is stricter than the OECD average; in particular, the protection of permanent workers against individual dismissal and the regulation of temporary employment are more stringent than in OECD member countries and most regional peers except China and Indonesia (Figure 1.9). More flexible labour market policies could thus help reduce the extent of informality. Such policy interventions have helped reduce informality in other countries. For example, Brazil coupled easier registration and lower taxation and social security contributions for small and micro-enterprises via an integrated tax and contribution payment system with improved incentive systems for labour inspectors, so as to enhance enforcement mechanisms (OECD, 2017d). Similarly, Colombia unified its health and pension payments in 2006-07, which encouraged formalisation (Calderón-Mejía and Marinescu, 2012).

Figure 1.9. **Thailand's employment protection policies are comparatively strict**

Scale from 0 (least restrictive) to 6 (most restrictive), 2014

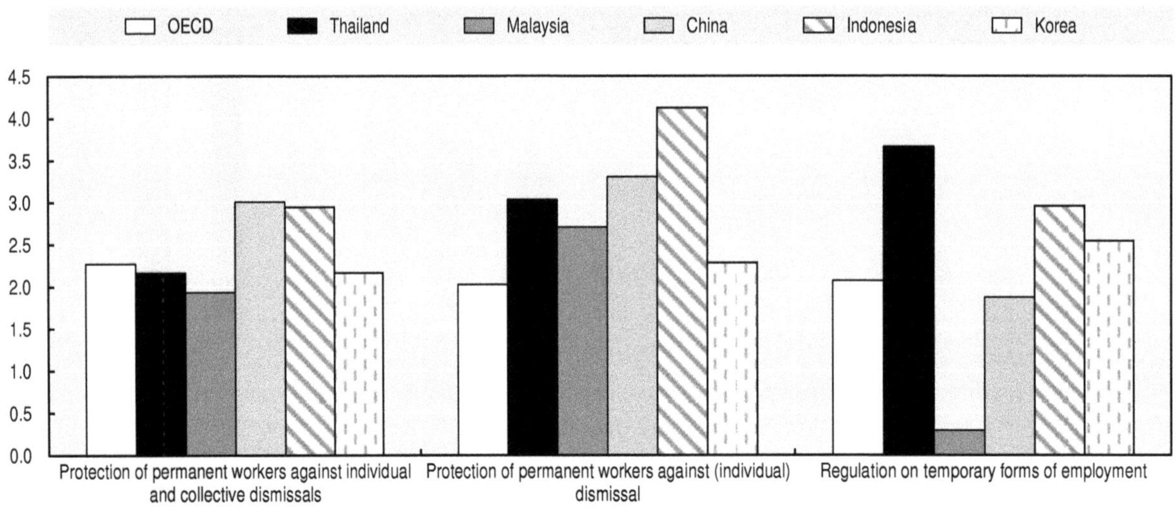

Note: Data for Thailand refer to 2014, China to 2012, and all other countries to 2013. OECD indicators of employment protection legislation measure the procedures and costs involved in dismissing individuals or groups of workers and the procedures involved in hiring workers on fixed-term or temporary work agency contracts.

Source: OECD (2017e), *Indicators of Employment Protection Legislation, www.oecd.org/els/emp/oecdindicatorsofemploymentprotection.htm.*

StatLink http://dx.doi.org/10.1787/888933691572

Minimum wage legislation only partially protects workers

After the introduction of regional minimum wages in the mid-1970s, Thailand moved to a national rate of THB 300 per day in 2013, aligning the minimum wage level in rural regions with the Bangkok area. This resulted in larger minimum wage hikes in rural regions. The government tried to mitigate the associated impacts via tax concessions and policy loans, in particular for SMEs (OSMEP, 2013). Different minimum wages for individual provinces were eventually reintroduced in January 2017 and revised as from April 2018, but the narrow range – THB 308 to THB 330 only partially reflects differences in living costs. OECD experience suggests that minimum wages should take into account regional differences in economic conditions. It also shows that adjustments in the minimum wage level should follow a regular schedule and be duly informed by objective assessments of potential impacts on the low-skilled and on living conditions (OECD, 2015a). At 63% of the average wage of manual workers in the manufacturing sector, the current minimum wage is lower than that in regional peer countries such as Indonesia, the Philippines or Malaysia (JETRO, 2017).

In practice, however, non-compliance with the minimum wage is substantial in Thailand and, more generally, the enforcement of labour protection measures needs to be improved. One third of private sector workers and over half of young and low-skilled workers received wages below the minimum rate in 2013 (Lathapipat and Poggi, 2016). An education and professional qualification system that inadequately prepares workers for the labour market (described below) as well as low productivity levels (Chapter 2) are likely to be contributing factors to low wages. Meanwhile, there is room to improve other forms of labour protection, which are less developed than in OECD countries. For instance, unemployment insurance (with a replacement rate for involuntary unemployment of 50% for six months) is only available to employees in the formal sector. Unionisation rates are low, at 3.6% of total employment in 2010, not only relative to the OECD average of 16.7% in 2014, but also compared to regional peers such as Malaysia (8% in 2013) and Indonesia (8.5% in 2009) (ILO, 2015; OECD, 2016a).

Further improving social protection

A comprehensive social protection system covers the entire life cycle ranging from child and maternity benefits, support for workers through unemployment and work injury insurance, all the way to pensions for the elderly. It also includes access to healthcare and disability benefits. The main challenges for Thailand's social protection system in the years to come will be to further extend coverage to the large informal sector, expand the social safety net for people at the bottom of the income distribution, and adapt the pension and healthcare systems to take into account population ageing and changing disease profiles.

Informal workers and the most vulnerable need better coverage

The evolution of Thailand's social security schemes has resulted in a relatively comprehensive but fragmented system. Recent initiatives for informal sector workers were not integrated into existing programmes for formal workers and civil servants, but established separately (Box 1.2). The co-existence of multiple schemes, many of them administrated by different government agencies, contributes to inefficiencies and administrative burdens, and benefits are not always portable across schemes.

Simplification of schemes would improve coverage for the most vulnerable. Lack of information and confusing regulations make it harder for the rural poor and commonly stigmatised groups, such as people living with a disability or HIV/AIDS, to access available support. Geographical distance to registration centres and cultural reluctance to deal with government officials are additional complicating factors (ADB, 2012). A key consideration going forward, as mentioned in the 12th Plan, is to establish how to best design easy access and well-targeted publicity for vulnerable beneficiaries. Easier registration procedures would help in this regard, including flexibility on the required documents, the opportunity to register and claim in different localities, and the development of an online registration system.

Box 1.2. The evolution of Thailand's social security system

Thailand's social protection schemes have grown and evolved over time, resulting in a relatively comprehensive but fragmented system with many very different schemes. Some are based on social insurance contributions, some are tax-financed and some are partially subsidised voluntary social insurance schemes. Benefit eligibility is largely tied to employment status, with different programmes for civil servants, people with formal jobs and the large share of informal sector workers (Table 1.1).

Table 1.1. Overview of social security schemes by eligibility group

Type	Benefit	Institution	Agency	Participation	Created in	Financed by
			Government officials			
Old age	Old-age pension or lump sum	Government officials' pension system	Controller General Department, Ministry of Finance	Compulsory	1951	Tax revenues
Old age	Old-age lump sum	Government Pension Fund	Government Pension Fund Board of Directors	Compulsory for officials who joined government after 1997, voluntary for others	1997	Contributions by workers and the government
Health	Medical care	Civil Servants' Medical Benefit Scheme	Controller General Department, Ministry of Finance	Compulsory	2010	Tax revenues
			Formal sector workers			
Working age	Work injury and work-related sickness	Workmen's Compensation Fund	Social Security Office, Ministry of Labour	Compulsory	1994	Contributions by employers
Working age and old age	Non-occupational injury or sickness benefits, maternity, invalidity, death, unemployment, old-age, child support grant	Social Security Fund (SSF) (Social Security Act Section 33)	Social Security Office, Ministry of Labour	Compulsory	1990	Contributions by employers, workers and the government
Working age and old age	Non-occupational injury or sickness benefits, maternity, invalidity, death, old-age, child support grant	Social Security Fund (SSF) (Social Security Act Section 39)	Social Security Office, Ministry of Labour	Voluntary for those previously insured under Social Security Act Section 33)	1990	Contributions by workers and the government
Old age	Lump sum upon retirement or termination of employment	Provident funds	Securities and Exchange Commission	Voluntary	1987	Contributions by employers and workers
			Informal sector workers			
Working age and old age	Package 1: Sickness, invalidity and death Package 2: Package 1 + old age lump sum	Social Security Fund (SSF) (Social Security Act Section 40)	Social Security Office, Ministry of Labour	Voluntary	1990	Contributions by workers, since 2010 by the government
Health	Medical care	Universal Coverage Scheme (UCS)	National Health Security Office, Ministry of Public Health	Universal	2002	Tax revenues
Working age	Disability allowance	Universal Non-contributory Allowance for People with Disabilities	Local administration under the umbrella of the Ministry of Interior	Universal	2010	Tax revenues
Working age	HIV/AIDS allowance	Universal Non-contributory Allowance for People with HIV/AIDS	Local administration under the umbrella of the Ministry of Interior	Universal	2003	Tax revenues
Old age	Old-age allowance	Universal Non-contributory Allowance for Older People	Local administration under the umbrella of the Ministry of Interior	Universal	2009	Tax revenues
Old age	Old-age pension or lump sum	National Savings Fund	Fiscal Policy Office, Ministry of Finance	Voluntary for those without old-age pension	2015	Contributions by workers and the government
			People living in poverty			
Maternity	Child allowance	Child Support Grant for poor families with newborn children	Office of Social Development and Human Security	Universal	2015	Tax revenues
Working age	Living and transport allowance	Welfare Card for low-income earners	Fiscal Policy Office, Ministry of Finance	Universal	2017	Tax revenues

Box 1.2. **The evolution of Thailand's social security system** *(cont.)*

Since 2002, informal workers have gradually been able to access the social security system: the Universal Coverage Scheme (UCS) represented a landmark move towards universal basic healthcare. In 2009, Thailand established a universal monthly old-age allowance for the elderly. In 2010, the government also extended the social security system to informal and self-employed workers by offering a partial subsidy to people who voluntarily sign up for the Social Security Fund (SSF), which covers sickness, invalidity, death and a lump-sum old-age pension. A matching-based National Savings Fund that can be accessed by informal workers on a voluntary basis was also established in 2015.

Note: Table 1.1. does not include SEP model villages, educational loans, school meal and material subsidy programmes, housing projects for the homeless, community social assistance centres or social protection schemes for migrants. Legal rights to participation do not imply actual beneficiary coverage since registration is required for many schemes.

Source: Compilation based on EIU (2015a); Schmitt, Sakunphanit and Prasitsiriphon (2013); United Nations (2017); UNICEF (2016) and World Bank (2012).

The recent addition of means-tested benefits that specifically target poor households is an encouraging step towards reducing inequality. In Thailand, as well as other countries in the region, social security systems that are either tied to formal employment and/or dominated by large universal schemes have disproportionately benefited the non-poor (Figure 1.10). Similarly, the redistribution effect of social protection programmes in Thailand is weak compared to the OECD average: the difference in the Gini coefficient of household disposable income pre- and post- social transfers is 0.9 percentage points in the former and 15.2 in the latter (Solt, 2016). In view of this, the government launched a child support grant for poor families with newborn children in 2015. More recently, a digital welfare card with a living allowance, access to consumer goods at designated shops and a transport stipend for low-income earners was introduced. Up to 12 million Thai citizens who earn below THB 100 000 (USD 3 000) a year could potentially qualify for this flagship project under the 12th Plan. The welfare card could exemplify the successful digitalisation of public service delivery, if reported technical glitches with card-reading machines can be resolved after the roll-out phase.

Pension system coverage needs to improve, notably for informal sector workers

Elderly people are currently not well prepared to cope financially with old age, with only a small proportion of workers having access to compulsory pension programmes. While pension replacement rates for formal-sector workers under the Social Security Fund (SSF Sections 33 and 39) are relatively high, at close to 50% (Figure 1.11), only a third of the overall active labour force is covered by these schemes. Already today, old-age poverty rates are higher than the national average, with 13% of people aged 60 to 74 and 14.6% of people over 75 living below the national poverty line (World Bank, 2016a). Moreover, 42% of Thais are unable to maintain their living standards after retirement and a third have no savings (EIU, 2015a).

Informal workers have recently been encouraged to prepare for retirement via voluntary pension and savings schemes, but more efforts to boost participation and contribution rates are needed. Under SSF Section 40, informal workers can opt into a pension programme. However, overall sign-up rates are low at only 10.4% in 2016 (SSO, 2017). Although participation increased following the 2010 introduction of a partial government subsidy of THB 50 per month, in addition to the worker's THB 100 contribution, only 54% of active members pay regular contributions (Schmitt et al., 2013). International experience with applications of behavioural insights may help to devise solutions (Box 1.3).

Figure 1.10. **Social protection schemes disproportionately benefit the non-poor**

Social Protection Index, 2013

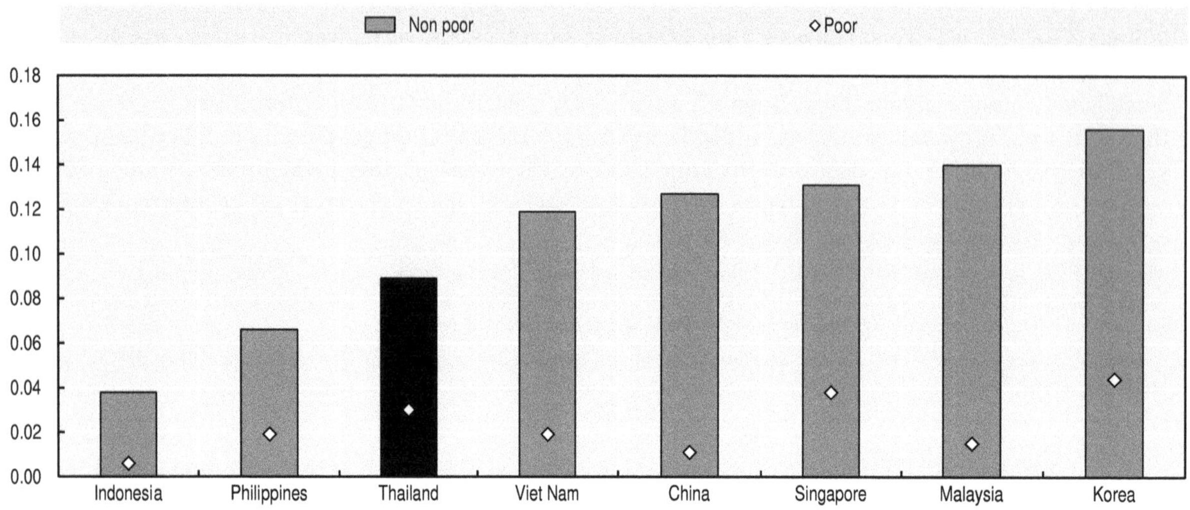

Note: The Social Protection Index (SPI) equals total expenditures on social protection divided by the total number of intended beneficiaries of all social protection programmes, normalised by poverty-line expenditures (which for cross-country comparability purposes are set uniformly at 25% of GDP per capita). An SPI of 0.10 would thus be equivalent to 2.5% of GDP per capita. A higher SPI denotes better social protection.

Source: ADB (2013), The Social Protection Index Assessing Results for Asia and the Pacific, Mandaluyong.

StatLink http://dx.doi.org/10.1787/888933691591

Figure 1.11. **Pension replacement rates in Thailand are close to 50% in the formal sector**

Pension net replacement rates for mean formal-sector earners, 2013

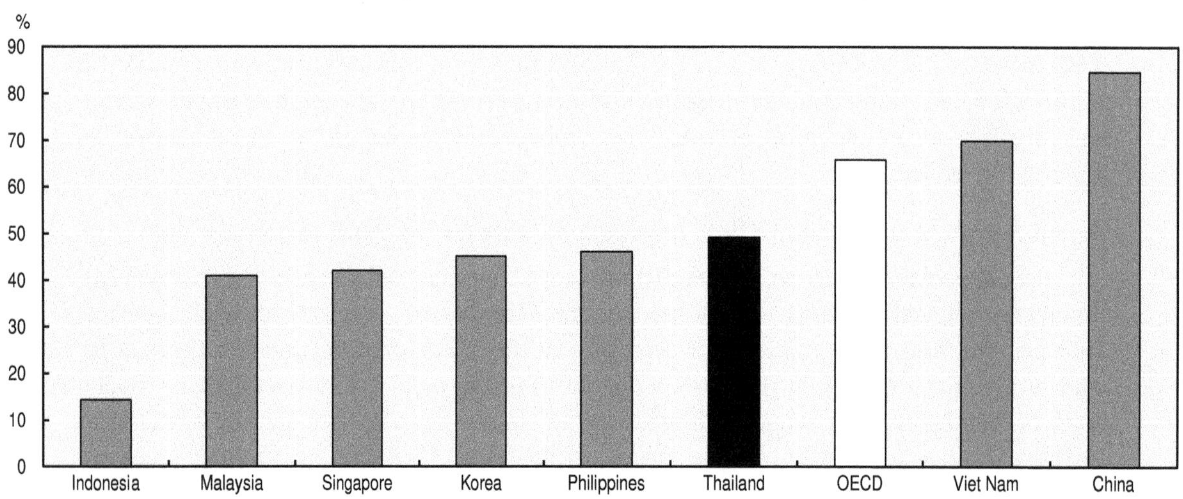

Source: OECD (2013b), *Pensions at a Glance Asia/Pacific, www.oecd-ilibrary.org/finance-and-investment/pensions-at-a-glance-asia-pacific-2013/net-replacement-rates_pension_asia-2013-6-en.*

StatLink http://dx.doi.org/10.1787/888933691610

A National Savings Fund was established in 2015 to increase retirement savings and supplement the inadequate provision of long-term old age protection under the SSF (Knodel et al., 2015). Since the SSF and the National Savings Fund are managed by different ministries, which each separately market their own programme, it is essential that information on the terms and conditions of both schemes be readily accessible and legible to ensure informal workers can make well-informed decisions.

Box 1.3. **Using behavioural insights to increase retirement savings**

Evidence from the emerging and increasingly popular field of behavioural science has been used by policy makers around the world to design better programmes and improve implementation, providing useful lessons on how to boost participation and contribution rates for pension and savings schemes. Behavioural science draws on insights from psychology, cognitive and neuroscience, and design thinking, as well as organisational and group behaviour to better understand human behaviour. While traditional models of human decision-making suggest that people seamlessly consider all their options and choose to do what is best for them, they often fail to predict what actually happens with complex decisions such as those around retirement savings.

Several successful examples demonstrate how taking into account cognitive biases in policy design can aid the adaptation of schemes at low cost, providing that these applications are appropriately tested and adapted to the specific country and policy context:

- In Kenya, informal worker contributions to a voluntary savings scheme doubled after participants were given a gold-coloured coin inscribed with numbers to help them track their weekly deposits. The tangibility of the coin helped to remind people to save and produced better results than a financial matching scheme.
- In the United Kingdom, the government successfully boosted employee pension savings rates by switching the default option from one in which employees had to actively choose to sign up for a pension scheme (opt in) to one in which they are automatically enrolled into workplace pension schemes but can choose to opt out if they so desire (opt out). This change resulted in a considerable reduction in opt-out rates.
- In the Philippines, Peru and Bolivia, targeted text message reminders helped poor bank clients who had recently signed up for commitment savings accounts to reach their savings targets. Messages that mentioned both savings goals and financial incentives were particularly effective.

Source: Akbas et al. (2016); Fertig, Lefkowitz and Fishbane (2015); Halpern and King (2016); Karlan et al. (2016) and OECD (2017f).

A universal old-age allowance supports informal workers without pension coverage, but the adequacy of benefits can be further improved. In 2009, the government expanded the entitlement for the non-contributory allowance for older people to all those not currently participating in pension schemes and significantly increased actual coverage. In 2016, 82% of persons over 60 received an allowance, up from fewer than 25% in 2007 (Department of Provincial Administration, 2017). The scheme was expanded in 2011 to accommodate benefit stratification by age, with monthly options of THB 600 (60-69 years), THB 700 (70-79 years), THB 800 (80-89 years) and THB 1 000 (90 years and above). Nevertheless, available support remains below the THB 1 300 national poverty line for the minimum monthly cost of basic food. Indeed, when asked to self-assess their economic situation, elderly Thai citizens who depend mainly on the old age allowance rated their situation least favourably (Knodel et al., 2015). In order for the scheme to fully guarantee income security in old age, benefits will have to rise further and could be indexed to the minimum required living costs. Financing reforms will have to complement this expansion of social benefits to ensure fiscal sustainability (Chapter 3).

Thailand's universal healthcare system needs to adapt to a modernising and ageing society

Thailand has received international praise for establishing universal healthcare in 2002. The Universal Coverage Scheme (UCS) provides access to comprehensive and free healthcare at the point of service for the large majority of the population (76%) not covered by existing formal sector schemes (ILO, 2016b). However, while an impressive network of village health volunteers spans the country, constituting a regular part of Thailand's health system since the 1960s, there is a shortage of qualified doctors and nurses particularly in rural areas. Furthermore, no additional support in terms of transport options and non-medical costs is provided for those living far from healthcare facilities (Rajatanavin, 2015; World Bank, 2016b).

Both objective and subjective health outcomes confirm the solid performance of the Thai health system. A life expectancy of 75 years is above what would be expected given Thailand's level of development. In 2016, Thailand became the first country in Asia to eliminate the mother-to-child transmission of HIV and syphilis (United Nations, 2017). Maternal and child mortality rates have dropped significantly since 1990 (Figure 1.12) and less than 10% of pre-school children were underweight in 2006 (Chavasit et al., 2013). Moreover, the large majority of people, and more than in any comparator country bar Singapore, are satisfied with the healthcare system in their area (Figure 1.13).

Figure 1.12. **Maternal and child mortality rates have more than halved since 1990**

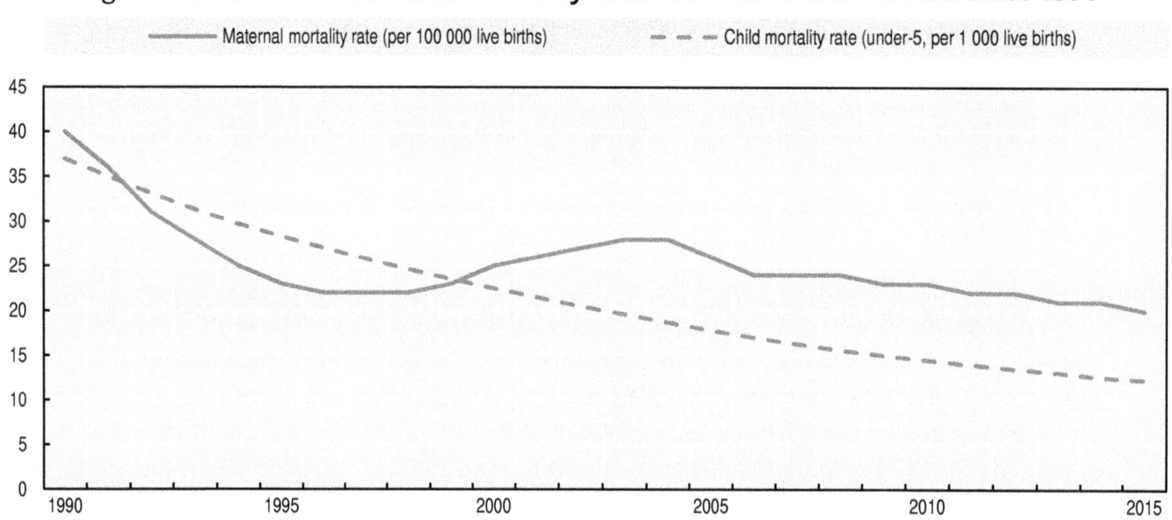

Source: World Bank (2017a), *World Development Indicators* (database), *https://data.worldbank.org/data-catalog/world-development-indicators.*

StatLink http://dx.doi.org/10.1787/888933691629

Disease profiles have been evolving alongside changing lifestyle patterns, as in many developing and middle-income countries. Non-communicable chronic diseases now account for 78% of total mortality rates, up from 64% in 2000 (World Bank, 2017a). Of particular concern is obesity: one in three adults and one in ten children are overweight and thus at risk of diabetes, cardiovascular diseases and some cancers (Figure 1.14). Increasingly urban lifestyles, with more sedentary activities and the consumption of now widely available calorie-dense food outside the home, have been blamed for this trend, but obesity also affects rural areas (Teerawattananon, 2017). Although more children in cities are obese (13%), childhood obesity is increasing faster in rural areas (Mohsuwan et al., 2011). The 12th Plan recognises the challenge of fighting obesity, as does the Thailand Healthy Lifestyle Strategic Plan (2011-2020). A range of initiatives to encourage healthier diets and more active lifestyles are being implemented or planned, including nutrition guidelines, awareness campaigns, subsidies for organic food production and consumption, and compulsory weekly workouts for civil servants in Bangkok. In September 2017, the government introduced a tax on sugary and alcoholic beverages.

Figure 1.13. **The majority of Thais are satisfied with the healthcare they receive**

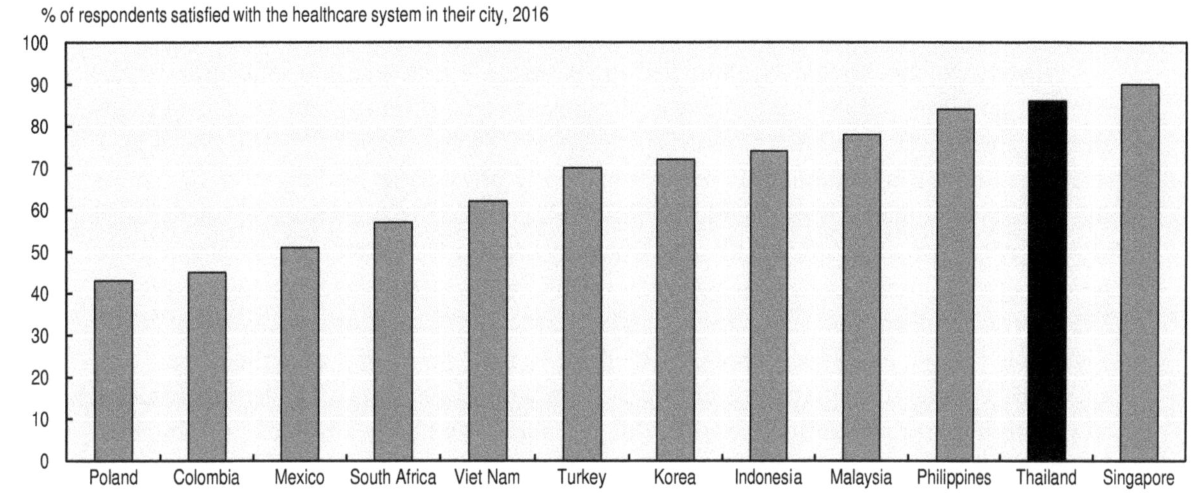

Source: Gallup (2017), *Gallup World Poll*, *www.gallup.com/services/170945/world-poll.aspx.*

StatLink http://dx.doi.org/10.1787/888933691648

Figure 1.14. **Obesity is more prevalent in Thailand than in most comparator countries**

Overweight prevalence (%) for adults of both sexes, 2016

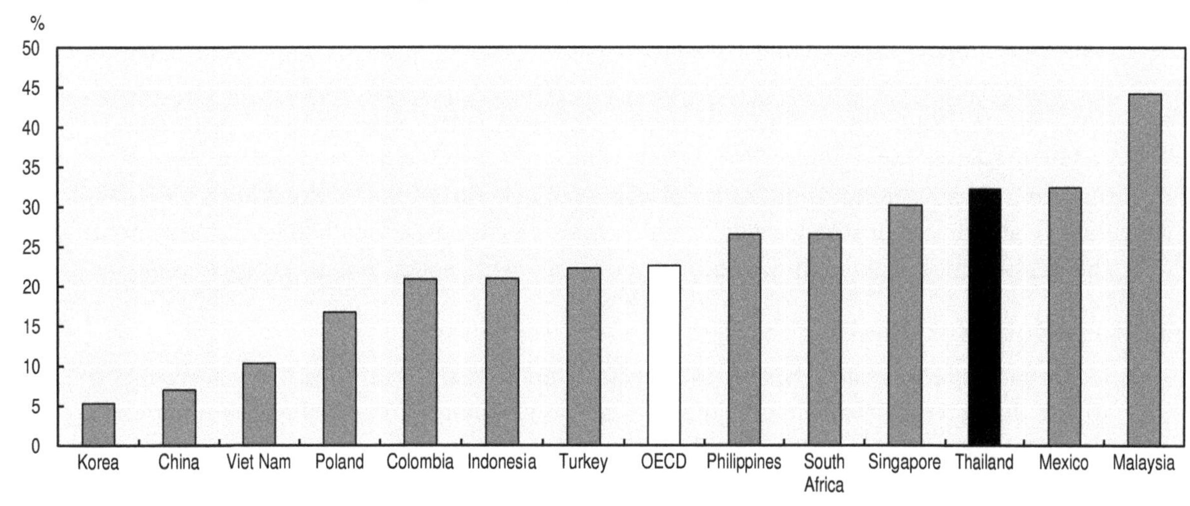

Note: "Overweight" is defined as BMI>25 kg/m^2 for Southeast Asian countries, and as BMI>30 kg/m^2 for other countries according to WHO standards.

Source: Data for Southeast Asian countries are from World Health Organisation (2016), *Global Health Observatory www.who.int/gho/ncd/risk_factors/overweight/en*; data for OECD countries, China, South Africa and Colombia are from OECD (2017g), *OECD Health Statistics Database*, *http://stats.oecd.org/index.aspx?DataSetCode=HEALTH_STAT*.

StatLink http://dx.doi.org/10.1787/888933691667

Looking ahead, Thailand's healthcare system will need to include a long-term care system (LTC) to cater to the growing share of the elderly population. While the 12th Plan recognises the need to develop such a system, both public and private LTC services are still embryonic and there is limited evidence that proposed policies aiming to integrate family and community care into the LTC system are feasible (Knodel et al., 2016). Moreover, LTC and rising curative costs of treating non-communicable diseases are likely to strain healthcare budgets into the future. As such, targeted supply-side reforms combined with financing reforms (Chapter 3) are needed in this area to ensure fiscal sustainability.

Greater recourse to primary care, prevention and ICT can reduce costs and improve quality

Provision of healthcare is often performed more effectively and efficiently at the primary care level, while the incidence of many chronic diseases can be substantially reduced through prevention. Currently, patients can access medical specialists without prior consultation of general practitioners or family physicians, leading to inefficiencies and unnecessary diagnostics and treatments. This situation is exacerbated by a shortage of primary care providers: it is estimated that only around 5% of medical school graduates are opting to become primary care doctors, resulting in an estimated shortage of around 5 600 physicians (Feige and Tiavongsuvon, 2015; Leavitt, 2015). Boosting the number of family physicians and general practitioners, particularly in rural areas, will ease the pressure on tertiary care providers and help prevent the overburdening of hospitals. In addition, focusing on prevention and population-based health promotion will be key to reducing the need for costly treatments in the future (OECD, 2015b). Although preventive health-promotion programmes are included in the UCS via the Thai Health Promotion Fund (ThaiHealth), the government has not allocated the originally pledged 20% of public health financing.

Consistent with Thailand's broader digitalisation strategy, increased use of ICT can promote efficiency gains by providing digital access to primary care consultations, especially in remote areas. This is achieved by optimising the workflows of clinicians and administrators and improving the management of patients' health-related information. With over 10 000 health ICT units across Thailand, consolidating the health ICT infrastructure could expedite the exchange of information. In this regard, the Ministry of Public Health has announced plans to consolidate its ICT infrastructure to achieve better management, performance and increased savings on operational expenditure. ICT also has a role to play in improving the administrative systems of Thailand's three publicly funded health insurance schemes. Harmonising health insurance data on entitlements, usage of service, budget disbursement and performance evaluation can boost administrative efficiency and aid policy making.

Boosting education quality

Improving education outcomes is essential to address inequality and to boost economic growth through the development of human capital (Chapter 2). Indeed, the government has identified the need to improve the education system as a means for realising Thailand 4.0 (Overview).

Participation rates in basic education are nearly universal, but quality remains a challenge

Thailand has made substantial progress in improving access to education, increasing enrolment rates at all levels, but early education is lagging. Access to primary, lower secondary and upper secondary education is now nearly universal. Non-formal education plays an important role in this regard by providing access to disadvantaged students in remote areas or from minority communities. In 2014, 20% of students were enrolled in the non-formal system. Enrolment in pre-primary education has also risen considerably as a result of government policy to expand free access. However, improvements are still required with as many as one-quarter of 3-5 year-olds not enrolled (NESDB, 2017b). Moreover, disadvantaged students who stand to benefit the most from pre-primary education account for the majority of the unenrolled. Pre-primary education helps to prepare children for school and improves lifelong education outcomes. Indeed, the OECD's 2015 Programme for International Student Assessment (PISA) shows that Thai students who attended two to three years of pre-primary education score 30 points higher on average than those who did not (OECD, 2016b). Beyond access, the quality of early childhood education remains a concern (UNICEF, 2017). The government is seeking to boost the quality of pre-primary education by raising teacher qualifications, improving the curriculum and creating a standardised evaluation system for all early childhood development centres.

At around 4% of GDP, Thailand's public expenditure on education is among the highest in the region. However, inefficient and inequitable allocation of resources has undermined investment effectiveness and ultimately hampered learning outcomes (OECD and UNESCO, 2016). Data from PISA 2015 show that the performance of Thai students trails most comparator countries and is far below the OECD average: out of 69 countries surveyed, Thailand ranked 52nd in mathematics, 56th in reading and 53rd in science.

Moreover, compared with PISA 2012, Thailand's scores declined significantly in science and reading, with performance in 2015 below Thailand's lowest-ever recorded scores (Figure 1.15). Reading performance is particularly worrisome, with only around half of Thailand's 15 year-olds demonstrating reading skills that would classify them as functionally literate – that is, able to locate information and understand the main idea in a text. Furthermore, very few students reach the highest proficiency levels. In PISA 2015, only 0.1% of students were classified as top performers (i.e. PISA levels 5 and 6) in all three tested subjects. Without significant improvement in basic skills, Thailand's labour force will struggle to do well in a more knowledge-based economy.

Figure 1.15. **Student performance is low and deteriorating**

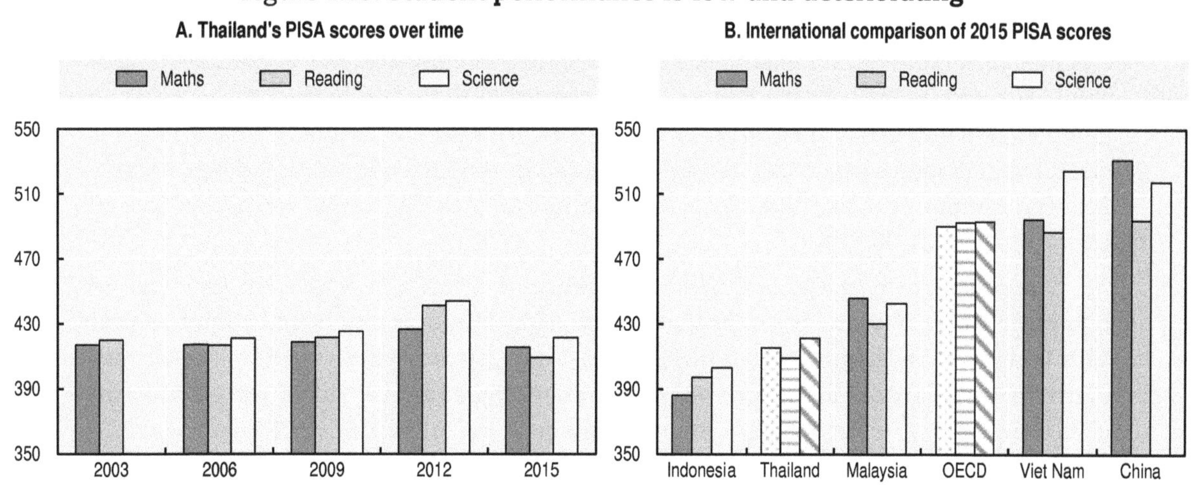

Note: China refers to the four PISA-participating Chinese entities: Beijing, Guangdong, Jiangsu and Shanghai. Coverage of Malaysian schools in PISA 2015 fell short of the standard PISA response rate, so results may not be comparable to those of other countries.

Source: OECD (2016c), PISA: Programme for International Student Assessment; OECD Education Statistics (database).

StatLink http://dx.doi.org/10.1787/888933691686

According to PISA 2015, Thailand performs better than many countries with respect to educational equity (e.g. gender, the extent to which differences in socio-economic status impact performance and whether disadvantaged students are more likely to repeat a grade), but disadvantaged students, who historically underperform, have failed to catch up in recent years. Instead, performance among Thailand's youth has deteriorated in general, with the share of low-performing students in science and reading increasing significantly, while the share of high-performing reading students fell significantly (Figure 1.16).

Figure 1.16. **The share of low performers has grown, while that of high performers has fallen**

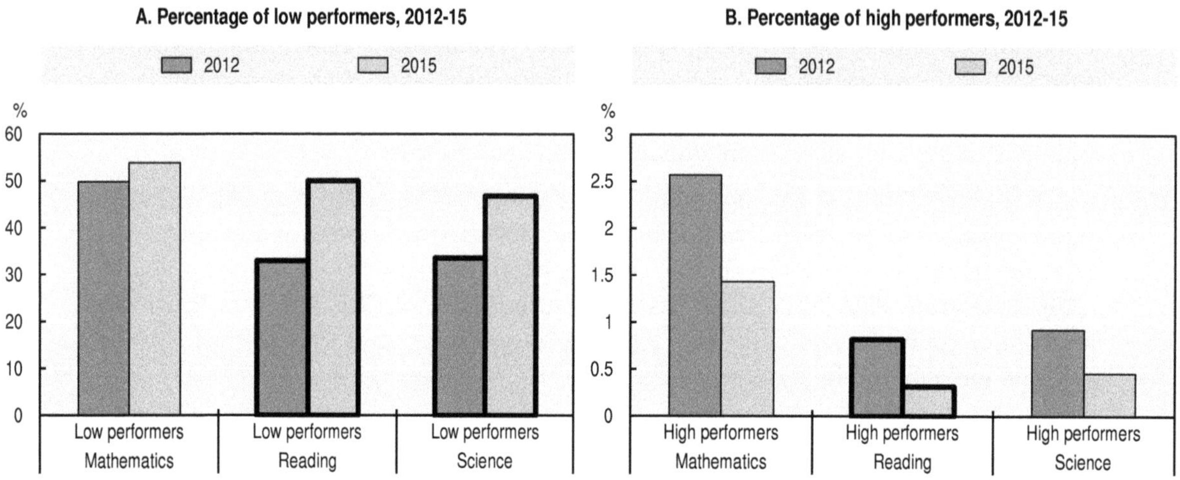

Note: Bold borders indicate that the percentage change in performers between 2012 and 2015 is statistically significant.

Source: OECD (2016b), *PISA 2015 Results (Volume II): Policies and Practices for Successful Schools*, OECD Publishing, Paris, *http://dx.doi.org/10.1787/9789264267510-en*.

StatLink http://dx.doi.org/10.1787/888933691705

Nevertheless, inequalities remain. Students from poorer, often rural, backgrounds are less likely to have access to quality schools with quality teachers. An evaluation by the Office for National Education Standards and Quality Assessment revealed that around one-fifth of Thai schools do not pass minimum quality standards and that most of these schools were in rural areas (OECD, 2014a). One factor is the shortage of skilled teachers in rural areas: for example, 20% of teachers in Bangkok have a graduate degree compared with only 9% in the remote province of Mae Hong Son in the northern region (Sondergaard and Lathapipat, 2017). While the divide between urban and rural schools is stark, other disparities are also deeply embedded in the Thai education system, notably between communities, social groups and education streams (e.g. formal versus non-formal education) (OECD, 2017h).

The government recognises the shortcomings of the education system and has put into place a new 20-year Education Master Plan (2017-2036), underpinned by the five-year 12th Education Development Plan (MOE, 2017). These plans seek to overhaul the current system in accordance with a long-term reform vision aligned with Thailand's broader reform objectives outlined in the 20-year National Strategic Plan (2017-2036) and Thailand 4.0. The government has also established an Independent Committee for Education Reform, which will conduct a study and offer suggestions to the Cabinet on child development, teacher development, education management, the restructuring of education-related agencies and the reduction of disparities in education.

While details of future policies are still being determined, the government has recently outlined some initial reform priorities. In relation to the teaching profession, the government plans to increase quality by reforming professional development policies. Currently, the Ministry of Education determines these based on school survey data. This has contributed to inefficiencies and ineffectiveness in training programmes (OECD and UNESCO, 2016). The government is therefore dismantling top-down centralised directives and instead providing a THB 10 000 (around USD 300) coupon directly to teachers. The coupon will enable them to attend available courses that best suit their needs. The government also recently implemented reforms to improve teaching incentives. Teacher pay and promotions are now linked to teaching hours rather than research work. The reforms stipulate a minimum number of teaching hours with bonuses for additional hours. The government should also consider addressing teacher shortages in specific subject areas (e.g. mathematics, science and foreign languages), by expanding teaching licencing arrangements to allow specialists from in-demand fields to enter the profession more easily.

The Ministry of Education also plans to consolidate close to 11 000 smaller rural schools by 2020 in order to reduce disparities between urban and rural schools. Schools with less than 120 students located within 6 km of another bigger school will be merged. Indeed, the excessive number of extremely small village schools stretches teaching and financial resources and contributes to under-performance (OECD and UNESCO, 2016). The provision of affordable transportation for students will be important to ensure that these changes do not impede access to schools.

Beyond these initiatives, further reforms are needed to implement the improvements to the school system outlined in the 12th Plan. A recent policy review by the OECD and UNESCO set out an extensive set of recommendations to support the development of a high-quality education system in Thailand, centred on the four priority areas outlined below. However, to effectively implement these reforms Thailand needs to concurrently improve educational governance arrangements, particularly by enhancing co-ordination and better allocating responsibilities between the school, local and central level. Indeed a lack of coordination across institutions is cited as a key reason for the stilted implementation of the 2008 curriculum (OECD and UNESCO, 2016).

1. *Curriculum*: Thailand has shifted its content-based curriculum to a modern standards-based approach that describes what students should know and be able to do in each subject area. However, implementation has been hampered by a lack of coherence in the new curriculum, lack of capacity among teachers and schools to implement it, and limited capacity to assess how well the curriculum has delivered on its intended outcomes.
2. *Student assessment*: While Thailand makes extensive use of standardised tests, capacity constraints, lack of comparability and a failure to address the full range of skills students require undermine the effectiveness of the assessment system. Thailand should enhance the rigour of its test development process and broaden its assessment mix. It should also build capacity to support the effective design and implementation of assessment procedures at all levels of education.
3. *Teachers and school leaders*: High-quality teachers and school leaders are key for education outcomes. Despite extensive efforts over recent decades, teacher development is still impeded by inadequate teacher preparation programmes, a lack of strategic approach

for teachers' professional development, administrative burdens, the absence of a framework to support the development of school leaders, and a fragmented approach to teacher deployment making it harder to tackle shortages. Thailand should develop a holistic strategy to build capacity among teachers and school leaders, in consultation with teachers, school leaders and their associations. Additionally, teacher funding and deployment should better reflect local needs to ensure that more students are taught by qualified and high-quality teachers.

4. *Information and communication technology*: Good ICT skills are increasingly important for effective participation in the economy. Despite significant investment, Thai students lag behind their peers in this area. Uneven infrastructure provision, limited relevant digital learning materials and teacher capacity to use ICT, lack of effective monitoring of ICT policies and the absence of a coherent ICT investment framework have all contributed to under-performance in this area. Thailand should develop a national strategy to enhance and integrate ICTs into teaching, including the development of appropriate learning materials and improved internet access in rural areas (Box 1.4).

Higher education and lifelong learning need to better equip individuals for the labour market

Human capital development is crucial for the success of Thailand 4.0. Improving the skills and education attainment of the labour force will increase Thailand's attractiveness for higher value-added activities, raise productivity and ultimately create higher-paying jobs. Despite growth in the number of graduates over time, skill shortages still persist. Two main factors contribute to this trend. First, Thai students tend not to enrol in courses that teach skills required by industry: the number of social science and humanities graduates is on the rise, while far fewer students are graduating in science, technology, engineering and mathematics (STEM). This problem is exacerbated by the shortage of places available in STEM fields (Figure 1.18). Second, the overall quality of tertiary education is inadequate. According to QS World University Rankings 2018, only one institution in Thailand is ranked among the world's top 300 universities (Chulalongkorn University, ranked 245th). In contrast, neighbouring Malaysia has five universities listed within the top 300.

The government recognises the need to raise the quality and relevance of university programmes. It has outlined ambitious goals to boost the number of papers published in international journals and to have at least seven universities ranked among the world's top 200 by 2036. Through the Cooperative Education Programme, the Ministry of Education fosters partnerships between Thai universities and prospective employers to adopt a work-learning system which integrates students' academic studies with hands-on work experience. It is also pursuing a reform strategy that devolves decision-making to universities, with a voucher system enabling institutions to offer tailored courses. This will give universities the flexibility to develop programmes in line with both industry and student demands, which over time should improve the relevance and quality of courses. Moreover, Thailand will host a STEM Education Centre to develop policies to improve STEM education and act as a regional information-sharing and learning hub for Southeast Asian economies. The government has also recently allowed foreign education institutions to offer their services in the eastern economic corridor.

Box 1.4. **Using ICTs to boost education outcomes**

Given Thailand's shortage of suitably skilled teachers in remote areas, embracing digital technologies can help to boost the educational quality provided to rural students and teaching skills. Indeed, OECD experience has shown that technology-supported education can widen teacher and student teaching and learning opportunities. For instance, online laboratories (remote or virtual) provide a wider range of experimentation and learning-by-doing than would be possible without technological support. Moreover, e-learning is viewed not only as a format for delivering education, but also as a means of acquainting students with the use of ICT in a context where digital literacy is increasingly important (OECD, 2016d). However, this will not be feasible without increased access to school computers. Availability of these has fallen since 2012, with Thailand currently lagging behind some comparator countries and the OECD average (Figure 1.17).

Figure 1.17. **Availability of computers in schools is insufficient**

Computers per student

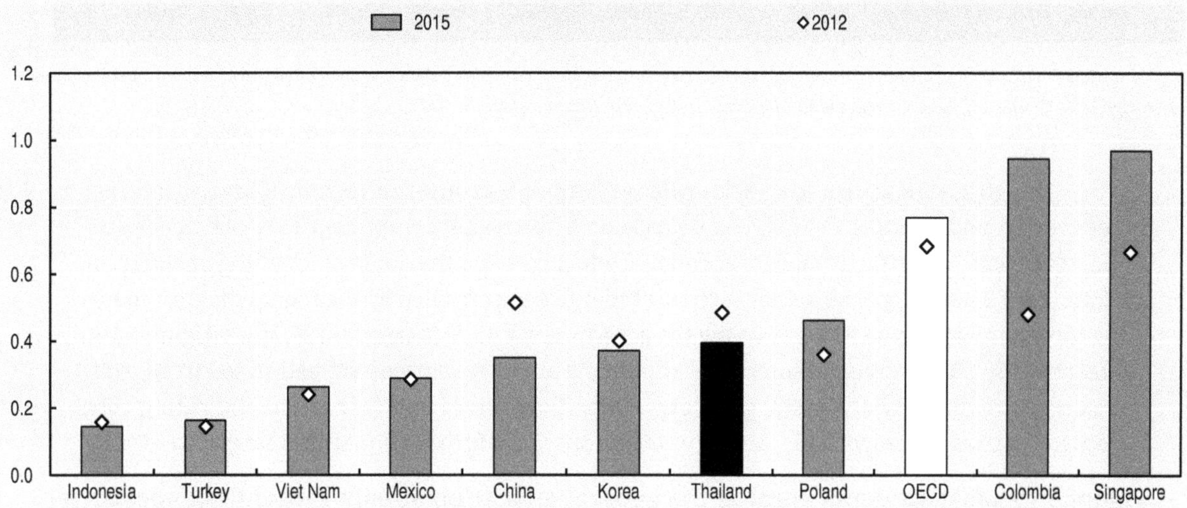

Note: China refers to the four PISA-participating Chinese entities: Beijing, Guangdong, Jiangsu and Shanghai. Figures for 2012 refer to Shanghai only.

Source: OECD (2015c), *PISA Database, www.oecd.org/pisa/data/2015database;* and OECD (2016d), *Innovating Education and Educating for Innovation – The Power of Digital Technologies and Skills*, OECD Publishing, Paris, *http://dx.doi.org/10.1787/9789264265097-en.*

StatLink http://dx.doi.org/10.1787/888933691724

Thailand's teachers and students need access to better-quality digital learning materials in order to improve the quality of education, particularly in disadvantaged rural areas. ICTs can support innovative teaching practices and the creation of learning environments intended to develop student competencies, such as problem solving and critical thinking. Rather than being used solely to transmit information and content to students, ICTs can serve as a tool to support higher-order learning (OECD and UNESCO, 2016). In this regard, Thailand should increase the availability of Thai-language open education resources. Such resources are particularly beneficial when textbooks are unaffordable, access to classrooms is limited and professional learning programmes for teachers are lacking. Thailand's higher education sector already makes use of similar technology through the promotion of Thailand Massive Open Online Courses (MOOCS) as part of the Thailand Cyber University Project. Thai MOOCS are improving access to higher education and lifelong learning opportunities.

Figure 1.18. **Thailand has a relatively low proportion of students enrolled in STEM courses**

Enrolment ratio in STEM subjects, latest available year

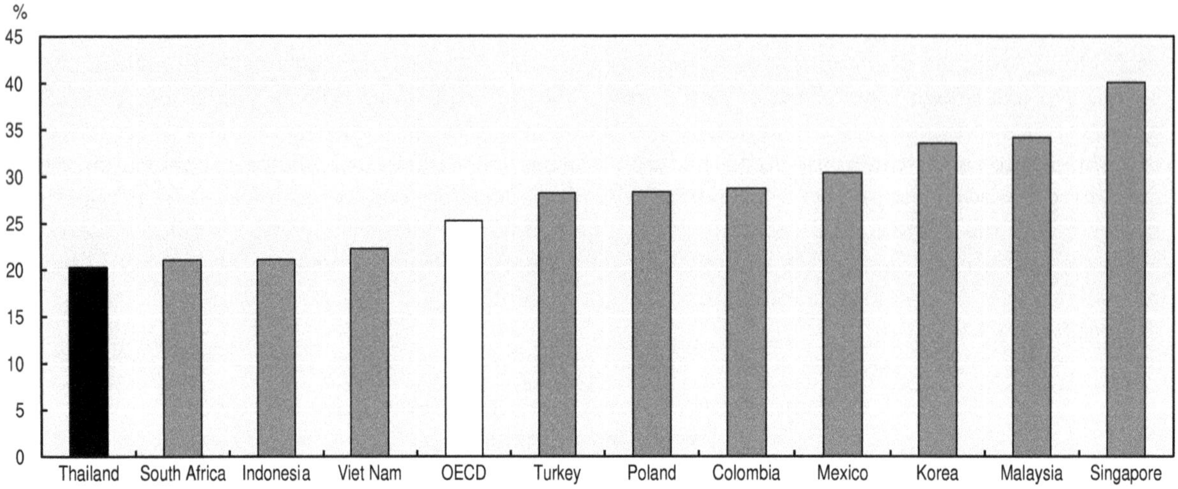

Note: STEM courses include natural sciences, mathematics and statistics programmes; information and communication technology programmes; and engineering, manufacturing and construction programmes. Enrolment data are not available for China and Philippines.

Source: UNESCO-UIS (2017), *Education* (dataset), UIS Data Centre, *http://data.uis.unesco.org/*.

StatLink *http://dx.doi.org/10.1787/888933691743*

The government has long acknowledged the importance of technical and vocational education and training (TVET), but despite its efforts, more improvements are needed to increase both the attractiveness of vocational education and the quality of training provided. In 2015, only 34% of upper secondary school students were enrolled in vocational programmes – down from 36% in 2011 and well below the government's 45-55% target (MOE, 2017) (Figure 1.19). Meanwhile, skill shortages among vocationally trained employees are estimated to be even more acute than for university graduates. One study found a 23% shortfall, indicating that only 77 recruits were available for every 100 job openings for vocational graduates (EIU, 2015b).

Figure 1.19. **Most students enrol in the general education stream rather than vocational programmes**

Share of upper secondary students enrolled in vocational programmes, latest available year

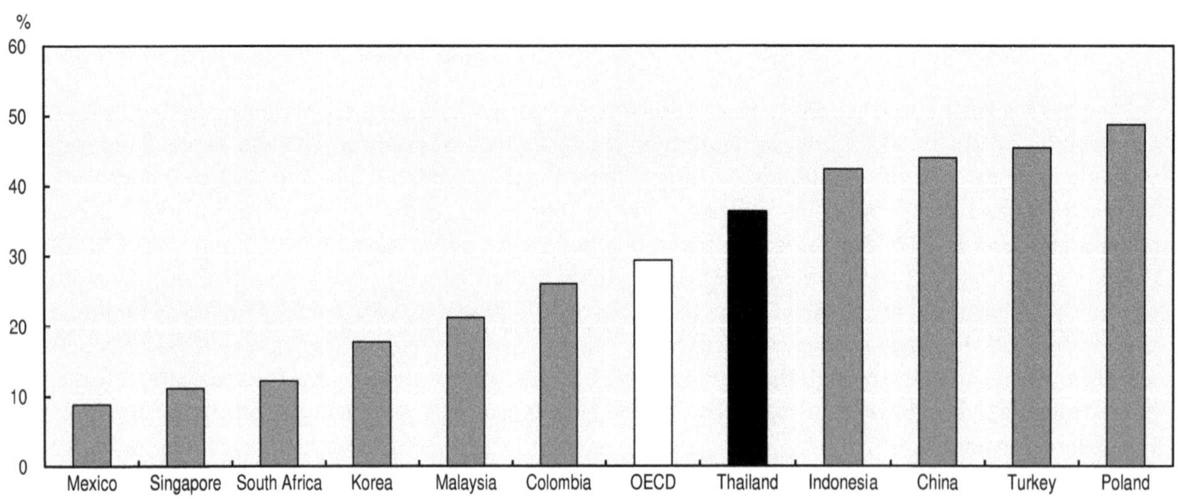

Note: Data for Thailand refer to 2015; data for China, Colombia, Indonesia, Malaysia, South Africa and the OECD average refer to 2014; data for Korea, Poland and Turkey refer to 2013; data for Mexico refer to 2012; and data for Singapore refer to 2009.

Source: World Bank (2017), *Education Statistics*, *https://data.worldbank.org/data-catalog/ed-stats*; MOE (2017).

StatLink *http://dx.doi.org/10.1787/888933691762*

The government is taking action under the aegis of the 12th Educational Development Plan. It will expand co-operation between vocational institutions, the private sector and academia to develop courses that better meet industry needs. It also plans to boost participation in Dual Vocational Training through the provision of incentives to both students and medium-sized workplaces (NESDB, 2017b). Thailand is further establishing vocational education schemes on a bilateral basis between regional chambers of commerce and relevant public institutions in an effort to meet labour demands in the agricultural and services sectors. This includes developing new curricula to respond to the needs of the ASEAN Community and industries within special economic zones (Chapter 2) (United Nations, 2017). Although the government's programmes are promising, TVET students need to acquire generic, transferrable skills (particularly in numeracy and literacy) alongside the specific on-the-job training. This is vital to support future occupational mobility and lifelong learning.

In relation to skills training for those already employed, the 2002 Skills Development Promotion Act requires enterprises with more than 100 staff to provide training to at least half of employees once a year. Training expenses are reimbursed via income tax benefits. Skills Development Centres are also operated at the regional and provincial level for workers wishing to upgrade their skills and for the unemployed (Wannagatesiri et al., 2015).

Addressing the lack of interest in skills training among employees is a further challenge. Responses to the 2016 Thailand Skill Development Survey indicate that 92.7% employees are reluctant to develop their skills, up from 90% in 2012 (NSO, 2016b). Obstacles to participation in lifelong learning exist in all countries and include lack of time, family responsibilities, the cost of training programmes and the remoteness of education providers. Many countries have attempted to address these challenges by implementing a range of measures targeted at low-skilled adults. In this vein, the Thailand Professional Qualification Institute, established in 2012, brings together government and private sector representatives to develop occupational standards and test individual competencies that can lead to formal qualifications.

Ensuring the social inclusion of women

The importance of gender equality is embedded in the SDGs and backed by empirical evidence. Women and men are happier when living in a country guaranteeing equal rights and opportunities to women and men (Ferrant et al., 2017). Discriminatory social institutions hamper growth by lowering both female levels of education and labour force participation, as well as productivity (Ferrant and Kolev, 2016). Increasing the labour force participation rate of educated women will be particularly important in countries with ageing populations such as Thailand, as witnessed in the case of Japan (Kawaguchi and Mori, 2017).

Thailand is promoting gender equality via a range of recent legislative initiatives. These include the landmark 2015 Gender Equality Act and a separate Women's Development Plan under the 12th Plan. Since 2001, all ministries are required to appoint a Chief Gender Equality Officer to act as gender focal point. Currently, gender-responsive budgeting is being piloted in government departments, as required by the current Constitution, and plans are underway to develop a gender-disaggregated database within the national statistical system (United Nations, 2017). The Gender Equality Act has also recently been expanded to cover LGBTI anti-discrimination provisions - indeed, LGBTI individuals in Thailand frequently report experiencing discrimination when buying property and in the labour market, including harassment at work and during application processes and promotions (ILO, 2014; World Bank, 2017c).

Women are active in the private sector, including in senior management, but few are engaged in politics

As in many other countries, gender inequities exist in female labour force participation and pay, although they are smaller than in comparator countries. At 16.7%, the gender gap in labour force participation is below the OECD average of 23.2% (Figure 1.20). In 2015, Thai women earned approximately 15% less than men, compared to a gender wage gap of 18% in OECD countries (OECD, 2017i).

Women also occupy a significant share of business leadership roles. Indeed, Thailand ranks highest among comparator countries in terms of the female share of senior and middle management roles (30.5%) and percentage of firms with female top managers (65% in 2017) (Figure 1.21). Thailand also made the top 10 of the 2017 Mastercard Index of Women Entrepreneurs, a composite index assessing female advancement outcomes in business, knowledge and financial assets, as well as the country's entrepreneurial environment (Mastercard, 2017).

Figure 1.20. **Thailand's gender gap in labour force participation is small relative to comparator countries**

Labour force participation rate (%), by sex, 2016

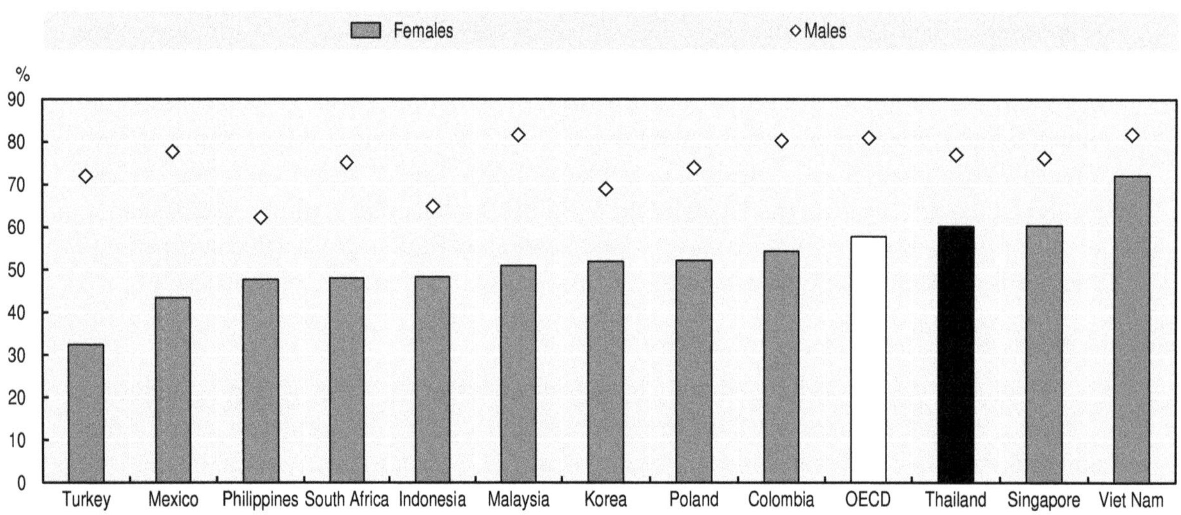

Note: The labour force participation rate refers to the working age population, for ages 15-64. No data are available for China.

Source: ILO (2017a), *Key Indicators of the Labour Market*, *www.ilo.org/global/statistics-and-databases/research-and-databases/kilm/lang--en/index.htm*. Data for the OECD average drawn from OECD (2017i), *Gender Portal*, *www.oecd.org/gender/data/labour-force-participation-by-sex-age.htm*.

StatLink http://dx.doi.org/10.1787/888933691781

In contrast, a major gender gap exists in political empowerment. Women hold only 6% of seats in national parliament, significantly fewer than in all comparator countries in 2017 (Figure 1.21). Slightly more women hold office at the provincial administrative level, but numbers are still low at 11.4% of seats (Department of Local Administration, 2017). The recent 2017 Global Gender Gap report ranked Thailand 127th out of 144 countries for political empowerment (World Economic Forum, 2017). This discrepancy between female leadership in the private and public sector extends beyond elected office: women fill only a minority of executive roles for various civil service functions (e.g. police administrators and public sector attorneys) (Table 1.2).

Figure 1.21. **The contrast between female leadership in the private and public sector is stark**

Female leadership, 2017

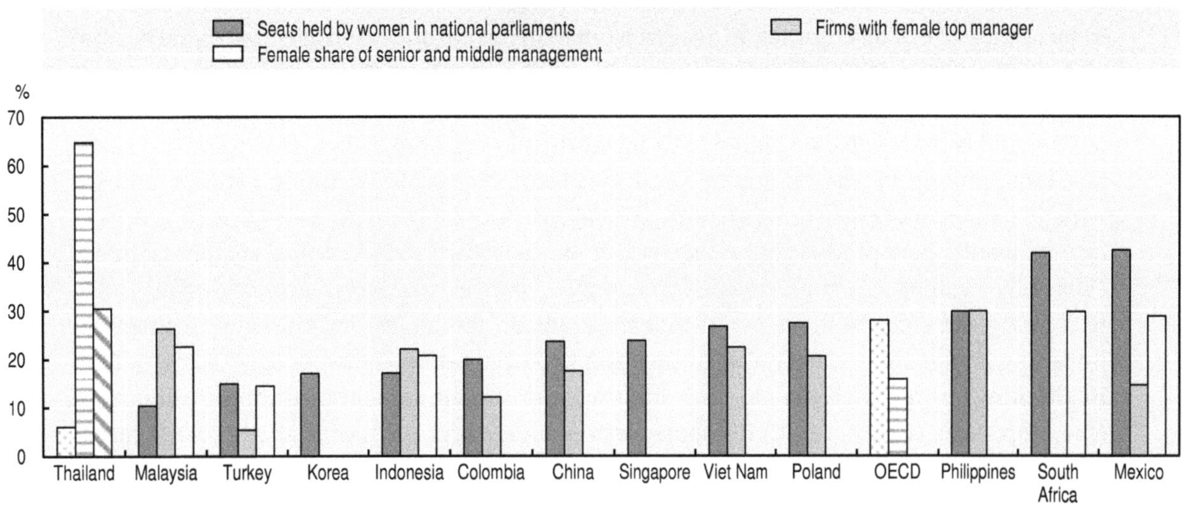

Note: No data are available on firms with female top managers for Korea, Singapore and South Africa, or on the female share of senior and middle management for China, Colombia, Korea, the OECD average, Philippines, Poland, Singapore and Viet Nam.

Source: Data on parliamentary representation are drawn from the Inter-Parliamentary Union (2017), *Women in Parliament*, *www.ipu.org/wmn-e/world.htm*; data on private sector representation are drawn from ILO (2017a), *ILOSTAT database*, *www.ilo.org/ilostat*, and the World Bank (2017b), Enterprise Surveys, *www.enterprisesurveys.org*.

StatLink http://dx.doi.org/10.1787/888933691800

Table 1.2. **Women are under-represented in the wider public sector**

Function	Female share of the workforce (%), 2015
Executives in public organisations	25.6
Executives in the ordinary civil service	17.8
Public sector attorneys	12.6
Judicial management in the public sector	17.3
Administration in the police	0

Source: NSO (2017), *Social Indicators 2017*, *http://service.nso.go.th/nso/nsopublish/pubs/e-book/Indicators_Social_2560/index.html*.

The lack of women in political life might be due in part to an engrained cultural belief that political leadership is reserved for men. Women wishing to stand for office face considerable hurdles in the form of discouragement from their families against entering a "male domain", lack of access to patronage networks, and violence or the threat thereof (UN Convention on the Elimination of all Forms of Discrimination Against Women, cited in OECD, 2014b). The experience of India, which since 1993 has required states to reserve a certain proportion of all council chief seats in its villages for women, suggests that political quotas increase female political leadership, but also raise adolescent girls' career aspirations, as well as their parents' aspirations for them, contributing to a reduction in gender discrimination over the long term (Beamam et al., 2012; Pande and Ford, 2011). Political quotas also exist at the subnational or national level in various OECD countries, such as Belgium, France, Greece and Slovakia (OECD, 2014b).

Violence against women remains a significant problem

While overall gender-based discrimination in Thailand's social institutions is relatively low, women face continued domestic violence. The OECD Social Institutions and Gender Index, a measure of discrimination against women in formal and informal laws, social norms and practices restricting women's agency and well-being, places Thailand at 0.11 on a scale from 0 for very low to 1 for very high discrimination. Overall gender-based discrimination in Thailand is therefore considered to be lower than in regional comparator countries such as China, Indonesia, the Philippines and Viet Nam. Areas of remaining concern and in which Thailand underperforms in international comparison include acceptance of violence against women and prevalence of domestic violence (Figure 1.22). Violence against women, especially intimate partner violence, not only negatively impacts women's health and well-being, but can also have major repercussions on female labour market outcomes by impeding female human capital accumulation and occupational choices (OECD, 2017j). The Health Ministry reported that 102 269 adult women sought assistance from the Ministry's One Stop Crisis Centre (OSCC) for abuse between 2007 and 2015, with about 10 000 cases reported in 2016 (NESDB, 2016). Out of all survivors of violence who physically reported to the OSCC, 22% indicated physical abuse and 72% sexual abuse (NSO, 2015). Intimate partner violence, as opposed to violence outside the family, accounted for almost four times as many calls to the OSCC 1300 hotline for women in 2017 (Department of Social Development and Welfare, 2017). Although the 2007 Act on the Prevention and Resolution of Domestic Violence criminalises perpetrators, it tends to prioritise mediation and family reunification, rather than encouraging victims of violence to speak up, which has reportedly led to a low overall conviction rate (OECD, 2014c).

Figure 1.22. **Overall gender-based discrimination in Thailand is low, but violence against women remains a concern**

OECD Social Institutions and Gender Index, 2014

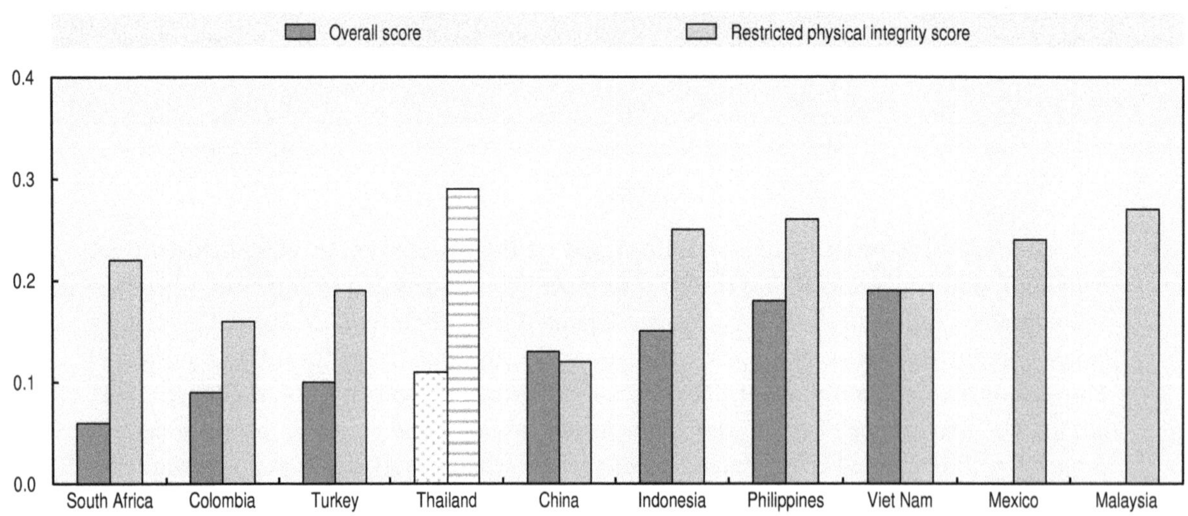

Note: The OECD Social Institutions and Gender Index is the unweighted average of a quadratic function of five sub-indices: discriminatory family code, restricted physical integrity, son bias, restricted resources and assets and restricted civil liberties. Both the overall index and the sub-indices range from 0 for very low to 1 for very high discrimination against women. The scores in each consider qualitative and quantitative information about legislative frameworks, de facto situations and practices (customary laws and practices, implementation of laws, etc.) through prevalence and attitudinal data. The overall Social Institutions and Gender Index score is not available for Malaysia and Mexico.

Source: OECD (2014c), "Social Institutions and Gender Index" (database), *www.genderindex.org*.

StatLink *http://dx.doi.org/10.1787/888933691819*

Human trafficking and forced labour, especially in the commercial sex industry and domestic work sector, represents another form of gender-based violence, affecting both Thai citizens and female migrants. In addition, despite government efforts to address illegal, unreported and unregulated fishing activities, male migrants from neighbouring Southeast Asian countries remain vulnerable to forced labour in Thailand's fishing industry (EC, 2017). Thailand's 12th Plan identifies the fight against human trafficking as priority and the government has passed strong anti-trafficking laws with harsh criminal penalties (NESDB, 2017b), resulting in an upgrade to Tier 2 Watch List status in the Trafficking in Persons report in 2016 (US Department of State, 2017). Further efforts are needed in legal enforcement and to reduce official complicity in trafficking. The OECD Guiding Principles on Combating Corruption related to Trafficking in Persons – the application of which was piloted in Thailand in 2015 – also underline the fundamental role that corruption plays in the trafficking process and stress the importance of tackling both issues together (OECD, 2016e).

References

ADB (2013), *The Social Protection Index Assessing Results for Asia and the Pacific*, Asian Development Bank, Mandaluyong City, *www.adb.org/publications/social-protection-index-assessing-results-asia-and-pacific*.

ADB (2012), *Thailand: Updating and Improving the Social Protection Index*, Asian Development Bank, Mandaluyong City, *www.adb.org/projects/documents/thailand-updating-and-improving-social-protection-index-tacr*.

Akbas, M. et al. (2016), "How to help poor informal workers to save a bit: Evidence from a field experiment in Kenya", *IZA Discussion Paper*, No. 10024, *http://ftp.iza.org/dp10024.pdf*.

Beaman, L. et al. (2012), "Female leadership raises aspirations and educational attainment for girls: A policy experiment in India", *Science*, Vol. 335/6068, pp. 582-586, doi:10.1126/science.1212382.

Calderón-Mejía, V. and I. Marinescu (2012), "The impact of Colombia's pension and health insurance systems on informality", *IZA Discussion Paper*, No. 6439, *http://ftp.iza.org/dp6439.pdf*.

Chavasit, V., V. Kasemsup and K. Tontisirin (2013), "Thailand conquered under-nutrition very successfully but has not slowed obesity", *Obesity Reviews*, Vol. 14, pp. 96–105, doi:10.1111/obr.12091.

Credit Suisse (2017), *Global Wealth Report 2017*, *https://www.credit-suisse.com/corporate/en/research/research-institute/global-wealth-report.html*

Department of Local Administration (2017), *Provincial Administrative Organization (PAO)*, Ministry of Interior, Bangkok, *www.dla.go.th/index.jsp*.

Department of Provincial Administration (2017), *Non-contributory Allowance for Older People*, Ministry of Interior, Bangkok.

Department of Social Development and Welfare (2017), *Women Abuse Statistics*, Ministry of Social Development and Human Security, Bangkok.

EC (2017), *Question and Answers on the EU's fight against illegal, unreported and unregulated (IUU) fishing*, European Commission, *https://ec.europa.eu/fisheries/question-and-answers-eus-fight-against-illegal-unreported-and-unregulated-iuu-fishing-5_en*.

EIU (2015a), *National Savings Fund is Established in Thailand*, Economic Intelligence Unit, Siam Commercial Bank, Bangkok.

EIU (2015b), *Insight: Bridging Thailand's Labor Gap*, Economic Intelligence Unit, Siam Commercial Bank, Bangkok.

Feige, M., and W. Tiavongsuvon (2015), *The Future of Thailand's Healthcare Industries in Tier 2 Cities. Outlook for 2015-2020*, Solidiance, Bangkok, *www.solidiance.com/whitepaper/future-of-thailands-healthcare-industry-in-tier-2-cities.pdf*.

Ferrant, G. and A. Kolev (2016), "Does gender discrimination in social institutions matter for long-term growth? Cross-country evidence", *OECD Development Centre Working Papers*, No. 330, OECD Publishing, Paris, *http://dx.doi.org/10.1787/5jm2hz8dgls6-en*.

Ferrant, G., A. Kolev and C. Tassot (2017), "The pursuit of happiness: Does gender parity in social institutions matter?", *OECD Development Centre Working Papers*, No. 337, OECD Publishing, Paris, *http://dx.doi.org/10.1787/f7e0c69c-en*.

Gallup (2017), "Gallup World Poll", *www.gallup.com/services/170945/world-poll.aspx*.

Halpern, D. and K. King (6 October 2016), "Setting smarter defaults for workplace pensions", Behavioural Insights Team blog, *www.behaviouralinsights.co.uk/uncategorized/setting-smarter-defaults-for-workplace-pensions*.

Fertig, A., J. Lefkowitz and A. Fishbane (2015), *Using Behavioral Science to Increase Retirement Savings: A New Look at Voluntary Pension Contributions in Mexico*, Ideas42, New York, *www.ideas42.org/wp-content/uploads/2015/11/I42_571_MexicoPensionsReport_ENG_final_digital.pdf*.

ILO (2017a), "Key indicators of the labour market" (database), *www.ilo.org/global/statistics-and-databases/research-and-databases/kilm/lang--en/index.htm*.

ILO (2017b), "Thailand", ILO Social Protection Platform, *www.social-protection.org/gimi/gess/ShowCountryProfile.action?id=404&lang=EN*.

ILO (2016a), "Thailand", *TRIANGLE II Quarterly Briefing Note* (January-March), ILO and Australian AID, Bangkok, *www.ilo.org/wcmsp5/groups/public/---asia/---ro-bangkok/documents/briefingnote/wcms_469497.pdf*.

ILO (2016b), *Thailand: Universal Health-care Coverage Scheme*, ILO, Geneva, *www.social-protection.org/gimi/gess/RessourcePDF.action?ressource.ressourceId=54059*.

ILO (2015), "Industrial Relations Data (IRData)" (database), *www.ilo.org/global/docs/WCMS_408983/lang--en/index.htm*.

ILO (2014), *Gender Identity and Sexual Orientation in Thailand*, ILO, Bangkok, *www.ilo.org/wcmsp5/groups/public/---asia/---ro-bangkok/---sro-bangkok/documents/publication/wcms_356950.pdf*.

Inter-Parliamentary Union (2017), "Women in Parliament" (database), *www.ipu.org/wmn-e/world.htm*.

IOM (2017), "Labour migration", *IOM Thailand*, International Organization for Migration, Bangkok, *https://thailand.iom.int/labour-migration*.

JETRO (2017), "Investment cost comparison", (database), Japan External Trade Organization, Tokyo, *www.jetro.go.jp/world/search/cost.html*.

Karlan, D. et al. (2016), "Getting to the top of mind: How reminders increase saving", Management *Science*, Vol. 62/12, pp. 3393-3411, doi.org/10.1287/mnsc.2015.2296.

Kawaguchi, D. and H. Mori (2017), "The labor market in Japan, 2000–2016", *IZA World of Labor*, *https://wol.iza.org/articles/the-labor-market-in-japan/long*.

Knodel, J., B. Teerawichitchainan and W. Pothisiri (2016), "Caring for Thai older persons with long-term care needs", *Research Collection School of Social Sciences*, No. 1945, *http://ink.library.smu.edu.sg/cgi/viewcontent.cgi?article=3202&context=soss_research*.

Knodel, J. et al. (2015), "The situation of Thailand's older population: An update based on the 2014 Survey of Older Persons in Thailand", *Population Studies Center Research Reports*, 15-847, University of Michigan Institute for Social Research, Ann Arbor, MI, *www.psc.isr.umich.edu/pubs/pdf/rr15-847.pdf*.

Lathapipat, D. and C. Poggi (2016), "From many to one: Minimum wage effects in Thailand", *PIER Discussion Papers*, No. 41, Puey Ungphakorn Institute for Economic Research, Bangkok, *www.pier.or.th/wp-content/uploads/2016/08/pier_dp_041.pdf*.

Leavitt, N. (11 May 2015), "Thailand seeks to address shortage of rural health care providers", *Harvard Chan School of Public Health*, *www.hsph.harvard.edu/news/features/thailand-seeks-to-address-shortage-of-rural-health-care-providers*.

Mastercard (2017), *Mastercard Index of Women Entrepreneurs*, Mastercard, New York, *https://newsroom.mastercard.com/wp-content/uploads/2017/03/Report-Mastercard-Index-of-Women-Entrepreneurs-2017-Mar-3.pdf*.

MOE (2017), *Education Development Plan 2017-2021* (in Thai), Ministry of Education, Bangkok, *http://waa.inter.nstda.or.th/stks/pub/2017/20170313-Education-Development-Plan-12.pdf*.

Mohsuwan, L. et al. (2011), *Report of Thai Health Survey 4th 2008-9: Child Health*, National Health Examination Survey Office, Ministry of Public Health, Nonthaburi.

NESDB (2017a), *Thailand Human Achievement Index 2017*, Office of the National Economic and Social Development Board, Bangkok, *www.nesdb.go.th/nesdb_en/download/article/social2-2560-eng.pdf*.

NESDB (2017b), *The Twelfth Economic and Social Development Plan (2017-2021)*, Office of the National Economic and Social Development Board, Bangkok, *www.nesdb.go.th/nesdb_en/ewt_w3c/ewt_dl_link.php?nid=4345*.

NESDB (2016), *Thailand's Social Development in Q4/2016 and Overall Situations in 2016*, Office of the National Economic and Social Development Board, Bangkok, *www.nesdb.go.th/nesdb_en/download/article/Social%20Press_Eng_Q4-2559.pdf*.

NESDB (2015), *Gross Regional and Provincial Product Chain Volume Measures*, Office of the National Economic and Social Development Board, Bangkok, *www.nesdb.go.th/nesdb_th/main.php?filename=gross_regional*.

NSO (2016a), *The Informal Employment Survey 2016*, National Statistical Office of Thailand, Bangkok, *http://web.nso.go.th/en/survey/lfs/imp/imp09.htm*.

NSO (2016b), *The Skills Development Survey*, National Statistical Office of Thailand, Bangkok, *http://web.nso.go.th/en/survey/desire/data/Full_Report2016.pdf*.

NSO (2015), *Social Indicators 2015*, National Statistical Office of Thailand, Bangkok, *http://service.nso.go.th/nso/nsopublish/pubs/e-book/e070759/index.html*.

OECD (2017a), "OECD Income Distribution Database (IDD): GINI, Poverty, Income, Methods and Concepts" (database), *www.oecd.org/social/income-distribution-database.htm*.

OECD (2017b), "OECD Labour Force Statistics" (database), *www.oecd.org/std/labour-stats*.

OECD (2017c), *How Immigrants Contribute to Thailand's Economy*, OECD Publishing, Paris, *http://dx.doi.org/10.1787/9789264287747-en*.

OECD (2017d), *OECD Economic Surveys: Mexico*, OECD Publishing, Paris, *http://dx.doi.org/10.1787/eco_surveys-mex-2017-en*.

OECD (2017e), "Indicators of Employment Protection Legislation" (database), *www.oecd.org/els/emp/oecdindicatorsofemploymentprotection.htm*.

OECD (2017f), *Behavioural Insights and Public Policy: Lessons from Around the World*, OECD Publishing, Paris, *http://dx.doi.org/10.1787/9789264270480-en*.

OECD (2017g), "OECD Health Statistics Database" (database), *http://stats.oecd.org/index.aspx?DataSetCode=HEALTH_STAT*.

OECD (2017h), *Economic Outlook for Southeast Asia, China and India: Addressing Energy Challenges*, OECD Publishing, Paris, *http://dx.doi.org/10.1787/saeo-2017-en*.

OECD (2017i), "Gender Portal" (database), *www.oecd.org/gender/data/labour-force-participation-by-sex-age.htm*.

OECD (2017j), *Strengthening Women's Entrepreneurship in ASEAN: Towards Increasing Women's Participation in Economic Activity*, OECD Publishing, Paris, *www.oecd.org/southeast-asia/regional-programme/Strengthening_Womens_Entrepreneurship_ASEAN.pdf*.

OECD (2016a), "OECD Employment and Labour Market Statistics" (database), *www.oecd-ilibrary.org/employment/data/trade-unions/trade-unions-trade-union-density-edition-2016_fbf99961-en*.

OECD (2016b), *PISA 2015 Results (Volume II): Policies and Practices for Successful Schools*, OECD Publishing, Paris. *http://dx.doi.org/10.1787/9789264267510-en*.

OECD (2016c), *PISA 2015 Results (Volume I): Excellence and Equity in Education*, OECD Publishing, Paris, *http://dx.doi.org/10.1787/9789264266490-en*.

OECD (2016d), *Innovating Education and Educating for Innovation: The Power of Digital Technologies and Skills*, OECD Publishing, Paris, *http://dx.doi.org/10.1787/9789264265097-en*.

OECD (2016e), *Trafficking in Persons and Corruption: Breaking the Chain*, OECD Publishing, Paris, *http://dx.doi.org/10.1787/9789264253728-en*.

OECD (2015a), *OECD Employment Outlook 2015*, OECD Publishing, Paris, *http://dx.doi.org/10.1787/empl_outlook-2015-en*.

OECD (2015b), *Fiscal Sustainability of Health Systems: Bridging Health and Financing Perspectives*, OECD Publishing, Paris, *http://dx.doi.org/10.1787/9789264233386-en*.

OECD (2015c), "PISA Database" (database), *www.oecd.org/pisa/data/2015database*.

OECD (2014a), *Southeast Asian Economic Outlook 2013 – With Perspectives on China and India*, OECD Publishing, Paris, *http://dx.doi.org/10.1787/saeo-2013-en*.

OECD (2014b), "Women in Politics" (database), *https://data.oecd.org/inequality/women-in-politics.htm*.

OECD (2014c), "Social Institutions and Gender Index" (database), *www.genderindex.org*.

OECD (2013a), "OECD Regional Database" (database), *http://stats.oecd.org/Index.aspx?DataSetCode=REGION_DEMOGR*.

OECD (2013b), *Pensions at a Glance Asia/Pacific 2013*, OECD Publishing, Paris, *http://dx.doi.org/10.1787/pension_asia-2013-en*.

OECD (2004), *OECD Employment Outlook*, OECD Publishing, Paris, *www.oecd.org/employment/emp/34846912.pdf*.

OECD and UNESCO (2016), *Education in Thailand: An OECD-UNESCO Perspective*, Review of National Policies for Education, OECD Publishing, Paris, *http://dx.doi.org/10.1787/9789264259119-en*.

OSMEP (2013), *White Paper on Small and Medium Enterprises of Thailand*, Office of Small and Medium Enterprise Promotion, Bangkok, *www.sme.go.th/upload/mod_download/Eng_04-20171018153410.pdf*.

Pande, R. and D. Ford (2011), "Gender quotas and female leadership: A review", Background Paper for the World Development Report on Gender Equality and Development, Washington, DC, *http://scholar.harvard.edu/files/rpande/files/gender_quotas_-_april_2011.pdf*.

QS (2018), "World University Rankings 2018" (database), QS TopUniversities, *www.topuniversities.com/university-rankings/world-university-rankings/2018*.

Rajatanavin, R. (2015), "Innovating Professional Education for Universal Health Coverage: Lessons from Thailand", *Dean's Distinguished Lecture Series*, April 28, Harvard School of Public Health, Boston. *www.hsph.harvard.edu/news/features/thailand-seeks-to-address-shortage-of-rural-health-care-providers*.

Schmitt, V., T. Sakunphanit and O. Prasitsiriphon (2013), *Social Protection Assessment Based National Dialogue: Towards a Nationally Defined Social Protection Floor in Thailand*, ILO, Bangkok, *www.ilo.org/wcmsp5/groups/public/---ed_protect/---soc_sec/documents/publication/wcms_213264.pdf*.

Solt, F. (2016), "The Standardized World Income Inequality Database", *Social Science Quarterly*, Vol. 97/5, pp. 1267-1281.

Sondergaard, L. and D. Lathapipat (2017), *Providing Quality Education to One Million Students in Thailand's Small Schools*, Washington, DC, World Bank, *http://blogs.worldbank.org/eastasiapacific/providing-quality-education-to-one-million-students-in-thailand-small-schools*.

SSO (2017), *Statistics for Social Fund*, Social Security Office, Bangkok, *www.sso.go.th/wpr/category.jsp?lang=th&cat=800*.

Teerawattananon, Y. (2017), "Obesity in Thailand and Its Economic Cost Estimation", *ADBI Working Paper Series*, No. 703, *www.adb.org/sites/default/files/publication/236536/adbi-wp703.pdf*.

UNDP (2014), *Advancing Human Development through the ASEAN Community, Thailand Human Development Report 2014*, Bangkok, United Nations Development Programme. *http://hdr.undp.org/sites/default/files/thailand_nhdr_2014_0.pdf*.

UNICEF (2017), *Early Childhood Development*, Bangkok, United Nations Children's Fund, *www.unicef.org/thailand/education_14938.html*.

UNICEF (4 October 2016), "Thailand's child support grant helps vulnerable families", *UNICEF Connect*, *https://blogs.unicef.org/east-asia-pacific/thailands-child-support-grant-helps-vulnerable-families*.

United Nations (2017), *Thailand's Voluntary National Review of the Implementation of the 2030 Agenda for Sustainable Development*, New York, United Nations, *https://sustainabledevelopment.un.org/content/documents/16147Thailand.pdf*.

US Department of State (2017), 2017 Trafficking in Persons Report Thailand, *https://www.state.gov/j/tip/rls/tiprpt/countries/2017/271297.htm*

Wannagatesiri, T., N. Kruea and A. Thongperm (2015), "Situations and guidelines for enhancement of Thai labors' vocational rehabilitation and retraining", *Procedia – Social and Behavioural Science*, Vol. 197, pp. 1053-1058, *https://ac.els-cdn.com/S1877042815043189/1-s2.0-S1877042815043189-main.pdf?_tid=46390dda-fee2-11e7-8160-00000aab0f6c&acdnat=1516563525_e5158b43d83c2e9b4c8bce40a46d4ec6*.

World Bank (2017a), *World Development Indicators* (database), Washington, DC, *https://data.worldbank.org/data-catalog/world-development-indicators*.

World Bank (2017b), *Enterprise Surveys* (database), *www.enterprisesurveys.org*.

World Bank (2017c), *Economic Inclusion of LGBTI Groups in Thailand*, World Bank, Washington, DC, *http://documents.worldbank.org/curated/en/197901494585972561/pdf/114995-REVISED-Economic-Inclusion-of-LGBTI-Groups-in-Thailand-English.pdf*.

World Bank (2016a), *Getting Back on Track: Reviving Growth and Securing Prosperity for All, Thailand Systematic Country Diagnostic*, World Bank, Washington, DC, *http://documents.worldbank.org/curated/en/855161479736248522/pdf/110396-REVISED-v1-4-26-WB-TH-SCD-REPORT-BOOKLET-159PAGE-RevisedApr26.pdf*.

World Bank (2016b), *Closing the Health Gaps for the Elderly: Promoting Health Equity and Social Inclusion in Thailand*, World Bank, Washington, DC, *http://documents.worldbank.org/curated/en/148431468299339382/pdf/AUS13326-REVISED-TITLE-HAS-CHANGED-PUBLIC-Closing-the-Health-Gaps-for-the-Elderly-English-final-for-IDU.pdf*.

World Bank (2012), *Reducing Elderly Poverty in Thailand: The Role of Thailand's Pension and Social Assistance Programs*, World Bank, Washington, DC, *http://documents.worldbank.org/curated/en/949741468120871479/pdf/805270WP0P14350Box0379805B00PUBLIC0.pdf*.

World Economic Forum (2017), *The Global Gender Gap Report*, Cologny/Geneva, *www3.weforum.org/docs/WEF_GGGR_2017.pdf*.

World Health Organisation (2016), "Global Health Observatory" (database), *www.who.int/gho/ncd/risk_factors/overweight/en*.

Multi-dimensional Review of Thailand
Volume 1. Initial Assessment

Chapter 2

Prosperity: Boosting productivity

The Prosperity pillar of the 2030 Agenda for Sustainable Development calls for an integrated approach based on boosting productivity through diversification, upgrading technology and innovation, and increasing employment and entrepreneurship. Thailand needs to address all these challenges to achieve high-income country status by 2036. Over the past decade, limited structural reform and capital investment have held back productivity growth and improvements in well-being, and Thailand has lost ground vis-à-vis regional comparators. More recently, however, economic growth has started to regain momentum helped by a pick-up in global trade, which has supported exports, and by a substantial public infrastructure investment programme. Moving forward, Thailand will need to boost productive capacity in the face of intensified competition with regional peers and rapid demographic ageing. In addition, productivity gains will be increasingly necessary to drive growth. Key areas of focus include improving human resource development, encouraging technology diffusion via cluster development, promoting innovation and digitalisation, improving the SME policy framework and expanding regional integration, as emphasised in the government's 12th Plan and Thailand 4.0.

Thailand has made commendable socio-economic progress since the 1970s and has ambitions to become a high-income country by 2036. This will require stepping up structural reforms to boost economic potential and inclusiveness. Thailand needs to develop human capital, foster innovation, invest in infrastructure, support SMEs and remain open to global trade, in line with the Prosperity pillar of the Sustainable Development Goals (SDGs), which calls for strong economic foundations through sustained and inclusive growth.

This chapter reviews Thailand's macroeconomic fundamentals, recent developments and projections. It also discusses the main structural challenges to boosting productivity and economic growth. These include removing obstacles preventing labour reallocation to higher-productivity sectors, increasing technology diffusion through cluster development, fostering innovation and digitalisation, improving the SME policy framework and furthering regional integration (for further discussion of human capital development, competition and regulation, see Chapters 1 and 5).

Sound macroeconomic fundamentals will help Thailand achieve its long-term growth ambitions

Thailand's ambition to become a high-income economy by 2036 calls for a substantial acceleration in growth rates. Between 1970 and 2016, Thailand's GDP growth per capita averaged 4.2% per year in purchasing power parity terms, with income per head reaching 42% of the OECD average in 2016 (Figure 2.1A). Thailand's economic structure underwent major changes during this period, with the share of the primary sector in GDP falling from 26% in 1970 to 8% in 2016. Concurrently, the share of industry rose from 25% to 36% and that of services increased from 49% to 56%, while the share of exports grew from 15% to 69%.

Structural reforms played an important role in this transformation, with trade and investment liberalisation and business-friendly regulatory reforms encouraging participation in global value chains (GVCs). As a result of these efforts, Thailand has become an integral part of GVCs in the Asia-Pacific region, particularly for automobile and electronics, which account for some 30% and 20% of total manufacturing output, respectively, up from about 10% for both sectors in 1996. Thailand's important role in regional GVCs is also reflected in automobile and electronics exports, which together account for around 30% of Thailand's total goods exports. Over 70% of goods exports go to the Asia-Pacific region, with Southeast Asian countries alone accounting for around a quarter of total goods exports. Tourism dominates the service sector in Thailand, which is one of the world's top tourist destinations. Tourism generates close to 13% of GDP, up from 4% in 1996, providing a valuable source of foreign exchange earnings. In 2016, Thailand welcomed 32.6 million tourists, the ninth largest inflow globally according to the World Tourism Organization.

Figure 2.1. **Thailand has been catching up but faster growth is needed**

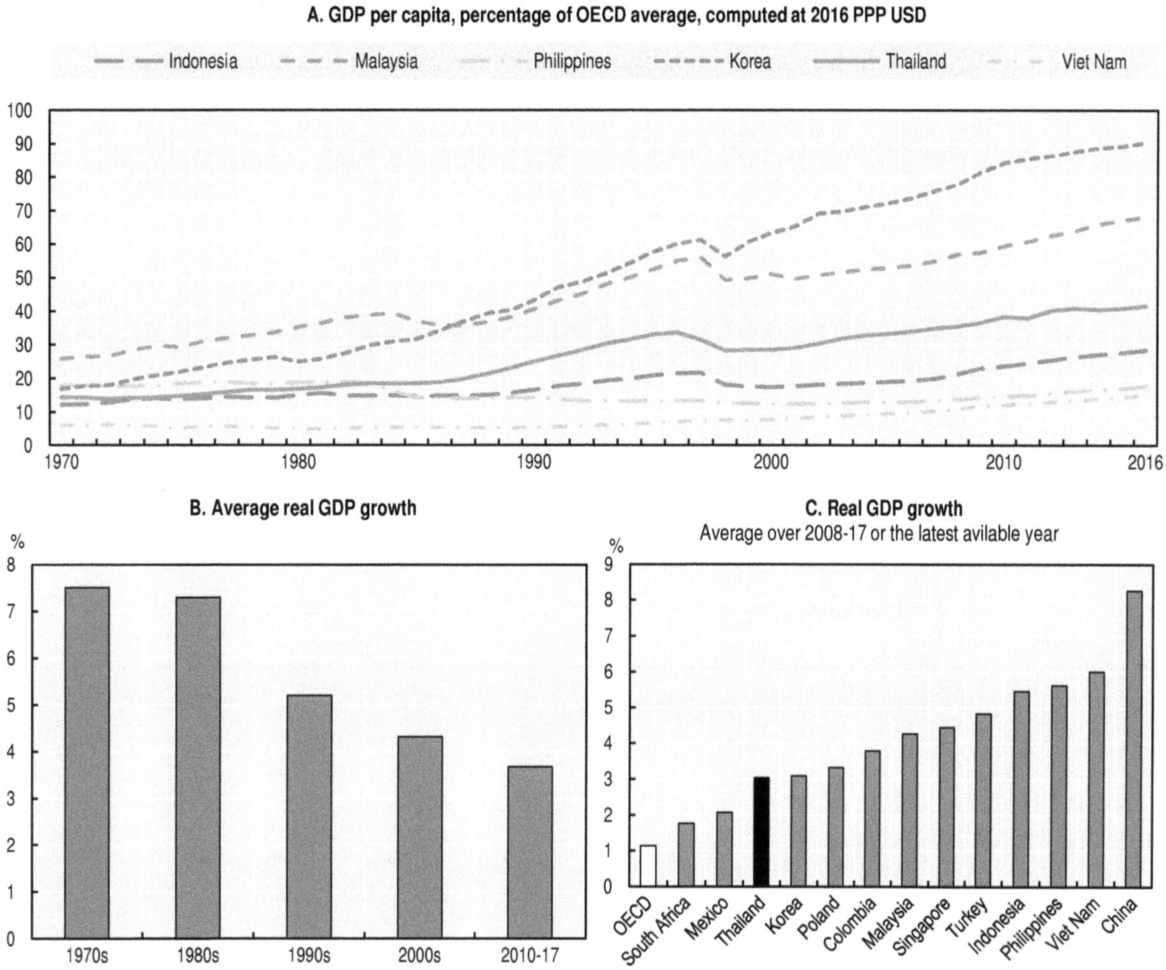

Note: In 2016, Thailand's per capita GDP in USD PPP was 17 359, versus an OECD average of 41 776.

Source: Conference Board (2017), *Total Economy Database*, May 2017, *www.conference-board.org/data/economydatabase*; Datastream and OECD calculations.

StatLink http://dx.doi.org/10.1787/888933691838

Growth has picked up in recent years

Trend GDP growth has declined progressively since the 1970s, due to unexpected shocks including the 1997-98 Asian financial crisis and the 2008 global financial crisis. In more recent times, growth has been hampered by the 2011 floods, which disrupted activities in key industrial areas, and broader political uncertainty, which affected investor confidence. Thailand's growth has thus remained below estimates of potential and is slower than in many comparator countries in East Asia (Figure 2.1B and 2.1C).

In recent years, growth has regained momentum, propelled by higher electronics exports, buoyant tourist arrivals and public investment (Figure 2.2A, C and D). Growth is projected to increase to 4.0% in 2018 and 4.1% in 2019 (Table 2.1). However, as the near-term outlook is largely supported by a cyclical uptick in global demand, Thailand will still need to undertake extensive structural reform to boost economic potential. The risks surrounding the projections are broadly balanced. On the one hand, exports and manufacturing performance could be stronger than foreseen, if global growth, and growth in ASEAN and China in particular, were to be faster. On the other hand, further implementation delays of the various planned infrastructure projects, increased global volatility from accelerated normalisation of monetary policy in advanced economies and a sharper slowdown in China, which accounts for around 11% of exports, could exert a drag on growth.

Figure 2.2. **Growth has been picking up, while investment has been lacklustre**

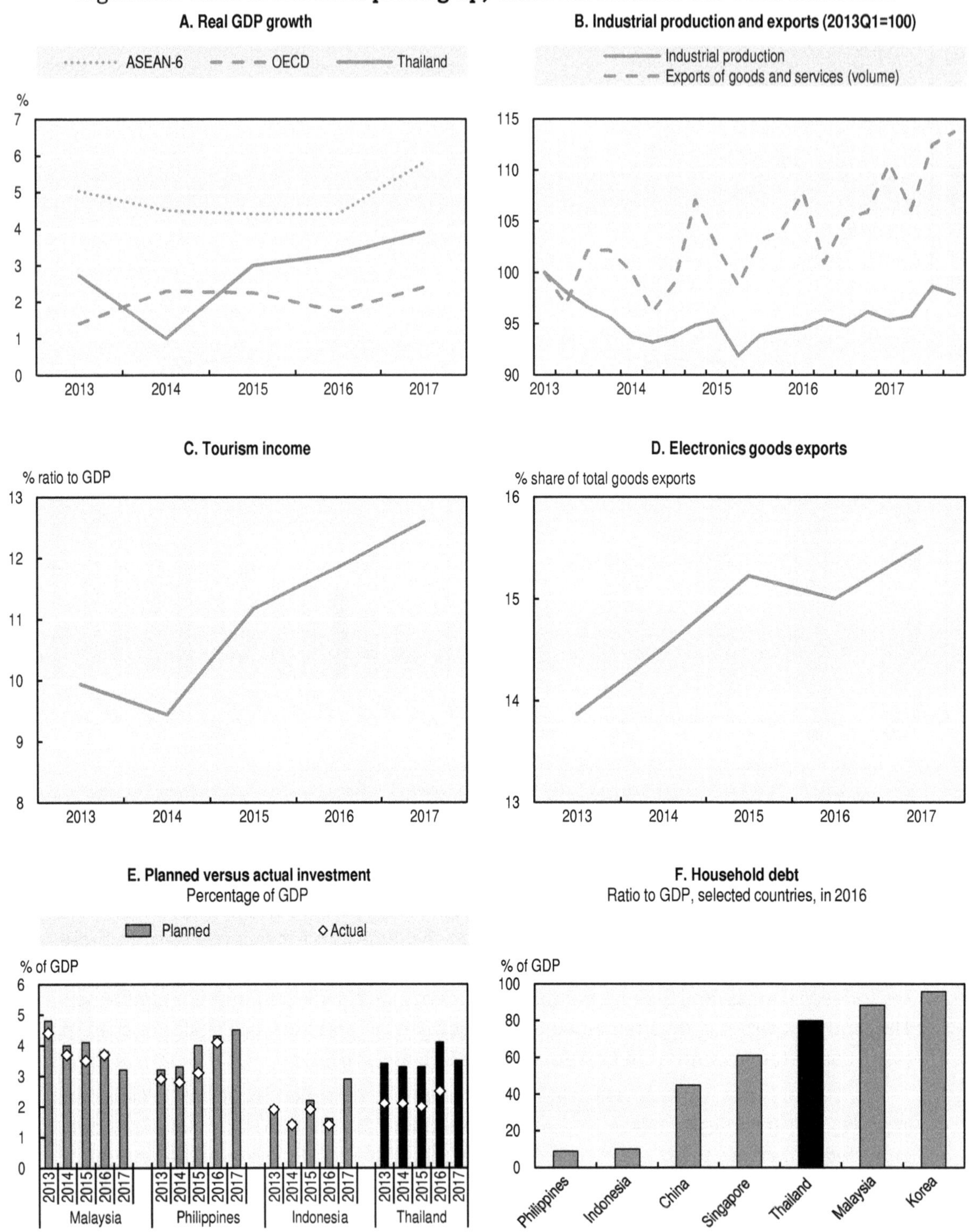

Note: ASEAN-6 is the weighted average growth rates of Indonesia, Malaysia, Philippines, Singapore, Thailand and Viet Nam. Tourism income refers to gross travel service receipts in the balance of payments.

Source: OECD (2017d), National Accounts database, *http://dx.doi.org/10.1787/na-data-en*; World Bank (2017), World Development Indicators, *http://databank.worldbank.org/data/home.aspx*; CEIC; Bank of Thailand; and Ministry of Commerce.

StatLink *http://dx.doi.org/10.1787/888933691857*

Table 2.1. **Macroeconomic indicators and projections**

Annual percentage changes unless specified

	2013	2014	2015	2016	2017	2018	2019
						Projection	
Real GDP	**2.7**	**1.0**	**3.0**	**3.3**	**3.9**	**4.0**	**4.1**
Private consumption	0.9	0.8	2.3	3.0	3.2	3.2	3.4
Public consumption	1.5	2.8	2.5	2.2	0.5	3.5	2.5
Gross fixed capital formation	-1.0	-2.2	4.3	2.8	0.9	4.2	4.7
- Private	-1.5	-0.9	-2.1	0.5	1.7	2.2	2.5
- Public	0.8	-6.6	28.4	9.5	-1.2	9.8	10.4
Exports (goods and services)	2.7	0.3	1.6	2.8	5.5	5.3	5.9
Imports (goods and services)	1.7	-5.3	0.0	-1.0	6.8	6.6	6.8
Consumer prices	2.2	1.9	-0.9	0.2	0.7	1.2	1.5
Policy interest rate (end-year, in %)	2.5	2.0	1.5	1.5	1.5	1.5	1.5
Unemployment rate (% of labour force)	0.7	0.8	0.9	1.0	1.2	1.2	1.2
Current account balance (% of GDP)	-1.2	3.7	8.1	11.7	10.8	8.5	8.0
General government fiscal balance (% of GDP, fiscal year)	0.5	-0.8	0.1	0.6	-1.7[1]	-1.8	-1.8
Public debt (% of GDP, fiscal year)[2]	42.2	43.4	42.5	41.8	41.9	41.2	40.6
Household debt (% of GDP)	76.6	79.9	81.2	79.9	78.3[3]	-	-
Gross official reserves (end-year, USD billion)	167.2	157.1	156.5	171.9	202.6	-	-
World trade growth (volume)	3.6	3.7	2.7	2.6	5.2	4.1	4.0
Oil price (spot, Brent, USD per tonne)	108.6	99.0	52.4	43.7	51.7	65.0	65.0

1. This figure is a projection. Final outcome was unavailable at the time of publication.
2. As of the end of the fiscal year (September). Includes general government and state-owned enterprises debt.
3. As of the end of 3Q 2017.

Source: OECD (2017k), Economic Outlook 102 database; CEIC database; NESDB; Bank of Thailand and Public Debt Management Office (February 2019).

Indeed, while exports have been accelerating in 2017, industrial production growth has been modest and domestic demand remains sluggish, with lacklustre private investment (Figure 2.2B), slow implementation of public infrastructure projects (Figure 2.2E), and consumption growth hampered by high household debt (Figure 2.2F). Accordingly, the current account surplus remains very large (Figure 2.3C). Looking further ahead, the Bank of Thailand (BoT) states that in the absence of structural reforms, export growth (in dollar value terms) will slow beyond 2018 to 2-3% per annum, down from an average of 10% over the past decade (BoT, 2017).

For trend growth to approach the 5-6% rate needed to achieve Thailand's high-income status ambitions under the 12th Plan, a revival in investment is needed. To this end, the government should prioritise investment spending. Reliance in recent years on consumer-related measures, such as income tax rebates, rural subsidies and cash handouts to low-income households, has provided relief to some groups as well as short-term stimulus, but has done little to increase longer-term productive capacity. Programmed higher public investment, particularly in infrastructure, may help lift the anaemic private investment rate. Although it is important Thailand remain fiscally prudent, undertaking targeted public investment in productivity-enhancing infrastructure is necessary to increase economic potential. Notwithstanding the government's ambitious infrastructure investment programme, public debt expected to remain around 41% of GDP in the coming years (see below). Some of the vulnerabilities that are difficult to assess in the context of this projection feature in Table 2.2.

Figure 2.3. **Inflation is low, the exchange rate has appreciated and the share of bad loans has risen**

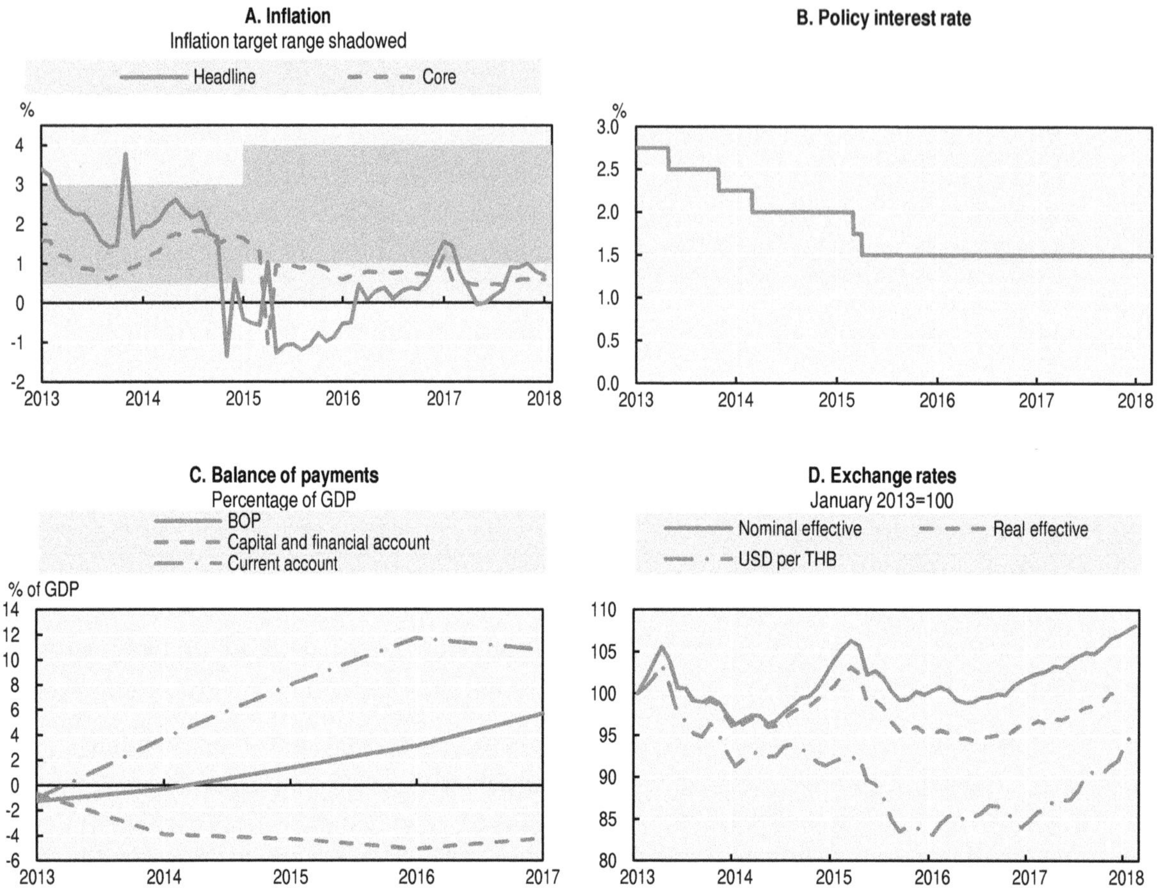

Note: A: The inflation target changed from the quarterly average of core inflation to an annual average headline rate in 2015.

Source: CEIC; Bank of Thailand.

StatLink http://dx.doi.org/10.1787/888933691876

Table 2.2. **Selected vulnerabilities**

Potential shock	Likely economic impact
More frequent natural disasters	Loss of assets, lower agricultural production and disruption of value chains
Hard landing for emerging economies, particularly China	Negative spillovers on growth through real and financial sector channels, amplified by close regional integration
Increase in protectionism	With foreign trade accounting for over 100% of GDP, growth would be affected
Intensified geopolitical tensions	Unexpected turbulence in the financial markets and weakening of business confidence
Turmoil in international financial markets	Tighter financing conditions and growth setback
More frequent or more harmful cyber-attacks	Economic and social disruptions

The government has long recognised the key role of infrastructure investment to boost both inclusivity and economic growth. While planning efforts in this area have been stepped up, implementation has lagged (Figure 2.2E). In the coming years, it will be important to ensure that unnecessary red tape does not slow down the approval and rollout of new infrastructure projects and improvements are made in both financing arrangements and public-private partnerships processes (Chapter 3). Public investment is expected to pick up soon with the resolution of land issues that will allow several mass-transit projects to proceed. In addition, the approval by Parliament of key Eastern Economic Corridor (EEC) legislation will incentivise inward foreign direct investment (FDI) to the area.

Monetary policy targets low inflation

Thailand's independent central bank, the Bank of Thailand (BoT), has a broad range of responsibilities including monetary policy, financial sector regulation and payment systems. It has been pursuing flexible inflation targeting since 2000, which has enhanced the credibility of the monetary policy framework, as is the case in a number of OECD countries. In 2015, the target changed from 0.5-3.0% for the quarterly average of core inflation to an annual average headline rate of 2.5% with a tolerance band of ± 1.5%. Monetary policy transparency is high, with edited minutes of the discussions of the Monetary Policy Committee, which meets eight times a year, released publicly two weeks after each meeting, as well as four press conferences per year. The Committee's membership is diverse and consists of four external experts, the BoT Governor and two Deputy Governors.

Since April 2015, the policy rate has remained at 1.5%, just 25 basis points above the record low reached in 2009 in the aftermath of the global financial crisis. Headline inflation, which turned negative in 2015, was below the target range, and underlying price pressures remain very subdued, with core inflation below 1% since November 2015. Even so, the policy rate is expected to remain unchanged in 2018 given the persistent appreciation of the Thai baht in recent years and high household debt.

Headline inflation is projected to inch up and to re-enter the policy target band in 2018. While output growth is on course to increase, not least thanks to the anticipated rollout in infrastructure spending, inflationary pressures are expected to remain contained, reflecting a variety of structural factors. These may include reduced agricultural output costs due to economies of scale and improved irrigation, continued globalisation and improvements in GVCs, and increased e-commerce amid a burgeoning digital economy (see below) (BoT, 2017).

Thailand has some strong buffers

Thailand has a long history of fiscal prudence and in the near term the fiscal outlook remains sound. Since 2013, the general government fiscal balance has averaged a slight surplus. Looking ahead, however, deficits are projected commensurate with the government's large public infrastructure investment programme and additional funding for farm sector reform and expanded social welfare included in the 2018 supplementary budget. Public debt-to-GDP is expected to edge down as a result of the projected uptick in economic growth. Ongoing fiscal reforms, such as the introduction of an inheritance tax and a land and building tax, will help raise revenue. On the spending side, the share in GDP of general government outlays, at around 21% of GDP, is only half of the OECD average, but similar to the levels in Malaysia (22%), Mexico (22%) and the Philippines (17%). Subsidies have been reduced substantially, in line with the government's commitment to rationalise non-productive subsidy programmes via fuel subsidy reform, and the replacement of the rice pledging scheme with a more targeted alternative. Over the longer term, however, ageing will be a major challenge for fiscal sustainability (Chapter 3).

On the external side, Thailand has sizeable buffers. The current account surplus was close to 11% of GDP in 2017, and foreign exchange reserves are equivalent to about 13 months of imports and three times short-term external debt (Figure 2.3C). The large current account surplus, driven by high tourism receipts and buoyant exports as well as a falling oil import bill following the oil price decline in 2014-15, has underpinned currency appreciation (Figure 2.3D). The anticipated pick-up in public investment in the coming years should help increase imports, easing one source of upward pressure on the Thai baht.

The pace and modalities of Thailand's financial liberalisation efforts will also have a bearing on the exchange rate. Since 2010, the central bank has embarked on a financial liberalisation strategy, focusing especially on the deregulation of the capital account and other foreign exchange measures. Going forward, it is considering further measures including lowering foreign exchange hedging requirements for financial institutions' offshore investments and encouraging outward FDI.

Thailand's financial sector is sound despite vulnerabilities in some areas

Overall, the financial sector is sound, notwithstanding the risks posed by high household debt, rising non-performing loans and possible vulnerabilities from the expanding shadow banking sector. Financial institutions are highly capitalised, in some cases exceeding the Basel III regulation standards (Figure 2.4A). In addition, the central bank is implementing the stricter net stable funding ratio, complementing the existing liquidity coverage ratio, across all financial institutions from January 2018. It has also been proactive in designating five major banks as of systemic domestic importance, with higher capital requirements to be phased in by 2020. However, the share of non-performing business loans has increased, especially for small and medium-sized enterprises (which accounted for over half of total non-performing loans as of end-2017) (Figure 2.4B). This could become a growing problem in the future when interest rates rise. Furthermore, households have been shifting deposits to more lightly regulated non-bank financial institutions, which offer higher-yielding instruments and cheaper funding. This has also favoured bond issuance by higher-rated firms. Harmonising regulatory treatment across all financial institutions, with integrated supervision of conglomerates and liquidity risk, may help preserve financial stability (IMF, 2017).

Figure 2.4. **Non-performing loans are on the rise**

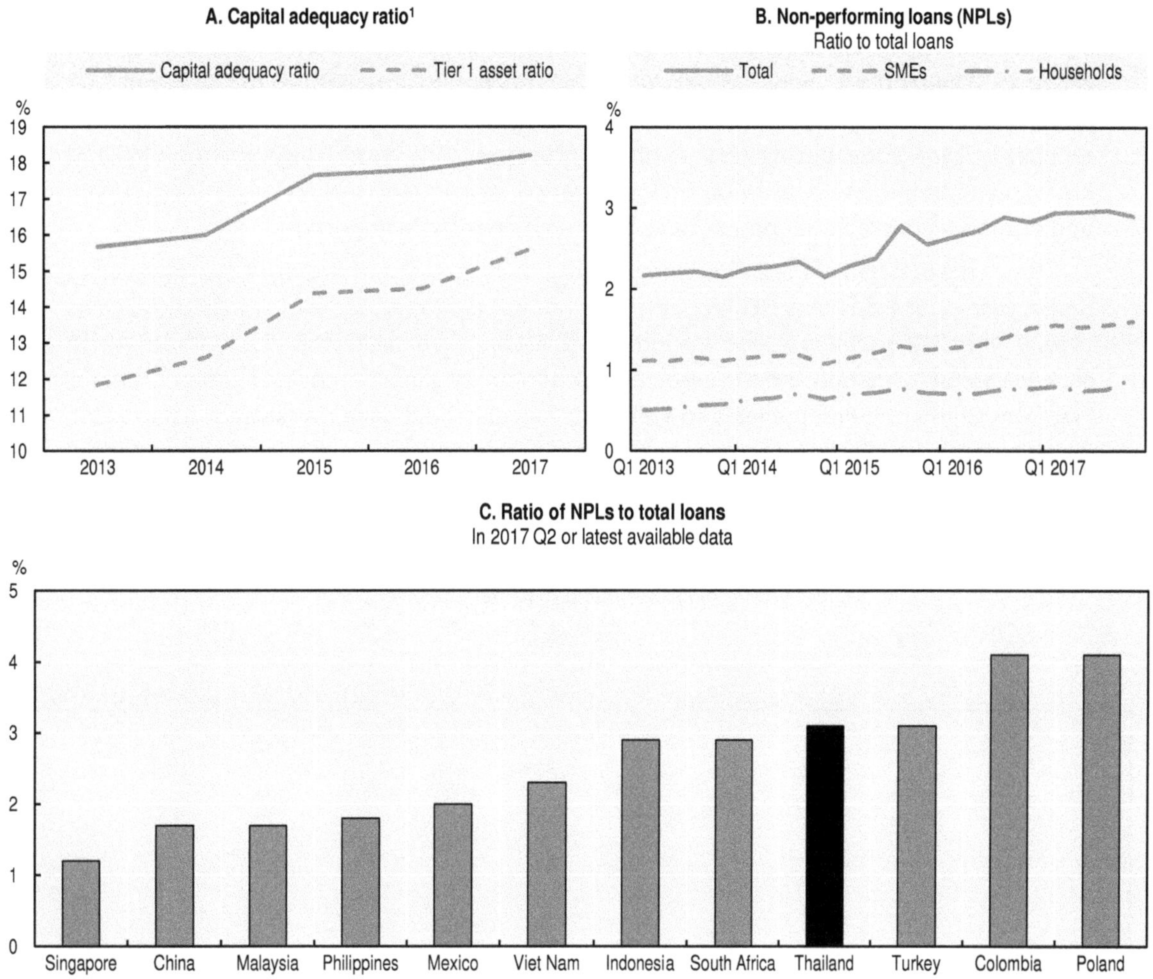

1. For domestically incorporated commercial banks.

Source: CEIC; Bank of Thailand; IMF (2017), Financial Soundness Indicators (database).

StatLink http://dx.doi.org/10.1787/888933691895

Boosting productivity on the way to Thailand 4.0

Improving labour productivity is key to Thailand 4.0

Productivity performance conditions long-run economic prosperity and well-being. Differences in labour productivity across countries are reflected in per capita income gaps. As in other East Asian emerging economies, productivity gains made during Thailand's early industrialisation phase came from the reallocation of under-utilised rural labour from agriculture to labour-intensive manufacturing, supported by capital accumulation and imported technology embodied in FDI. To attain high-income country status, Thailand's growth needs to be driven increasingly by productivity gains, rather than by the sheer accumulation of capital and labour inputs.

Thailand's 12th Plan sets a target of over 2.5% annual growth both for labour productivity and total factor productivity (TFP), enshrined in Thailand 4.0 and premised on innovation, human capital development, regulatory reform and infrastructure development.

This compares with a 1.1% average TFP growth rate experienced over 2011-15. Thailand 4.0 entails a transformation to a more productivity and technology-driven economy. It embodies a progression from the accumulation of capital and labour inputs led by the agricultural sector in "Thailand 1.0", light industry (e.g. food processing and textiles) in "Thailand 2.0", and heavy industry (e.g. petrochemicals and steel) in "Thailand 3.0". Gains from imported technology are contributing less to productivity growth, while high-technology and knowledge-intensive activities, domestic innovation, investment in knowledge-based capital and human resource development have become increasingly important.

Since the first half of the 2000s, labour productivity growth has averaged 3%. However, in recent years, and as in many OECD countries, it has not recovered to pre-global financial crisis rates (Figure 2.5), partially due to weak demand arising from lacklustre global trade, which slowed capital formation and the associated productivity gains. Intensified competition for FDI from China, the Philippines and Viet Nam has also held back investment (Figure 2.6), as have domestic political uncertainty, delays in public investment projects and widening skills gaps (Chapter 1).

Figure 2.5. **Thailand needs to further boost labour productivity growth**

Average growth of labour productivity per employee per year

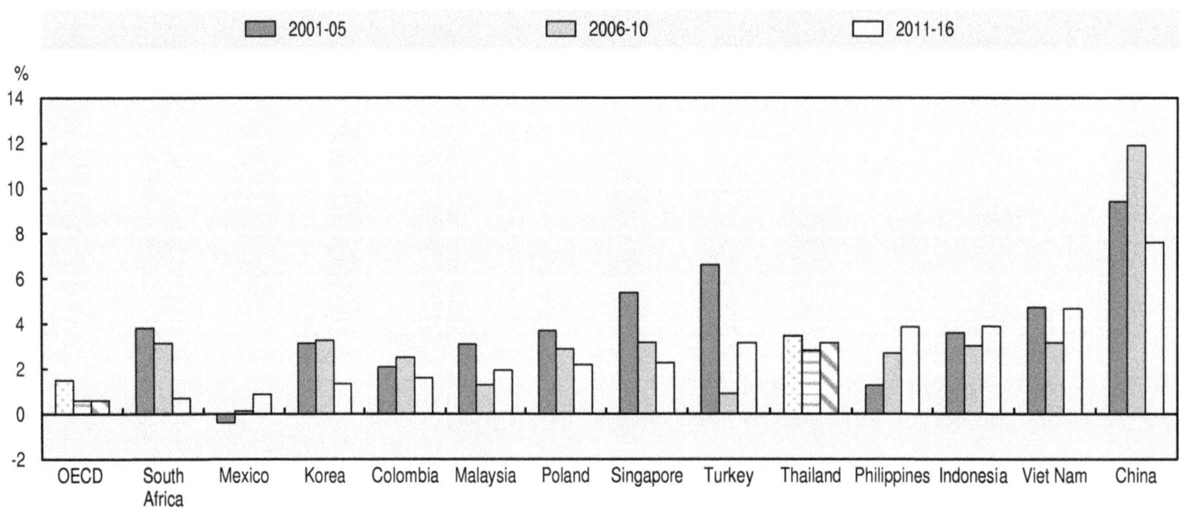

Source: OECD calculations based on data provided by the National Statistical Office and Datastream; OECD (2017e), Productivity Statistics database, *www.oecd.org/std/productivity-stats*

StatLink http://dx.doi.org/10.1787/888933691914

Thailand's historical competitive advantage in labour-intensive manufacturing is eroding due to higher wage costs, compared with regional peers such as Indonesia, the Philippines and Viet Nam. This partly reflects demographics: Thailand's population is ageing earlier than in other East Asian countries, which weighs on domestic labour supply. Indeed, the contribution of labour inputs to GDP growth was substantial through the 1990s, but declined gradually afterwards and even turned negative in 2011-15 (Figure 2.7).

Labour reallocation from the low-productivity agricultural sector in rural areas to higher-productivity sectors in urban areas is a key feature of catch-up growth and structural transformation. In Thailand, the share of the primary sector in GDP, at 8% in 2016, is not far above the average for upper middle-income countries, but its share of total employment (33%) is still high and closer to that of lower middle-income countries such as Indonesia and the Philippines (Figure 2.8A). Labour productivity in Thailand's agricultural sector relative to the manufacturing and services sectors has room to improve compared with other countries in the region (Figure 2.8B).

Figure 2.6. **Lacklustre capital formation has held back growth and productivity**

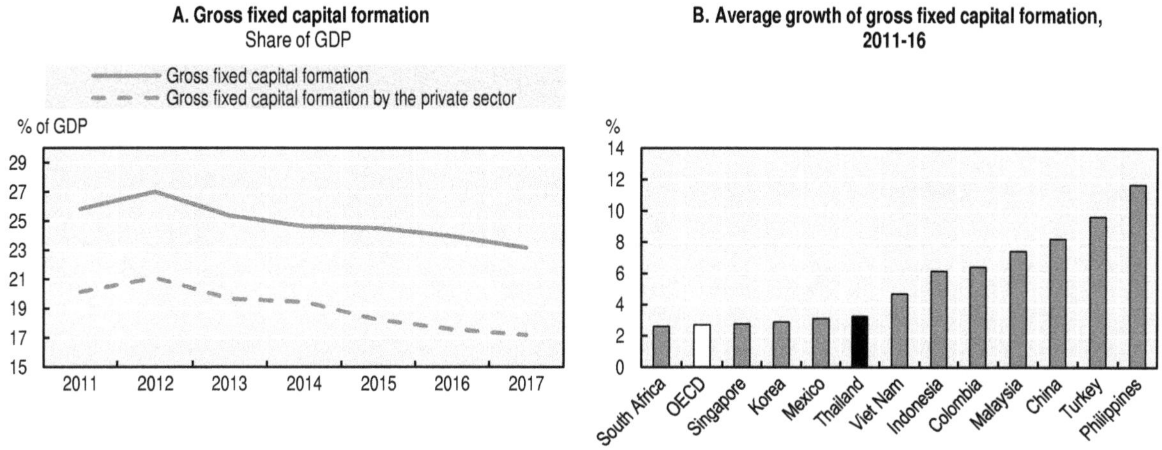

Source: NESDB; World Bank (2017), *World Development Indicators* (database), *http://databank.worldbank.org/data/home.aspx.*

StatLink *http://dx.doi.org/10.1787/888933691933*

Figure 2.7. **Labour input has not driven Thailand's recent growth**

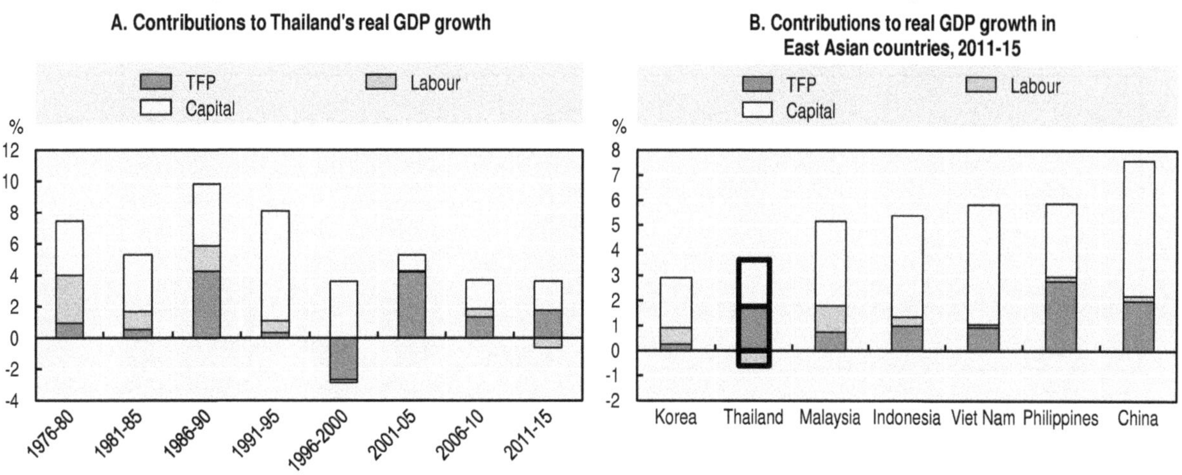

Source: Asia Productivity Organization (2017), Productivity database 2017 Version 1, *www.apo-tokyo.org/wedo/measurement.*

StatLink *http://dx.doi.org/10.1787/888933691952*

Over the past three decades, the contribution of labour reallocation to overall labour productivity growth has declined (Figure 2.9A). From 2001 to 2015, it was lower than in China and Viet Nam (Figure 2.9B), reflecting the impact of rising agricultural commodity prices in the world market and a widening skills mismatch for rural migrant workers. Additionally, rural development policy in the first half of the 2010s, notably a rice-pledging scheme launched in October 2011 and abolished in 2014 (under which the government bought rice at a considerably higher cost than the market price), may have discouraged labour reallocation by distorting its expected return (Egawa, 2015).

Figure 2.8. **Employment in the primary sector remains high and productivity low**

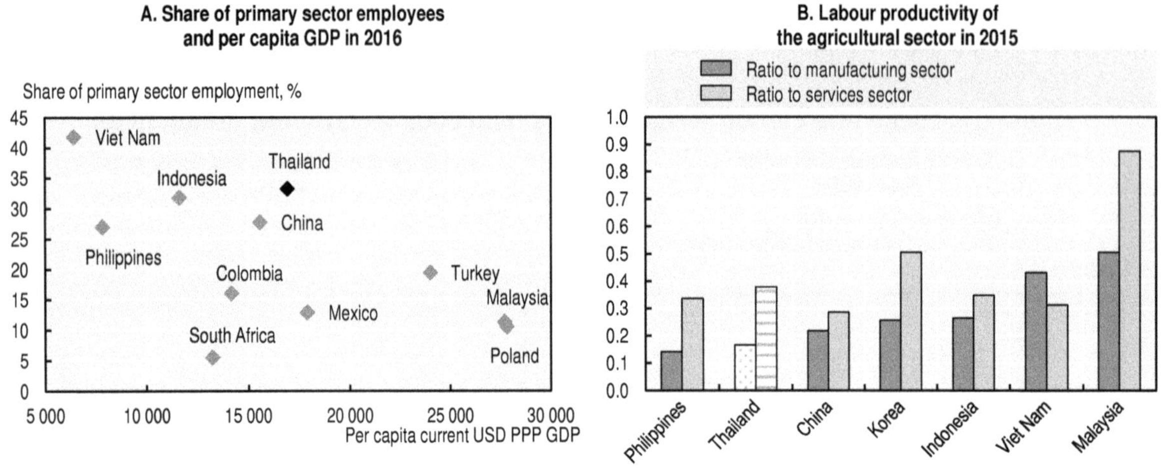

Source: World Bank (2017), World Development Indicators database, *http://databank.worldbank.org/data/home.aspx*; ILO (2017), ILO Stat (database), *www.ilo.org/global/statistics-and-databases/lang--en/index.htm*; and Asia Productivity Organization (2017), Productivity database 2017 Version 1, *www.apo-tokyo.org/wedo/measurement*.

StatLink http://dx.doi.org/10.1787/888933691971

Figure 2.9. **Labour reallocation has not boosted productivity substantially in Thailand**

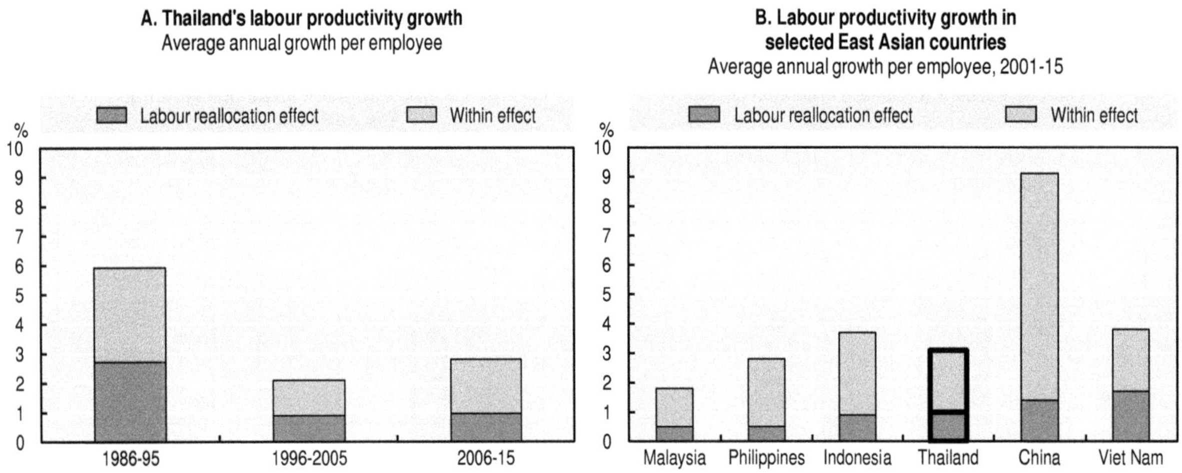

Note: The "within effect" refers to the contribution to total labour productivity growth from productivity growth within sectors. The "labour reallocation effect" refers to the contribution of the movement of labour from lower to higher-productivity sectors, where sectors are disaggregated into nine categories: (i) primary; (ii) mining; (iii) manufacturing; (iv) construction; (v) electricity, gas and water supply; (vi) wholesale and retail trade, and hotels and restaurants; (vii) transport and communications; (viii) financial intermediation, real estate and business activities; and (ix) community, social and personal services.

Source: OECD calculations based on Asia Productivity Organization (2017), Productivity database 2017 Version 1, *www.apo-tokyo.org/wedo/measurement*.

StatLink http://dx.doi.org/10.1787/888933691990

To remedy this, the government should encourage such reallocation by narrowing skills mismatches through lifelong learning and skills training. In addition, it should promote productivity gains in the agricultural sector by spurring the transformation of the traditional family-based and low technology model. In this regard, the 12th Plan aims to integrate fragmented farm land to facilitate the introduction of higher skills and technology and reap economies of scale. Thailand is also encouraging innovation through expanded ICT use, particularly through the Smart Agriculture Programme. The latter develops databases and knowledge management systems to provide useful data to farmers in specific localities and for specific agricultural products. OECD experience suggests that providing farmers with access to innovations that meet their diverse and complex needs, ensures that public spending on agricultural R&D raises agricultural productivity more effectively and sustainably, compared with other public expenditures in agriculture such as irrigation and fertiliser subsidies (OECD, 2015, 2017j). Agricultural policy should also be diversified from supporting rice production to promote more high value-added products such as livestock and horticultural products. In the process, it is important to avoid introducing incentives that would leave some rural groups behind.

The importance of food processing and food-related services will grow, particularly in rural areas, as primary agriculture becomes more capital and knowledge-intensive and less labour intensive. Thailand should strengthen the competitiveness of food industries that add value to primary agricultural products, bearing in mind that policies to boost the domestic prices of agricultural products are likely to have the opposite effect. The OECD's Trade in Value-Added database shows that value-added from Thailand's service sector is low in food and agriculture exports (OECD-WTO, 2017). Thailand should enhance the linkage between the agrifood sector and the service sector to promote high value-added food production, including the development of agriculture-related service industries such as technical services and farm machine services, and distribution via e-commerce of local specialities. Another policy area that merits attention is the regulatory environment. Strengthening food safety standards and the food labelling system, among others, will contribute to ensuring a fair market valuation for high-quality products.

To boost productivity gains, narrowing the productivity gap between frontier and lagging firms in the manufacturing and services sectors is also key. A large share of lagging firms is likely to be small businesses run by low-skilled entrepreneurs, employing low-skilled workers, and operating informally or semi-informally. OECD experience suggests that catch-up with high-productivity firms can be facilitated through human capital development, encouraging technology diffusion, promoting digitalisation, improving the SME policy framework and furthering regional integration (OECD, 2016b). These policies are prioritised in the 12th Plan and are discussed below.

A holistic approach is required for cluster development

In the context of Thailand 4.0, the government selected a set of priority sectors which builds off the existing industrial base in November 2015, comprising "First S-Curve" and "New S-Curve" industries (MOI, 2015). The "S-Curve" concept posits that during the infancy stage, an industry's growth is relatively slow due to limited market size; once economies of scale take hold and the market expands, output rises rapidly, and eventually growth levels off due to demand saturation. First S-curve industries aim to upgrade the existing industrial base and include sectors such as agro-products processing, automobile and electronics manufacturing, and tourism, with a view to maintaining growth momentum in the short and medium term. They include next-generation automotive (e.g. electronic vehicles), smart electronics (e.g. high value-added ICT products), medical and wellness tourism, agriculture and biotechnology, and food for the future (e.g. functional foods). New S-curve industries are found in sectors identified as promising drivers of growth in the long term, based upon further technological sophistication. They include robotics, aviation and logistics, biofuels and biochemicals, the digital industry and the medical hub.

To support the development of these priority sectors, the government has launched investment promotion measures in designated Special Economic Zones (SEZs), located in different areas and with specific purposes (Table 2.3). SEZs are based on the concept of clusters designed to improve industrial value chains by strengthening linkages among firms, research and academic institutions, and public organisations within a geographical area. The government designates the SEZs and provides financial incentives (e.g. tax reduction and subsidies to innovation and human resource development by firms), as well as non-financial stimuli (e.g. simplifying visa procedures for skilled foreign labour and easing the regulation of foreign equity and land ownership). In July 2016, the government designated three provinces in the east coast area as the Eastern Economic Corridor (EEC). This flagship SEZ builds on the existing manufacturing and energy industrial base. The government has an ambitious target for public and private investment in the EEC of THB 1.5 trillion (some 10% of 2016 nominal GDP) over 2017-21.

Although industrial cluster policies have been in place in Thailand since the early 2000s, their success in creating a base of high value-added industries has been limited. Moreover, policy measures have concentrated on providing financial incentives to investment such as tax breaks, but have not adequately promoted agglomeration within the cluster. In particular, weak collaboration and co-ordination at various levels, including the government, firms, and research and academic institutions, hampered the horizontal and vertical integration of stakeholders in the clusters (Fukuoka et al., 2016).

Table 2.3. **Thailand's Special Economic Zones**

Border area SEZs	Ten provinces close to the borders of neighbouring ASEAN countries aiming to boost cross-border trade and employment (started in 2016).
Super-clusters and other targeted clusters	Super cluster zones located in 32 provinces in total (including overlaps), mainly in the Central and Eastern regions. Targeted sectors include: automotive and parts, electrical and electronics, eco-friendly petrochemicals, digital services, food, aviation and aerospace, automation and robotics, and medical services. Other targeted clusters are located in rural regions and focus on agro-processing and textiles (started in 2016).
Eastern Economic Corridor (EEC)	Three coastal provinces (Cachengsao, Chonburi and Rayong) in the Eastern region aiming to promote 10 S-curve industries. The Act to develop the EEC passed in February 2018. FDI in the EEC will be encouraged through tax incentives, infrastructure development and zone-specific regulatory reform (e.g. easing visa restrictions for foreign workers).

Source: Board of Investment, Thailand (2017).

OECD experience shows that successful clusters are underpinned by good public governance characterised by the ability to respond adequately to industry needs, strengthen skills training for the local labour force and support the entry of innovative SMEs (OECD, 2009). In line with these observations, the government set up an EEC Policy Committee chaired by the Prime Minister. To ensure effective collaboration and communication among stakeholders, the Committee is composed of relevant ministers and private sector representatives. The Policy Committee is pursuing a range of initiatives; for example, it is seeking to halve the 20-month approval process for public-private partnership infrastructure projects by streamlining duplicative bureaucratic work.

To strengthen collaboration between research and academic institutions and firms in SEZs, the government has made access to investment incentives in some SEZs, most notably the EEC conditional on various forms of co-operation including participation in the Talent Mobility Programme and the government's human resource development programmes, such as the promotion of internship and dual systems that combine on-the-job training and school (see below).

While the government is undertaking high-profile promotion efforts targeted at foreign investors, clear and detailed plans and measures would help enhance linkages between foreign and domestic firms in the SEZs, notably the EEC. This would strengthen technology diffusion and ensure that the benefits of regional-based industrial cluster policies are shared, thereby promoting nationwide well-being and reducing regional inequality. Encouraging the entry of innovative domestic SMEs and their participation in horizontal and vertical agglomeration within the SEZs is key in this respect.

Fostering innovation will help Thailand move up the value-added ladder

Thailand needs to facilitate further domestic innovation to realise Thailand 4.0 and move up the value-added ladder. As industries and companies innovate, their competitiveness in international markets, participation in GVCs and the quality of their products improve. The efficient production of higher quality and higher value-added products leads to sustainable growth in real income and living standards. This is all the more important in a world of rapid technological progress and falling automation costs. However, Thailand's innovation performance, as measured for example by the Global Innovation Index, has either fallen behind or lost ground vis-à-vis some comparator East Asian countries.

To date, imported technology linked to FDI has been the major source of innovation. Given the lack of backward linkages, this foreign-sourced technology has not spilled over to domestic businesses. Indeed, while Thailand is exporting goods such as automobiles and hard disk drives, its input into the production of these goods tends to be at the lower value end, with higher-end components imported rather than produced domestically (ADB, 2015).

Recognising the importance of fostering innovation, the government put in place a ten-year National Science Technology and Innovation Master Plan 2012-2021 (STI Plan), which sets out societal, economic and environmental objectives based on the increased use of science, technology and innovation. It seeks to facilitate innovation by expanding the quantity and quality of research and development (R&D) and improving enabling institutions and infrastructure including human capital. So far, R&D investment, especially in applied research, has been modest and has held back innovation (NESDB, 2017). In addition, a constraining regulatory environment and poor human capital have hampered innovation (Chapter 1).

As part of the STI Plan and the 12th Plan, the government is seeking to boost R&D spending as a share of GDP to 1.5% by 2021, with 70% coming from the private sector. It also intends to increase the share of R&D personnel to 0.25% of full-time employees (NESDB, 2017; NSTIPO, 2014). Thus far, results have been mixed. Gross expenditure on R&D has increased in recent years, reaching 0.6% of GDP in 2015, but remains below target and lower than other countries in the region including Malaysia (1.3%), China (2.1%) and Singapore (2.2%), as well as the OECD average (2.4%) (Figure 2.10). Even so, its composition has improved, with the share of business innovation rising from 52% in 2011 to 66% in 2015 (UNESCO-UIS, 2017). Targeted policy measures over the past two years have also helped. The tax deduction available for R&D expenses was raised from an already high 200% to 300%, and the government established a competitiveness fund that provides matching grants for projects engaged in R&D and for those that undertake technology transfer or acquisition activities. Furthermore, the share of R&D personnel has risen from 0.079% in 2011 to 0.132% in 2015 (UNESCO-UIS, 2017).

Promotion of innovation has been hindered, however, by governance issues including weak co-ordination and lack of clarity around institutional roles and responsibilities. This often leads to the dispersion of funds across multiple projects with insufficient critical mass. Moreover, the limited involvement of industry in public R&D activities hampers technology transfer and commercialisation potential (UNCTAD, 2015). The absence of a strategic approach at all levels of the process (including policy development, funding and research priorities) is creating overlaps in operations among concerned organisations, and delays in technology and innovation development (NESDB, 2017).

Figure 2.10. **Thailand's R&D expenditure is rising, but remains below many comparator countries**

Gross expenditure on R&D per cent, 2015

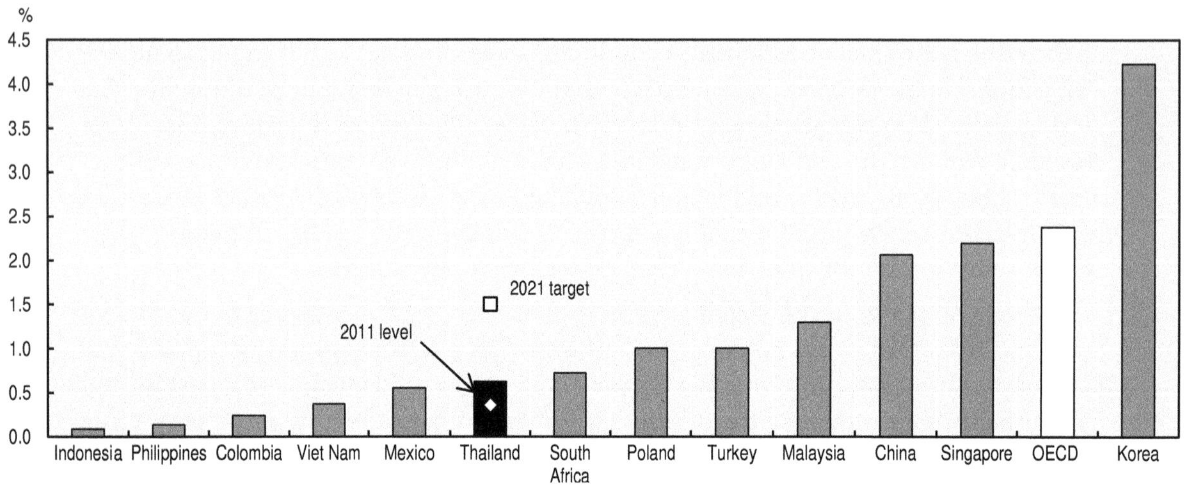

Note: The 2% R&D expenditure target included in the STI Plan was subsequently revised downwards in the 12th Plan to 1.5%. Data for Indonesia, the Philippines, Viet Nam and South Africa refer to 2013. Data for Turkey and Singapore refer to 2014.

Source: UNESCO-UIS (2017), Science, Technology and Innovation (dataset), UIS Data Centre, *http://data.uis.unesco.org*; and OECD (2017f), Gross domestic spending on R&D, *https://data.oecd.org/rd/gross-domestic-spending-on-r-d.htm*.

StatLink http://dx.doi.org/10.1787/888933692009

To address these issues, the government established the National Research and Innovation Policy Council in late 2016 to establish the direction for research and innovation policy. Chaired by the Prime Minister, it consists of relevant ministers, independent experts, and representatives from state-owned enterprises, business and academia. The Council is currently undertaking a review of Thailand's research and innovation system and developing a new 20-year National Research and Innovation Policy Framework, which aims to boost competitiveness through the enhancement of S-curve industries (see above).

Another major barrier to innovation is access to talent, particularly in the case of business. Weak collaboration between academia and industry limits the flow of researchers between the two sectors. To help foster mobility, the government established a Talent Mobility Programme, which enables industry and/or the government to reimburse universities for access to talent, while universities allow academics to take leave and return without incurring any career penalties (Durongkaveroj, 2015). To further improve the human capital pool, the government is assisting industry to access talent from abroad, by setting up a one-stop shop where firms can source talent from ASEAN countries. This programme will also facilitate streamlined visa arrangements. Moreover, the government has launched the Eastern Economic Corridor of Innovation (EECi) project as part of the flagship EEC development plan. The EECi aims to create a regional innovation hub which will attract international talent and foster R&D in the public sector, private sector, academia and local communities. In 2016, the government also launched a campaign to support entrepreneurs and start-ups through financial aid programmes (e.g. the Research Gap Fund and the Technology and Innovation Enterprise Development Fund), and by expanding entrepreneurship education programmes, setting up innovation districts and revising commercial law to facilitate business operations for start-ups.

Beyond supply-side innovation policies, like many OECD countries, Thailand seeks to make greater use of demand-side policies where government action complements market mechanisms with minimal financial outlays. For instance, in 2016, the Government Procurement Programme to Support Local Innovation was introduced to fast-track local innovation products through the government procurement process and to foster technology spillovers to local firms. Although targeted procurement programmes can help spur business innovation, they are not without risk, as they can favour large firms over small, lead to technology lock-in and may not be compatible with "value for money" requirements (OECD, 2016c). As such, it is vitally important that efforts to facilitate efficient and fair domestic market conditions remain at the centre of Thailand's demand-side innovation policy settings. In this regard, Thailand should enhance competition and consumer laws and crack down on corruption (Chapter 5), ensure state-owned enterprises operate on a level playing field with private business and price/regulate externalities where appropriate.

Fostering the digital economy can help boost productivity and socio-economic development

Digitalisation can boost productivity and efficiency, as well as broader socio-economic development. It allows for better governance arrangements and a more inclusive society through improved access to and quality of key services such as health, education and banking. It aids innovation and helps countries move up value chains (OECD, 2017a). Moreover, having the means to participate in a global digital economy is essential, as cross-border digital flows continue to grow (Chakravorti and Chaturvedi, 2017). The government recognises the benefits of expanding the use of digital technologies and is seeking to increase the coverage of affordable digital services as part of the 12th Plan. While increased digitalisation offers tremendous opportunities, it is also highly disruptive and changing the ways in which people work and live their lives. Adequate plans therefore need to be in place to ensure Thai society is ready to embrace the digital revolution.

To ensure the benefits from the digital economy are spread equally, all individuals, businesses and governments must have reliable and affordable access to digital networks and services. Thailand is making progress in this area, but has room to improve. According to the 2016 Network Readiness Index, Thailand's information and communication technology (ICT) infrastructure is in the middle of the pack vis-à-vis comparator countries, but ahead of all regional comparators except Korea and Singapore (Figure 2.11A). However, the share of people using the internet, which reached 47.5% in 2016, is below most comparator economies. Meanwhile, despite efforts, the gap in urban/rural access to ICT remains wide: in 2016, 57% of people in urban areas were internet users versus 40% in rural areas (NSO, 2016). However, Thailand performs well with regard to mobile phones with over 81% of the population aged six and over using a phone in 2016 and over 176 connections per 100 people – the highest amongst comparator countries (NSO, 2016; ITU, 2016).

If ICT infrastructure is the vehicle to reach the digital economy, ICT literacy is the driver. According to the Network Readiness Index, Thailand's education system, including the quality of maths and science courses, is under-equipping Thai students with the skills required for effective ICT use. Indeed, Thailand's digital skills readiness ranks below most comparator countries (Figure 2.11B). Further efforts to address digital knowledge deficiencies are needed to ensure all people can participate and thrive in a digital economy.

Figure 2.11. **Thailand has room to improve in digital infrastructure and skills readiness**

Index, scale 1-7 from lowest to highest level of readiness, 2016

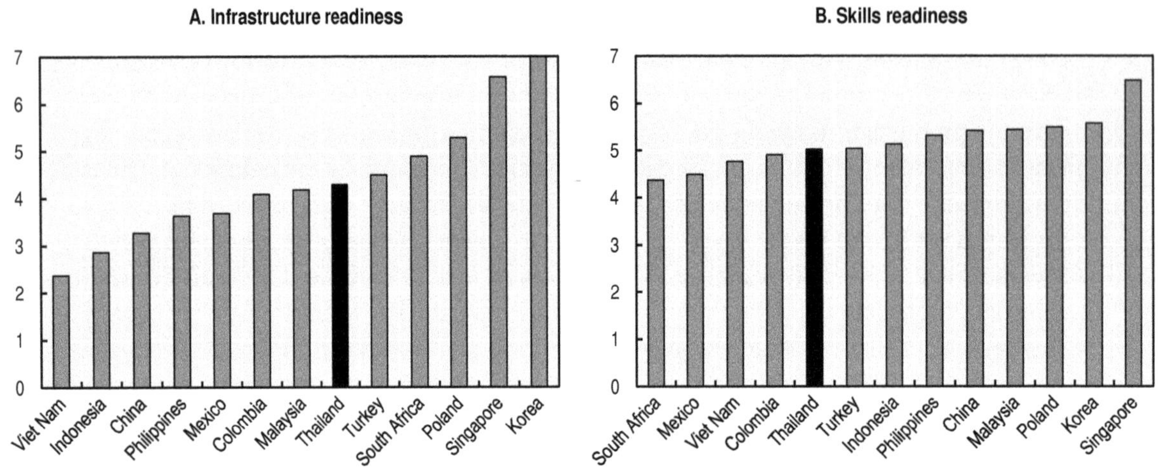

Source: WEF (2016), Network Readiness Index, *http://reports.weforum.org/global-information-technology-report-2016/networked-readiness-index.*

StatLink http://dx.doi.org/10.1787/888933692028

Thailand also faces challenges in relation to cyber security. In the first quarter of 2017, Thailand had a malware encounter rate (the number of computers that detect a malware or unwanted software threat) of 20%, one of the highest among comparator countries (Microsoft, 2017). Meanwhile, Thailand ranked tenth and seventh worldwide, respectively, for reported data breaches and the average lifespan of a bot-infected computer (Symantec, 2017). Boosting digital security is important to foster individual and business confidence in the use of digital technologies.

Thailand is implementing a number of initiatives to help overcome these obstacles. In 2016, the Ministry of Digital Economy and Society developed a Thailand Digital Economy and Society Development Plan, which consists of four phases over 20 years. As part of the first phase, the government seeks primarily to boost digital infrastructure (Table 2.4). Indeed, the number of broadband connections with speeds of 10 Mbps or higher soared in 2017 (Akamai, 2017). The government is also trying to leverage private investment in ICT infrastructure by offering tax incentives to encourage local and international businesses to establish data centres. Additionally, the Ministry of Digital Economy and Society is establishing a digital park to support digital businesses and offering a range of tax and non-tax incentives (e.g. simplified visa and work permit procedures).

Table 2.4. **Thailand's digital infrastructure targets**

Target	Time frame
Provide broadband access to all villages	Within two years
Provide broadband access to 90% of users in all municipalities and economic zones at speeds no less than 10 Mbps	Within three years
Provide broadband access to 95% of schools, sub-district health promotion hospitals, local administration organisations and digital community centres at speeds no less than 30 Mbps	Within five years

Source: MEDS (2016), *Thailand Digital Economy and Society Development Plan, 1st edition.*

While investment in necessary infrastructure is progressing, Thailand needs to focus on improving ICT literacy and skills. Established community learning centres can serve to build familiarity and knowledge of ICT. At the same time, ICT education in schools needs to improve, with ICT use integrated into teaching, including the development of appropriate learning materials (Chapter 1).

Digital technologies can promote social inclusion by facilitating better access to quality education, offering new opportunities for skills development, enhancing access to healthcare, and more generally improving access to free and low-cost information, knowledge and data. Mobile telephony in particular has been used intensively in a number of initiatives that aim to improve the welfare of lower-income and excluded groups in developing countries (OECD, 2017a).

SMEs need to be better financed, digitalised and properly incentivised

Small and medium enterprises (SMEs) represent about 42% of Thailand's GDP, mostly in services and manufacturing. In 2015, they accounted for 99.7% of the total number of enterprises in the country, 80% of employment and about a quarter of total exports. Addressing the obstacles faced by SMEs and promoting entry of innovative SMEs are crucial for economy-wide growth and reducing inequality between regions and individuals (Lee et al., 2017). While some Thai SMEs have benefited from linkages with GVCs in key manufacturing segments, particularly automotive and electronics, most SMEs are excluded.

SMEs face a number of interrelated problems, not least because of their often-informal status (Lathapipat and Poggi, 2016). These include inadequate financing, insufficient upgrading of capital stock and slower adoption of technology, as well as inadequate regional integration (Charoenrat and Harvie, 2017). The government has developed an SME Promotion Masterplan (2017-2021), with the objective to increase the SME share of GDP to at least 50% by 2021. To this end, it is prioritising regulatory reform by streamlining licensing procedures, initiating an experimental regulatory regime for FinTech firms, promoting skills training with an emphasis on ICT, and facilitating start-ups through the provision of entrepreneurship education and finance (Chapter 5). To adequately address these cross-cutting issues, improved co-ordination is needed across existing agencies responsible for delivering both financial and non-financial support to SMEs.

Better access to financing is key, as Thai SMEs often struggle in this area, as do their peers elsewhere. Even though collateral requirements for SME loans are much stricter, the share of non-performing loans has been rising for SMEs (see above). The bulk of SME loans are disbursed through specialised financial institutions, which may affect the degree of credit access between sectors and regions. While the government tried to alleviate the problem in 2008 by introducing a credit guarantee scheme through the Small Business Credit Guarantee Corporation (SBCGC), the take-up rate has been low (OECD, 2016a). Potential solutions that could help broaden its appeal include higher government funding for the SBCGC and more targeted guarantee-related products offered to SMEs, with lower rates and fees. In addition, reliance on bank financing could be reduced by encouraging SMEs to access the capital market via the creation of a special lower-cost bourse in the Thai Stock Exchange. In June 2017, Malaysia launched a similar instrument, the Leading Entrepreneur Accelerator Platform, to help its SMEs access the capital market (Bursa Malaysia, 2017).

SMEs also need to embrace the digital economy by tapping into the rapid development of e-commerce and e-payment. In this regard, the central bank has introduced measures such as PromptPay and standardised quick response (QR) code payments (Box 2.1).

Box 2.1. **Lowering the cost and improving the ease of financial transactions**

PromptPay is the first project to be rolled out under the government's National e-Payment Master Plan. Since early 2017, it has enabled registered individuals and businesses to more efficiently transfer funds between banks and e-wallets, by using mobile phones or citizen ID numbers instead of exchanging bank account details. PromptPay provides one of the cheapest rates globally, with free transfer services for transactions up to THB 5 000 (USD 150) and a top tier rate of THB 10 (USD 0.30) for transactions over THB 100 000 (USD 3 000). As of the end of 2017, over 37 million people had registered for PromptPay.

Thailand has also used the PromptPay system to launch a standardised QR code for payment services. This offers an efficient and cost-effective e-Payment alternative, whereby consumers can pay for goods and services instantly by scanning the QR code through a smartphone application. Thailand's performance is in line with global best practice in this area, as consumers need not scan different QR codes to make payments, while merchants only need to display one QR code. Aside from the expediency and convenience, increased use of QR code payments also helps to collect financial data on SMEs which could eventually be used to support access to credit. By the end of 2017, the Bank of Thailand had permitted eight Thai Banks to provide QR code payment services. Looking ahead, QR code payment services will be expanded to allow the use of alternative sources of funds including credit and debit cards.

The cost and convenience benefits of PromptPay and QR code payments are demonstrated by their rapid uptake across the economy (Figure 2.12). Spreading the use of these systems will help drive further efficiencies, incentivise SMEs to join the formal economy and provide a foundation for innovative financial services.

Figure 2.12. **Use of mobile phones to process financial transactions has grown rapidly**

Share of total e-payment transactions by method

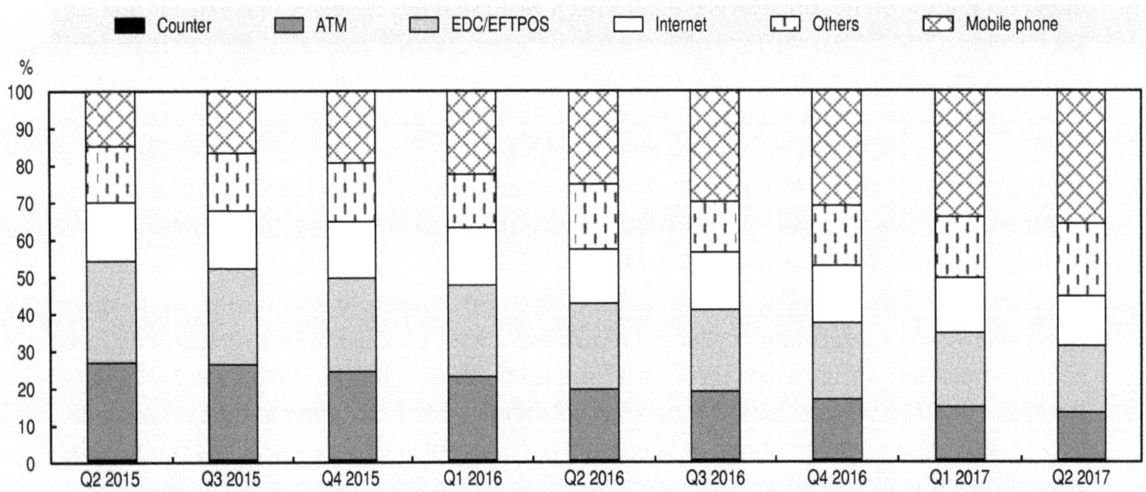

Source: Banchongduang (2017); Bank of Thailand (2017), Payment transactions statistics, *https://www.bot.or.th/English/Statistics/PaymentSystems/Pages/StatPaymentTransactions.aspx*; and Santiprabhob (2017a, b).

StatLink http://dx.doi.org/10.1787/888933692047

Over the slightly longer term, e-commerce offers many opportunities for SMEs. The government has launched a National e-Commerce Master Plan (2017-2021) whose measures include improving ICT access in rural areas and promoting an e-payment service for cheaper and easier transactions. Regional peers such as Malaysia and Singapore have pioneered specific incentives, reduced costs and set up clusters, such as the Digital Free Trade Zone in Malaysia, to help promote e-commerce among SMEs. Thailand could envisage such clusters for Thai SMEs, notably in under-served economic regions in the Northeast, North and South. This would help reduce regional economic imbalances through infrastructure development and take advantage of lower costs in these regions compared to the Bangkok Metropolitan Area and Eastern regions. In accordance with Thailand 4.0, the government should also step up the development of high-speed broadband network infrastructure in these regions, starting with 4G mobile broadband for a quicker rollout (Bangkok is expected to move to 5G mobile in 2018-19), while building a fixed broadband network in parallel, which may be slower to set up but is necessary.

Last but not least, SMEs face challenges with respect to taxation. Under the present tax regime, SMEs with paid-up capital below THB 3 million and annual income below THB 30 million qualify for a reduced corporate tax of 0%, 15% or 20%, depending on their net profit, against a 20% regular corporate tax rate. In 2015 and 2016, this was cut to 0-10%, to support SMEs amid the economic slowdown. In 2017, this support was temporarily continued to encourage greater tax compliance by SMEs and reduce the vast informal sector, but normal rates are due to be restored in 2018. While this approach led to an increase in tax registration among SMEs, it is important to offer greater certainty through the creation of a more stable corporate income tax rate structure. One option could be a permanently lower tax rate of 10% for qualifying SMEs. To mitigate any threshold effects and avoid discouraging expansion, a lower marginal tax rate could also be considered to reward more successful SMEs, as is the case in Malaysia. For example, SMEs with income growth exceeding 10% could be granted a five-percentage point reduction on the tax rate applicable to their incremental income.

Furthering global value chain participation and regional integration

Trade and foreign investment have been major drivers of Thailand's industrialisation since the second half of the 1970s. Foreign trade amounted to 123% of GDP in 2017, more than double the OECD average, reflecting active participation in GVCs. The share of foreign value-added in gross total exports (i.e. the proportion of imported intermediate goods in total exports) rose from 24% in 2001 to 37% in 2014, well above the OECD average of 26% (Figure 2.13). Thailand's participation in GVCs has also brought about significant productivity gains thanks to international technology and knowledge transfers. Participation in GVCs provides opportunities to diversify exports into sectors characterised by a faster pace of technological progress, and to attract FDI (OECD, 2013).

Making the best of opportunities created by participation in GVCs calls for efficient and cheap access to imported intermediate and capital goods. Thailand has made substantial progress in this regard, almost halving the weighted applied mean tariff rate for manufacturing goods between 2007 and 2015 (Figure 2.14). During the same period, a series of free trade agreements (FTAs) were concluded, either bilaterally or regionally through ASEAN, with major trade partners such as Australia, China, India, Korea, Japan and New Zealand. By 2010, tariffs had been almost completely eliminated for intra-regional trade with ASEAN countries (except Cambodia, Lao PDR, Myanmar and Viet Nam) as a consequence of the ASEAN Free Trade Area. Following the advent of the ASEAN Economic Community (AEC) in December 2015, remaining tariffs for these four countries have now been abolished. In addition, FTAs have contributed to reducing non-tariff trade barriers, notably by harmonising standards and streamlining rules of origin to reduce compliance costs. By 2016, 60% of Thailand's trade value was covered by FTAs (JETRO, 2017). These developments have strengthened regional linkages among ASEAN countries, including Thailand, with some traditional suppliers of intermediates in Europe, Japan and the United States being replaced by regional suppliers (Lopez Gonzales, 2016).

Figure 2.13. **GVC participation has improved**

Share of foreign value-added in gross total exports of goods and services

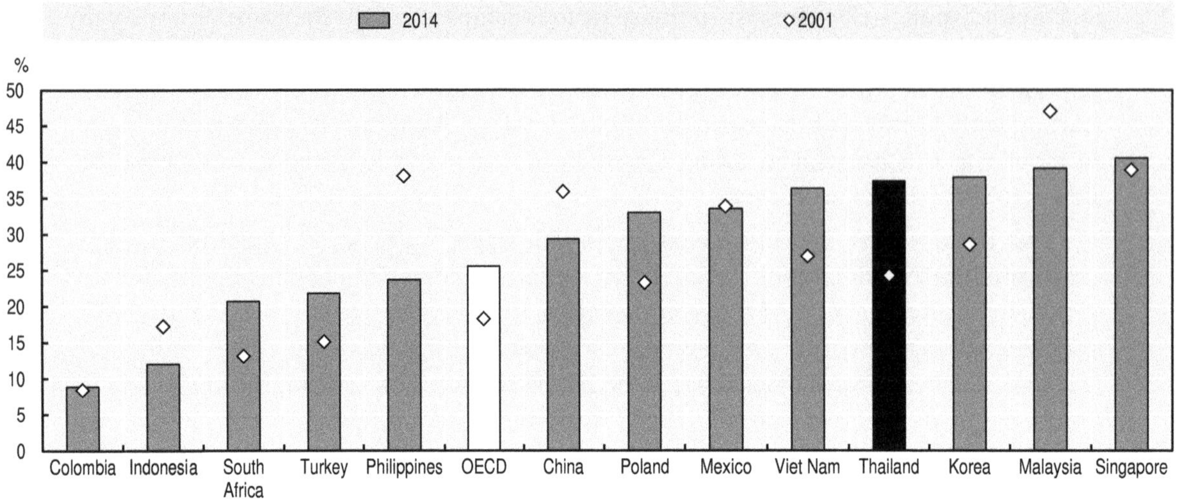

Source: OECD-WTO (2017), Trade in Value-added database, *https://stats.oecd.org/index.aspx?queryid=75537*.

StatLink http://dx.doi.org/10.1787/888933692066

Figure 2.14. **Thailand's average tariff rate fell in the past decade**

Weighted mean applied tariff rate for manufacturing goods

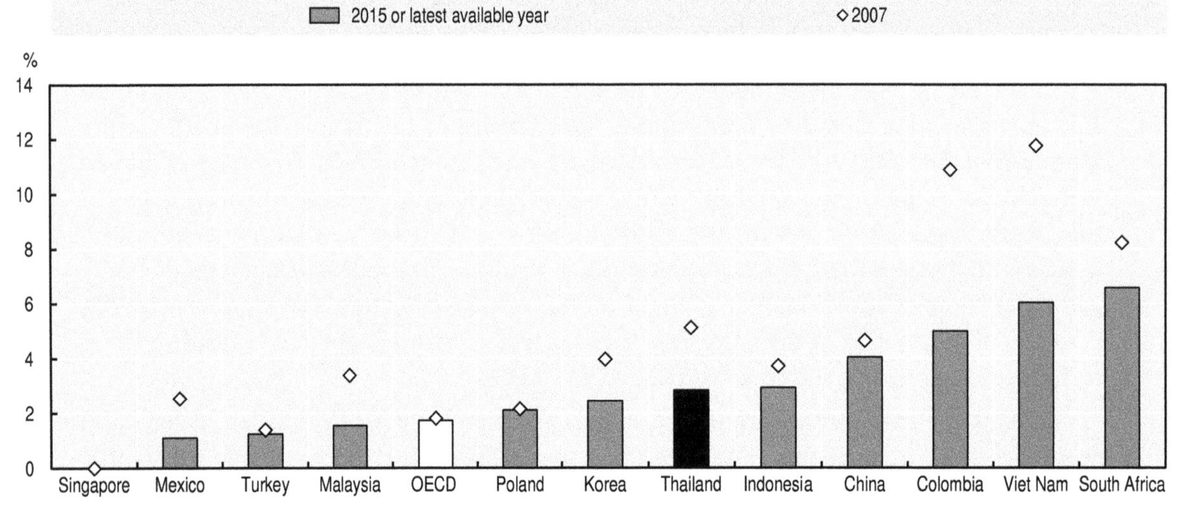

Source: UNCTAD (2017), Trade Analysis and Information System database, *http://unctad.org/en/Pages/DITC/Trade-Analysis/Non-Tariff-Measures/NTMs-trains.aspx*; World Bank (2017), World Development Indicators database, *http://databank.worldbank.org/data/home.aspx*.

StatLink http://dx.doi.org/10.1787/888933692085

Trade costs can also be reduced by streamlining trade-related procedures and enhancing the quality of related infrastructure and services. According to the OECD Trade Facilitation Indicators, Thailand compares favourably to the average Asian or upper-middle-income country in this respect. In fact, Thailand matches global best practice with respect to the involvement of the trade community, appeal procedures and formalities (documents, automation and procedures) (Figure 2.15). Further trade facilitation gains can be reaped by promoting this agenda multilaterally, in particular with neighbouring ASEAN countries with which Thailand's trade ties have strengthened, such as Cambodia, Lao PDR, Myanmar and Viet Nam.

Figure 2.15. **Thailand's trade facilitation has made good progress**

As of 2017; indicators range from 0 (worst) to 2 (best)

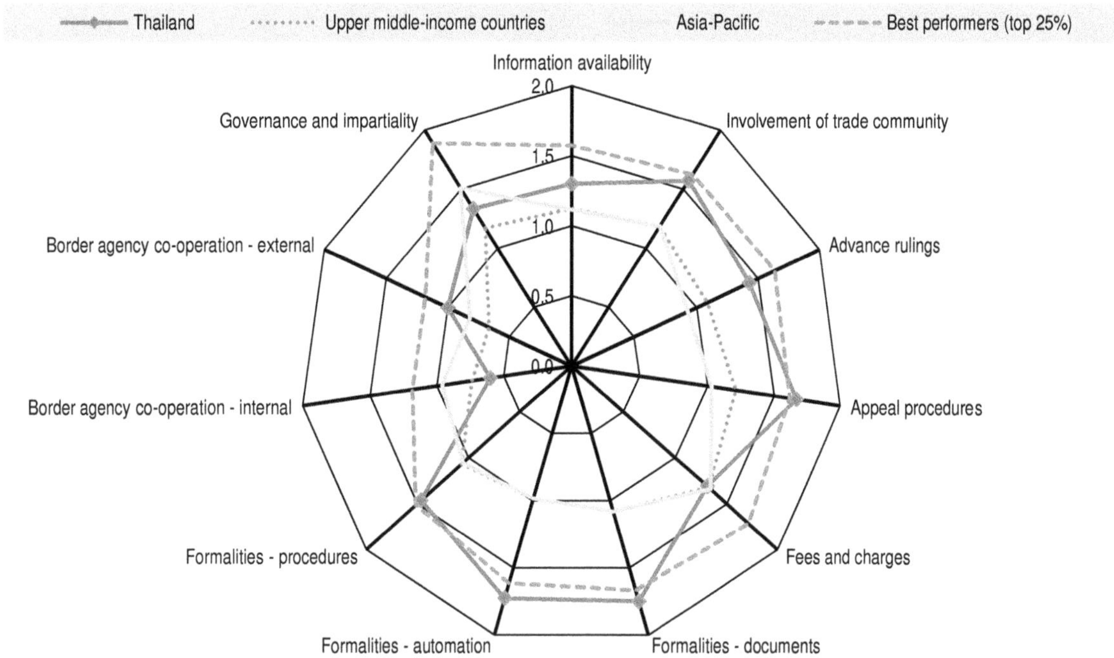

Source: OECD (2017g), Trade Facilitation Indicators database, *www.oecd.org/trade/facilitation/indicators.htm*.

StatLink *http://dx.doi.org/10.1787/888933692104*

Trade liberalisation and facilitation has lagged somewhat in the services sector, but is key for productivity and competitiveness. Open and well-regulated services markets are the gateway to GVCs, ensuring access to information, skills and technology, reducing costs and improving quality of services (OECD, 2017c). This is true in particular for digital, logistics and professional services used in high value-added activities. However, restrictions on services trade, in particular on telecommunication, transportation and professional services, remain high in Thailand (World Bank, 2016). While the ASEAN countries including Thailand have committed to services trade liberalisation by allowing higher foreign equity ownership in various areas (including business services, professional services, construction, healthcare and finance), progress is still limited due to delays in regulatory reform in each country (OECD, 2017b).

The OECD Services Trade Restrictiveness Index (STRI) quantifies barriers to services trade and helps identify regulatory bottlenecks and "low-hanging fruit" for policy reforms. The STRI for Thailand is being computed for the first time and is focusing on two services sectors – construction and architecture – between 2014 and 2017. These services provide key inputs and infrastructure for manufacturing and other sectors, and accounted for 3% of GDP and 6% of employment in 2016.

The STRI results show that Thailand's regulatory framework creates international trade impediments in both the construction and architecture service sectors (Figure 2.16). The impediments result from both economy-wide and sector specific regulations. The economy-wide regulations include residency requirements for boards of directors, foreign land acquisition restrictions and a 49% cap on foreign ownership for companies without a foreign business license. To obtain a foreign business licence companies must have investments screened by the government and meet minimum capital requirements. In public procurement markets, preference is given to local suppliers. Apart from the economy-wide implications, such limitations have a particular bearing on construction services providers given the importance of government demand for such services in infrastructure development. Concerning foreign workers seeking to provide services in Thailand, employers must first undertake labour market tests and give preference to Thai nationals. When foreign work permits are granted, they are limited to 12 months. In addition, companies must employ a minimum of four Thai nationals for every foreign worker. Combined, these requirements create a large disincentive for foreigners seeking to provide services in Thailand.

Figure 2.16. **Service trade restrictiveness is high in the construction and architecture sectors**

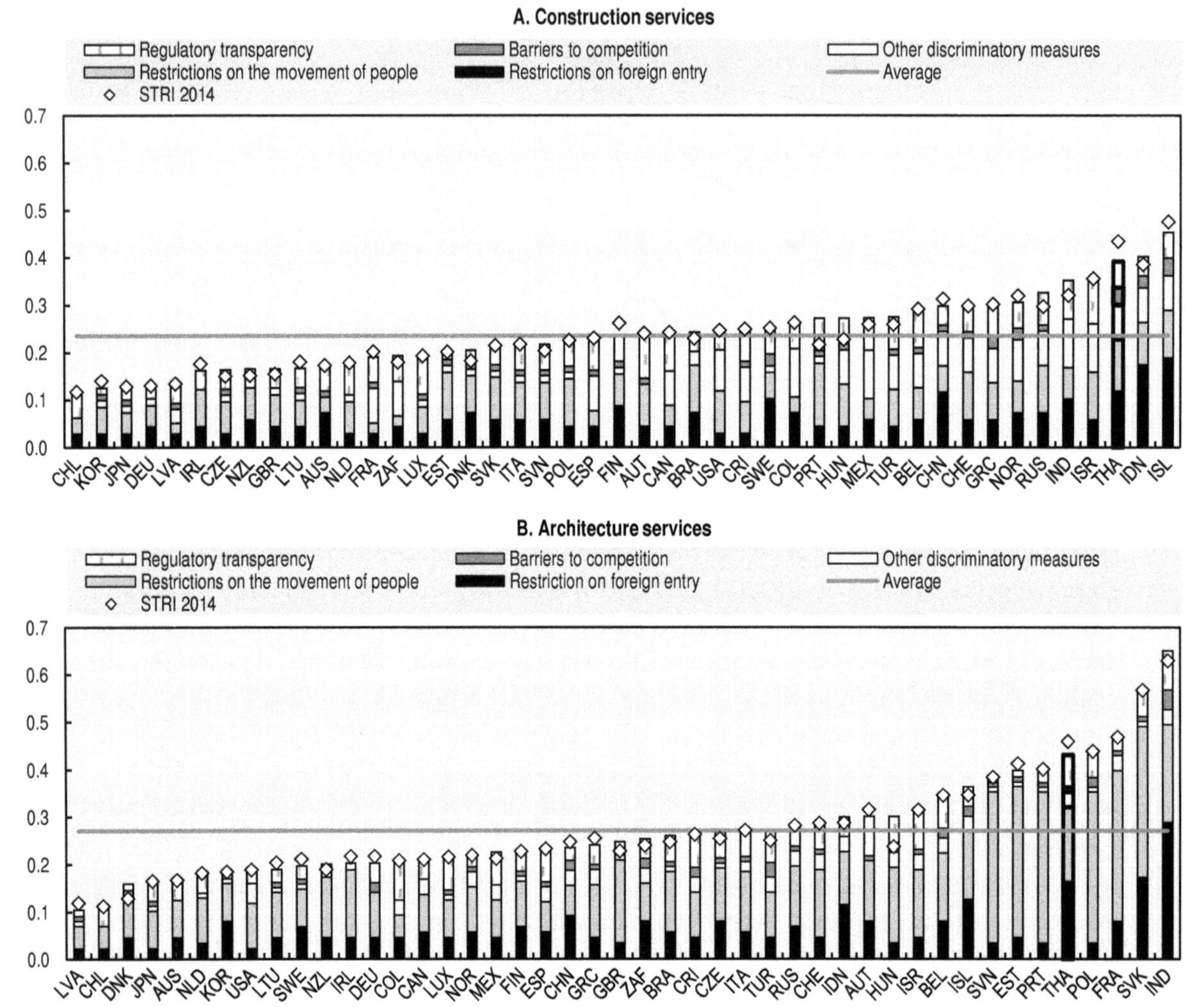

Note: The OECD Services Trade Restrictiveness Index (STRI) is a unique, diagnostic tool that inventories trade restrictions in 44 countries for 22 services sectors, allowing countries to benchmark their services regulations relative to global best practice, identify outlier restrictions and prioritise reform efforts. Composite indices quantify restrictions across five policy areas, with values between zero and one. Complete openness to trade in services gives a score of zero, while complete closure to foreign services providers yields a score of one. Since 2014, the STRI database monitors changes in services trade policies on an annual basis. It records measures on a Most Favoured Nations basis, so preferential trade agreements are not taken into account.

Source: OECD (2017h), Services Trade Restrictiveness index database, *www.oecd.org/tad/services-trade/services-trade-restrictiveness-index.htm*.

StatLink http://dx.doi.org/10.1787/888933692123

International trade in construction and architecture services is also impacted by sector-specific restrictions. For construction services, all professionals, such as civil engineers, must obtain local license. Although there are processes in place to recognise foreign qualifications, applicants for licenses must have a local residence and undergo additional testing for specific engineering professions. Civil engineering professions related to testing, supervising and consulting on construction activities are reserved to Thai nationals. Companies providing architecture services must have a commercial presence in Thailand and a majority of their board members need to be locally licensed professionals. Moreover, foreign architects cannot operate independently, and must form a joint venture with local architects. Foreign architects also have to be residents and pass additional testing to get their qualification recognised.

Certain policy changes were introduced in 2017 to ease the conditions for foreign services suppliers. Reforms include allowing foreign suppliers to challenge the public procurement procedures and incorporating a constitutional obligation on the part of the government to consult with stakeholders, including foreign services suppliers, in the area of proposing new legislation. With regard to construction services, a centralised system for licenses has been created, making application for license more transparent and efficient.

As noted above, FDI has played an essential role in Thailand's industrialisation and export growth through the provision of capital, technology and managerial skills, delivering major productivity gains. Thailand initiated investment liberalisation for the manufacturing sector in the 1970s, and liberalised the services sector in the early 1990s. In recent years, Thailand has become a major source of FDI to other Southeast Asian countries, notably Cambodia, Lao PDR and Myanmar, thereby contributing to regional integration. Nevertheless, the rules governing inward FDI remain comparatively restrictive (Figure 2.17).

Figure 2.17. **FDI is still subject to substantial restrictions**

As of 2016; index ranges from 0 (open) to 1 (closed)

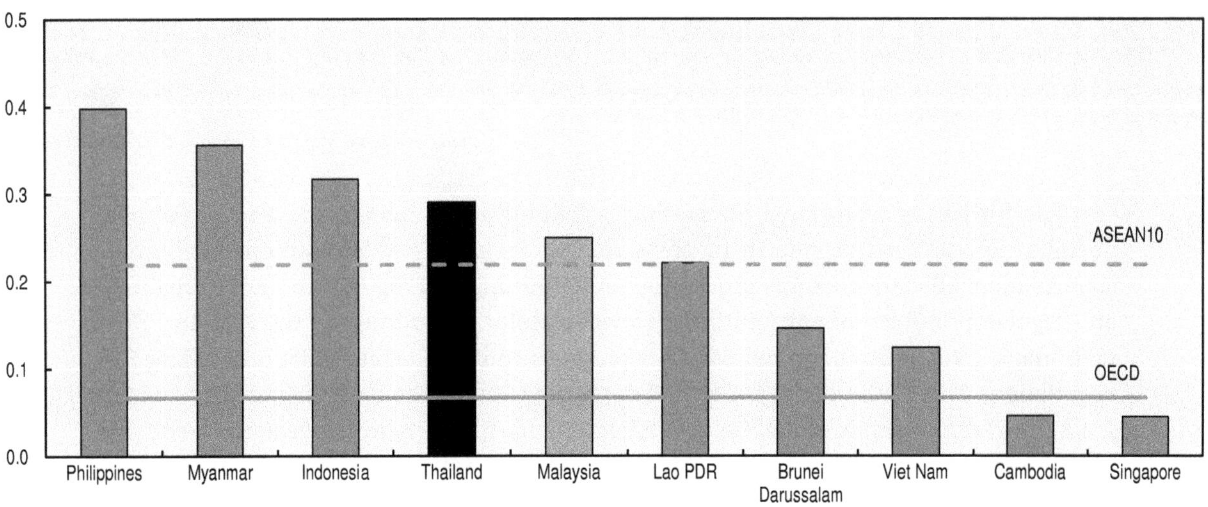

Note: The OECD FDI Regulatory Restrictiveness Index covers only statutory measures discriminating against foreign investors (e.g. foreign equity limits, screening and approval procedures, restrictions on key foreign personnel and other operational measures). Other important aspects of the investment climate (e.g. the implementation of regulations and state monopolies) are not considered. Data for Brunei Darussalam, Thailand and Singapore are preliminary.

ASEAN 10 comprises Brunei Darussalam, Cambodia, Indonesia, Lao PDR, Malaysia, Myanmar, Philippines, Singapore, Thailand and Viet Nam.

Source: OECD (2017i), FDI Regulatory Restrictiveness Index database, *www.oecd.org/investment/fdiindex.htm.*

StatLink http://dx.doi.org/10.1787/888933692142

Thailand's gross FDI inflows as a share of GDP have been comparatively high over the past 15 years, but have lost ground in relative terms vis-à-vis Indonesia, Malaysia and the

Philippines (Figure 2.18A). Amid intensified regional competition for FDI, Thailand may have been negatively affected by insufficient efforts to improve its business environment, even though the government has provided tax exemptions targeted to specific areas with a view to enhancing productivity gains (knowledge-based activities, human resource development and commercialisation of local R&D outputs). Despite these efforts, Thailand's performance improved only marginally between 2008 and 2017, according to the Global Competitiveness Index (Figure 2.18B). To address this lacklustre performance, the government conducted a series of regulatory reforms to promote FDI inflows. These include amendment of the Foreign Business Act allowing foreign majority ownership in financial and infrastructure sectors, and revision of the Licensing Facilitation Act to ensure accountability and transparency of business licensing (Chapter 5).

Figure 2.18. **Gross FDI inflows have slowed in recent years**

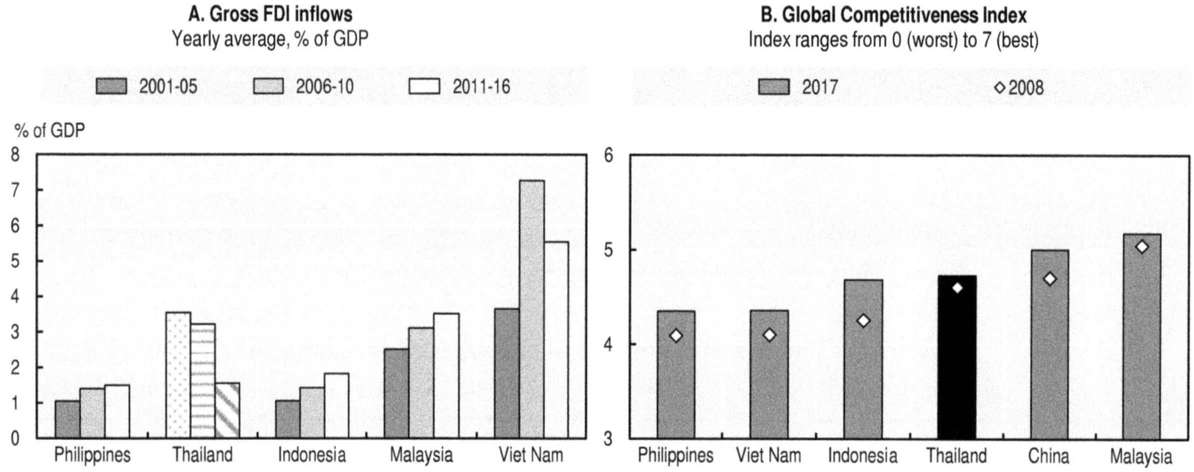

Source: UNCTAD (2017), UNCTADstat, *http://unctadstat.unctad.org*; WEF (2017), Global Competitiveness Index 2017-2018 database, *http://reports.weforum.org/global-competitiveness-index-2017-2018/#topic=data.*

StatLink *http://dx.doi.org/10.1787/888933692161*

The furthering of regional integration is helping to promote trade and investment liberalisation, as well as reform in areas related to trade and investment facilitation, such as more efficient customs procedures, streamlining and digitalisation of formalities, and regulatory reform of entry into the services sector. In addition to the AEC and FTAs with major trade partners in Asia, further progress could be achieved by concluding FTA negotiations with the European Union and the United States. Thailand's regional and wider-scale integration agenda would be well served by its participation in regional trade and investment fora such as Asia-Pacific Economic Cooperation and the Regional Comprehensive Economic Partnership.

References

ADB (2015), *Thailand Industrialisation and Economic Catch-Up*, Asian Development Bank, Mandaluyong City, *www.adb.org/sites/default/files/publication/178077/tha-industrialization-econ-catch.pdf.*

Akamai (2017), *State of the Internet: Q1, 2017 Report*, Vol. 10/1, Akamai, Paris, *www.akamai.com/fr/fr/multimedia/documents/state-of-the-internet/q1-2017-state-of-the-internet-connectivity-report.pdf.*

Asia Productivity Organization (2017), "Productivity Database 2017 Version 1" (database), Tokyo, *www.apo-tokyo.org/wedo/measurement.*

Banchongduang, S. (26 December 2017), "BoT governor to keep accommodative policy", *Bangkok Post*, *www.bangkokpost.com/business/news/1385742/bot-governor-to-keep-accommodative-policy*.

BOT (2017), *Monetary Policy Report 2Q 2017*, Bank of Thailand, Bangkok.

Board of Investment (2017), *A Guide to the Board of Investment 2017*, Bangkok, Board of Investment, *www.boi.go.th/upload/content/BOI-A%20Guide%202017-EN-20170419_72762.pdf*.

Bursa Malaysia (2017), *LEAP Market Listing Requirements*, Bursa Malaysia Berhad, Kuala Lumpur, *www.bursamalaysia.com/market/regulation/rules/listing-requirements/leap-market/listing-requirements*.

Chakravorti, B. and R. Chaturvedi (2017), *Digital Planet 2017: How Competitiveness and Trust in Digital Economies Vary Across the World*, The Fletcher School, Tufts University, *https://sites.tufts.edu/digitalplanet/files/2017/05/Digital_Planet_2017_FINAL.pdf*.

Charoenrat, T. and C. Harvie (2017), "Thailand's SME participation in ASEAN and East Asian regional economic integration", *Journal of Southeast Asian Economies*, Vol. 34/1, pp. 148-174.

Conference Board (2017), "Total Economy Database" (database), May 2017, *www.conference-board.org/data/economydatabase*.

Durongkaveroj, P. (2015), *Science, Technology and Innovation Policies in Thailand: Achievements and Challenges*, 18th Annual session of United Nations Commission on Science and Technology for Development, 6 May, *http://unctad.org/meetings/en/Presentation/ecn162015p15_Durongkaveroj_en.pdf*.

Egawa, A. (2015), "How should the Thai Government change its policy for narrowing income disparity among the provinces?", *St. Andrew's University Economic and Business Review*, Vol. 56/4, *https://ci.nii.ac.jp/els/contentscinii_20180122061911.pdf?id=ART0010429792*.

Fukuoka, N., R. Ochiai and S. Tada (2016), "Analysis on the macroeconomy and industrial policies toward industrial upgrading in Thailand and policy recommendations" (in Japanese with English summary), *RIETI Discussion Papers*, Research Institute of Economy, Trade and Industry, Tokyo, *www.rieti.go.jp/jp/publications/pdp/16p013.pdf*.

ILO (2017), "ILO Stat" (database), ILO, Geneva, *www.ilo.org/global/statistics-and-databases/lang--en/index.htm*.

IMF (2017), *Article IV Staff Report*, IMF Country Report No. 17/136, May, International Monetary Fund, Washington, DC.

ITU (2016), "Global and Regional ICT Data" (dataset), International Telecommunications Union, Geneva, *www.itu.int/en/ITU-D/Statistics/Pages/stat/default.aspx*.

JETRO (2017), *JETRO Global Trade and Investment Report 2017*, Japan External Trade Organisation, Tokyo.

Lathapipat, D. and C. Poggi (2016), "From many to one: Minimum wage effects in Thailand", *PIER Discussion Papers*, No. 41, Puey Ungphakorn Institute for Economic Research, Bangkok, *www.pier.or.th/wp-content/uploads/2016/08/pier_dp_041.pdf*.

Lee, C., D. Narjoko and S. Oum (2017), "Southeast Asian SMEs and regional economic integration", *Journal of Southeast Asian Economies*, Vol. 34/1, pp. 1-3.

Lopez Gonzalez, J. (2016), "Using foreign factors to enhance domestic export performance: A focus on Southeast Asia", *OECD Trade Policy Papers*, No. 191, OECD Publishing, Paris, *http://dx.doi.org/10.1787/18166873*.

Microsoft (2017), *Microsoft Security Intelligence Report*, Vol. 22, January-March, Microsoft Corporation, Redmond, WI, *www.microsoft.com/en-us/security/intelligence-report*.

MEDS (2016), *Thailand Digital Economy and Society Development Plan, 1st edition*, Ministry of Digital Economy and Society, Bangkok, *www.itu.int/en/ITU-D/Regional-Presence/AsiaPacific/Documents/Events/2016/Apr-Digital2016/S2_Present_Pansak_Siriruchatapong.pdf*.

MOI (2015), *Thailand Moving Ahead with Cluster Development*, Ministry of Industry, Bangkok, *www.boi.go.th/upload/content/Presentation%20by%20Minister%20of%20Industry_89274.pdf*.

NESDB (2017), *The Twelfth Economic and Social Development Plan (2017-2021)*, Office of the National Economic and Social Development Board, Bangkok, *www.nesdb.go.th/nesdb_en/ewt_w3c/ewt_dl_link.php?nid=4345*.

NSO (2016), *The 2016 Household Survey on the Use of Information and Communication Technology*, National Statistics Office, Ministry of Information and Communication Technology, Bangkok.

NSTIPO (2014), *Thailand's Science, Technology and Innovation Policy and Institutional Framework*, National Science Technology and Innovation Policy Office, Bangkok, *http://unctad.org/meetings/en/Presentation/MYEM2_2014_Durongkaveroj_Pichet.pdf*.

OECD (2017a), *Opportunities and Policy Challenges of Digitalisation in Southeast Asia*, OECD Publishing, Paris, *www.oecd.org/southeast-asia/events/regional-forum/Forum_Note_Digital_Transformation_STI.pdf*.

OECD (2017b), *Economic Outlook for Southeast Asia, China and India 2017*, OECD Publishing, Paris, *http://dx.doi.org/10.1787/saeo-2017-en*.

OECD (2017c), *Services Trade Policies and the Global Economy*, OECD Publishing, Paris, *http://dx.doi.org/10.1787/9789264275232-en*.

OECD (2017d), "National Accounts" (database), *http://dx.doi.org/10.1787/na-data-en*.

OECD (2017e), "Productivity Statistics" (database), *www.oecd.org/std/productivity-stats*.

OECD (2017f), "Gross domestic spending on R&D" (database), *http://dx.doi.org/10.1787/d8b068b4-en*.

OECD (2017g), "Trade Facilitation Indicators" (database), *www.oecd.org/trade/facilitation/indicators.htm*.

OECD (2017h), "Services Trade Restrictiveness Index" (database), *www.oecd.org/tad/services-trade/services-trade-restrictiveness-index.htm*.

OECD (2017i), "FDI Regulatory Restrictiveness Index" (database), *www.oecd.org/investment/fdiindex.htm*.

OECD (2017j), *Building Food Security and Managing Risk in Southeast Asia*, OECD Publishing, Paris, *http://dx.doi.org/10.1787/9789264272392-en*.

OECD (2017k), "OECD Economic Outlook No. 102 (Edition 2017/2)", *OECD Economic Outlook: Statistics and Projections* (database), *http://dx.doi.org/10.1787/05b705e7-en*.

OECD (2016a), *Financing SMEs and Entrepreneurs 2016: An OECD Scoreboard*, OECD Publishing, Paris, *http://dx.doi.org/10.1787/fin_sme_ent-2016-en*.

OECD (2016b), *OECD Economic Surveys: Turkey 2016*, OECD Publishing, Paris, *http://dx.doi.org/10.1787/eco_surveys-tur-2016-en*.

OECD (2016c), "Stimulating demand for innovation", in *OECD Science, Technology and Innovation* Outlook 2016, OECD Publishing, Paris, *http://dx.doi.org/10.1787/sti_in_outlook-2016-26-en*.

OECD (2015), *Analysing Policies to Improve Agricultural Productivity Growth, Sustainably: Revised Framework*, OECD Publishing, Paris, *www.oecd.org/agriculture/policies/innovation*.

OECD (2013), *Interconnected Economies: Benefitting Global Value Chains*, OECD Publishing, Paris, *http://dx.doi.org/10.1787/9789264189560-en*.

OECD (2009), *Clusters, Innovation and Entrepreneurship*, OECD Publishing, Paris, *http://dx.doi.org/10.1787/9789264044326-en*.

OECD-WTO (2017), "Trade in Value-added" (database), *https://stats.oecd.org/index.aspx?queryid=75537*.

Santiprabhob, V. (2017a), "Confidence in connectivity of the GMS", *Euromoney Conferences: The Greater Mekong Investment Forum*, Bangkok, *www.bis.org/review/r170629b.pdf*.

Santiprabhob, V. (2017b), "Navigating through uncertainties for Thailand's sustainability", *Association of International Banks Dinner Talk Series*, Bangkok, *www.bis.org/review/r170703d.pdf*.

Symantec (2017), *Internet Security Threat Report*, Vol. 22, Symantec Corporation, Mountain View, California.

UNCTAD (2017), "Trade Analysis and Information System" (database), United Nations Conference on Trade and Development, Geneva, *http://unctad.org/en/Pages/DITC/Trade-Analysis/Non-Tariff-Measures/NTMs-trains.aspx*.

UNCTAD (2015), *Science, Technology and Innovation Policy Review: Thailand*, United Nations Conference on Trade and Development, Geneva, *http://unctad.org/en/PublicationsLibrary/dtlstict2015d1_en.pdf*.

UNESCO-UIS (2017), "Science, Technology and Innovation" (dataset), UNESCO Institute of Statistics, *http://data.uis.unesco.org*.

World Bank (2017), "World Development Indicators" (database), *http://databank.worldbank.org/data/home.aspx*.

World Bank (2016), *Thailand Economic Monitor 2016: Services as a New Driver of Growth*, Washington DC, World Bank, *http://pubdocs.worldbank.org/en/660991482204992792/TEM2016-Services-as-a-New-Driver-of-Growth.pdf*.

WEF (2017), *Global Competitiveness Index 2017- 2018* (database), World Economic Forum, Geneva, *http://reports.weforum.org/global-competitiveness-index-2017-2018/#topic=data*.

WEF (2016), "Network Readiness Index" (database), World Economic Forum, *http://reports.weforum.org/global-information-technology-report-2016/networked-readiness-index*.

Multi-dimensional Review of Thailand
Volume 1. Initial Assessment

Chapter 3

Partnerships: Sustainably financing development

The Partnerships pillar of the 2030 Agenda for Sustainable Development cuts across all the goals focusing on the mobilisation of resources needed to implement the agenda.

Thailand's "sufficiency economy philosophy" encourages the prioritisation of long-term sustainability over short-term benefits. As such, Thailand has a long history of fiscal prudence that has served the country well in times of economic and political instability. However, relying on current fiscal buffers to finance foreseeable expenditure pressures is not sufficient or sustainable. A rapidly ageing population and shrinking workforce will weigh on future public finances and on the ability to achieve the Sustainable Development Goals.

To ensure that Thailand is well placed over the medium term to meet growing social, environmental and infrastructure requirements, the government should: (i) increase tax revenues by broadening the tax base and enhancing collection efficiency; (ii) facilitate greater private sector investment in productive infrastructure; and (iii) reform the healthcare and pension systems to increase their efficiency and effectiveness.

Thailand's current fiscal position is sound (Chapter 2), but its population is ageing much faster than in comparator countries. With rising life expectancy and low fertility rates (1.5 child per woman (World Bank, 2017b)), Thailand's dependency ratio is more in line with high-income countries such as Korea and Singapore, than other regional emerging economies such as Indonesia, the Philippines, Malaysia or Viet Nam (Figure 3.1). The drivers of Thailand's low fertility rates – increased education and career opportunities for women and high childrearing costs – are not dissimilar to those of East Asian high-income countries (UNFPA and NESDB, 2015). As a result, the cost of financial and social support for the elderly will rise considerably as demand for improved social outcomes and the weight of the elderly population both increase. Moreover, further investment in economic and social infrastructure is necessary to increase economic potential and ultimately attain high-income status. To this end, Thailand has to better marshal domestic resources by broadening the tax base and enhancing collection efficiency. At the same time, the private sector must play a greater role in financing productive infrastructure through enhanced public-private partnerships, while the social healthcare and pension system needs to be reformed without compromising quality and accessibility. This will help ensure Thailand achieves the objectives presented under the Partnerships pillar of the Sustainable Development Goals, which focuses on mobilising the resources needed to implement the agenda.

Figure 3.1. **Thailand's elderly dependency ratio is expected to exceed the OECD average by 2030**

Elderly dependency ratio

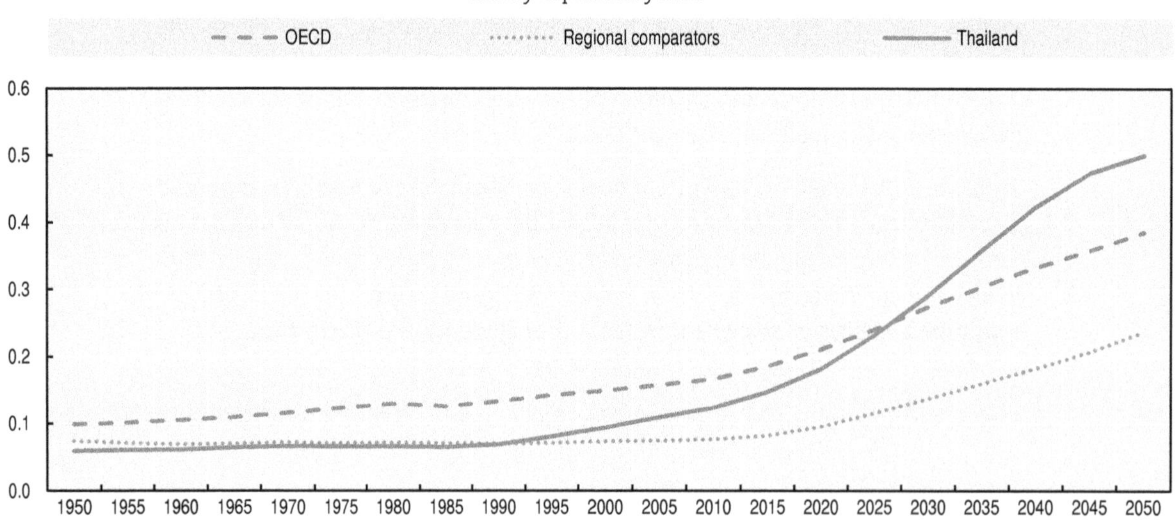

Note: The elderly dependency ratio refers to the number of persons (aged 65 and above) per working age population (aged 15 to 64). Regional comparators refer to the simple average elderly dependency ratio for Malaysia, Philippines, Indonesia and Viet Nam.

Source: UN Population projections, 2017 revision.

StatLink http://dx.doi.org/10.1787/888933692180

This chapter discusses the sustainability of Thailand's public finances, breaking down the structure of public revenue and assessing how revenues can be increased through future tax reform. It also discusses how to better fund long-term infrastructure projects, including through greater private sector participation. Building on the analysis presented in Chapter 1, it then reviews how to improve the financial sustainability of the pension and healthcare system.

The fiscal position is healthy, thanks to a record of fiscal prudence

Over the past 10 years, Thailand's public debt has averaged 40% of GDP (Figure 3.2). This is far below the 60% peak in 2000 and compares well with most countries in the region (in 2016, it stood at 53%, 42% and 62% in Malaysia, the Philippines and Viet Nam, respectively). Over the past four fiscal years, the general government fiscal balance has averaged a surplus of 0.1% of GDP, while the central government fiscal deficit has been relatively low, averaging 2.3% of GDP. The cyclically adjusted primary balance averaged a surplus of 0.9% of GDP over the same period.

Figure 3.2. **Thailand's gross public debt ratio has remained moderate**

Fiscal years, in % of GDP

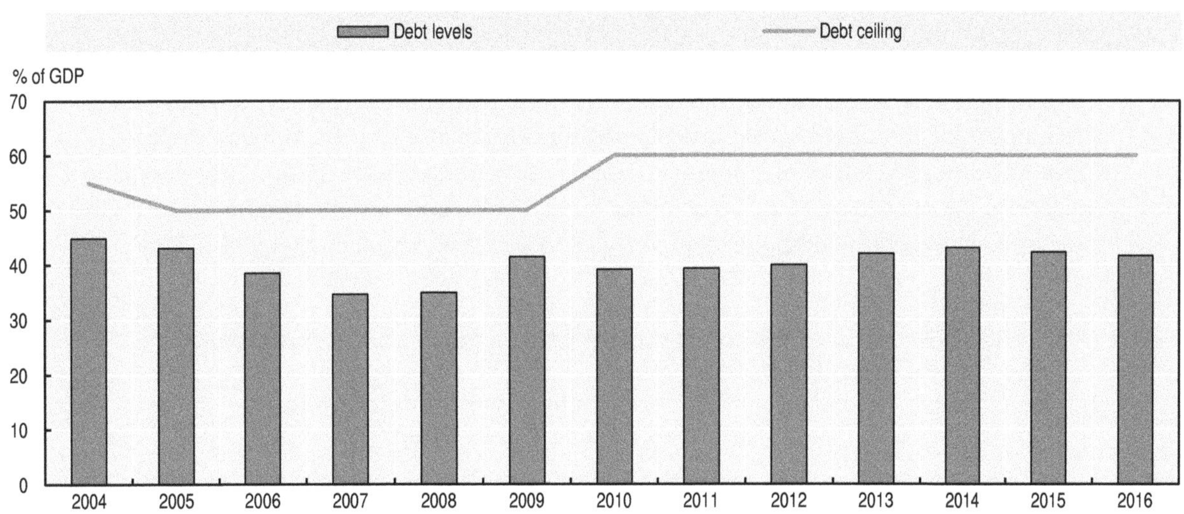

Note: The Ministry of Finance raised the debt ceiling in 2010 to 60% of GDP to ensure the availability of sufficient fiscal space in the event of a downturn. Public debt includes general government debt and state-owned enterprise debt. Fiscal year N runs from October in year N-1 to September in year N.

Source: Fiscal Policy Office and NESDB.

StatLink http://dx.doi.org/10.1787/888933692199

Looking ahead, there is room for ongoing fiscal stimulus without compromising longer-run sustainability. According to OECD model simulations, if nominal GDP growth and effective interest rates were to remain around current levels, there would be room for further fiscal expansion beyond the 2017 deficit without pushing gross public debt above 50% of GDP over the longer term, provided that the primary deficit is subsequently brought back gradually to around 0.5% of GDP (Figure 3.3). As long as the cost of debt financing remains low, borrowing to boost the productive capacity of the economy over the long term is a sensible strategy. However, interest rates are bound to rise from current low levels and without structural reform to boost economic potential, GDP growth could lose momentum. This would limit the available fiscal space and require a reversion to primary surpluses to safeguard debt sustainability.

Figure 3.3. **Thailand has fiscal space in the near term**

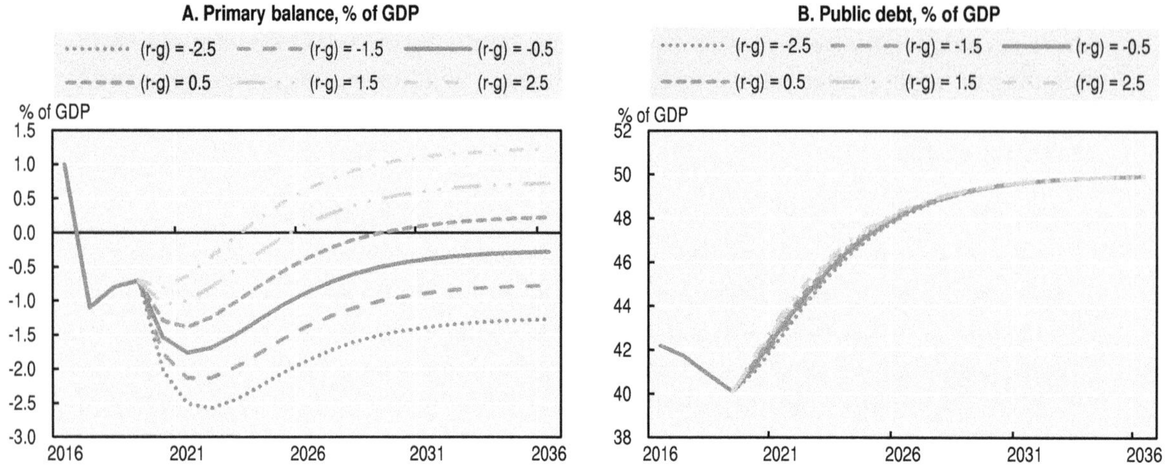

Note: r is the nominal implicit interest rate on government debt and g is the nominal potential growth. If current interest rates and economic potential are held constant *(r-g)* will be around -0.5. Figure 3.3A shows the evolution of the primary balance required under various assumptions about *(r-g)* to ensure longer-term convergence of the public debt ratio to 50%.

Source: OECD calculations; Datastream.

StatLink http://dx.doi.org/10.1787/888933692218

Since 2001, a formal sustainability framework has guided Thailand's fiscal policy. The framework includes four parameters periodically updated by the Ministry of Finance (Table 3.1). Since 2014, they are: (i) public debt not exceeding 60% of GDP, (ii) debt-servicing obligations not exceeding 15% of the annual budget, (iii) a balanced budget in the medium term, and (iv) capital spending reaching at least 25% of the annual budget (FPO, 2017a).

Table 3.1. **Thailand's self-imposed fiscal sustainability framework**

	2001-02	2002-03	2003-04	2004-09	2009-14	2014-21
Public debt/GDP (%)	≤ 65	≤ 60	≤ 55	≤ 50	≤ 60	≤ 60
Debt service/budget (%)	≤ 16	≤ 16	≤ 16	≤ 15	≤ 15	≤ 15
Budget balance	Balance in FY2009	Balance in FY2008	Balance in FY2005	Balance from FY2005 onwards	Maintain budget balance	Balance in medium term
Capital expenditure/budget (%)	-	-	-	≥ 25	≥ 25	≥ 25

Source: Fiscal Policy Office; Siksamat and Wanitthanankun (2015).

While not legally binding, Thailand has sought to adhere to this framework. It has never exceeded the public debt or debt servicing ceilings. The results are more mixed for the remaining parameters on capital expenditure and balanced budgets. To further strengthen fiscal discipline, the Cabinet recently approved a Fiscal Responsibility Bill, which is currently under review by the National Legislative Assembly. The Bill imposes a requirement for future governments to prepare medium-term economic forecasts of up to five years and projections for public debt, revenue, expenditure and contingent liabilities. The Bill also seeks to guard against open-ended populist measures by requiring future governments to calculate the costs of policy decisions and identify sources of funding prior to implementation.

Improved fiscal transparency has helped strengthen Thailand's credibility and performance

Thailand's prudent fiscal management is also a result of improved fiscal transparency across government. Key economic agencies including the Bank of Thailand and the Ministry of Finance have ensured that reporting on Thailand's public finances is accessible, reliable and timely. This has given successive governments the tools needed to make well-informed decisions on the economy, while also building fiscal credibility by providing citizens and markets, including foreign investors, with sound and consistent information.

Thailand has steadily increased the availability of budget documentation to meet international standards (Table 3.2). However, the comprehensiveness of the data can be improved. A recent study highlighted shortcomings in the provision of fiscal risk analysis, notably with respect to the disclosure of Thailand's financial derivative position, major and multi-annual contracts, environmental risks, and fiscal risks related to healthcare and social security funds (Siksamat and Wanitthanankun, 2015). In addition, the contingent liabilities and quasi-fiscal activities of some Specialised Financial Institutions are not well tracked. To further improve transparency and accountability Thailand should strengthen reporting in these areas. Against this background, the additional reporting requirements included in the aforementioned Fiscal Responsibility Bill are a welcome development.

Table 3.2. **The availability of budget documents has improved over time**

	2010	2012	2015	2017
Pre-budget statement	×	×	✓	✓
Executive's budget proposal	✓	✓	✓	✓
Enacted budget	✓	✓	✓	✓
Citizens budget	×	✓	✓	✓
In-year report	✓	✓	✓	✓
Mid-year review	×	×	×	✓
Year-end report	×	×	×	×
Audit report	✓	×	×	✓

Source: International Budget Partnership (2017, 2015, 2012 and 2010).

Revenue will need to increase to fund social protection and safeguard fiscal sustainability

The Fiscal Responsibility Bill will avoid excessive debt and deficit, but adhering to the Bill while also funding a foreseeable expansion in government outlays will require additional revenue. Total public revenues, at 21% of GDP, are largely in line with other countries in the region with similar income levels, although much lower than the OECD average (Figure 3.4). So are total tax collections, at 17% of GDP in 2016, which the government aims to raise to 20% of GDP by 2020 (RD, 2016).

Increasing tax revenue over the longer term is needed to sustainably fund social and economic development. This calls for tax reform, however, which should be designed in a way that supports innovation, investment and competitiveness. The government's recent reforms have helped in this regard, but greater effort will be required.

Figure 3.4. **General government revenue is broadly in line with regional comparators**

In % of GDP, average over 2011-15

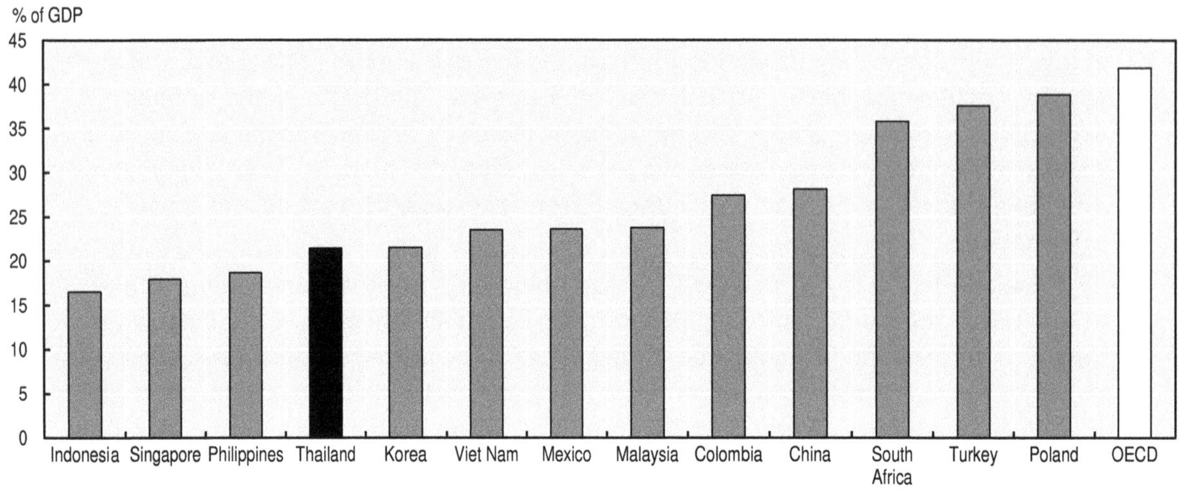

Source: Datastream, OECD Revenue Statistics (2017).

StatLink http://dx.doi.org/10.1787/888933692237

In relation to the tax mix, indirect and direct taxes accounted for 59% and 41% of total tax revenue, respectively, in 2016. Taxes on specific goods and services (which include a range of consumption taxes such as excises but exclude value-added tax (VAT)) are the largest contributor to indirect taxes and account for about a third of all tax collections (or 6% of GDP). This proportion is among the highest of all comparator countries. Corporate income tax is the largest contributor to direct taxes, accounting for a quarter of all tax revenues (4.6% of GDP). Social security contributions amounted to 1.2% of GDP – above most regional peers but well below the 9.1% OECD average (Figure 3.5). Meanwhile, taxes collected by local administrative organisations (LAOs) accounted for 8.4% of general government tax collection. Revenue redistributed from the central government is the primary funding source for LAOs (Box 3.1).

Figure 3.5. **Thailand relies more on specific goods and services taxes than most comparator countries**

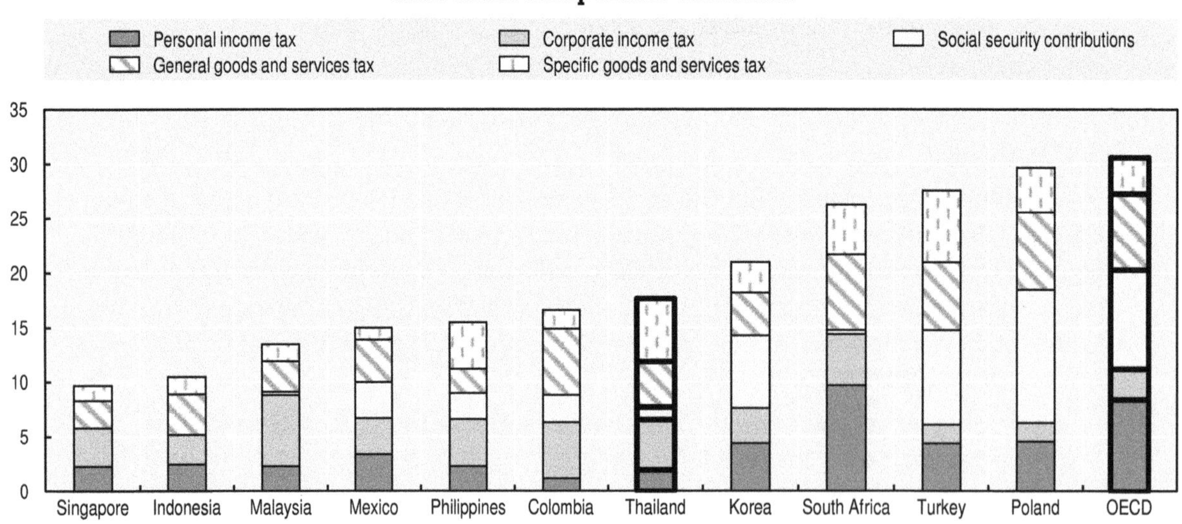

Note: Data for 2014 used for Poland and the OECD average. The figure does not include all sources of tax revenue. It excludes tax collections from international trade and transactions and other taxes.

Source: OECD Revenue Statistics database (2017); Thailand Ministry of Finance, Government Finance Statistics (2017).

StatLink http://dx.doi.org/10.1787/888933692256

Box 3.1. Working toward effective fiscal decentralisation in Thailand

The government has long sought to empower local municipalities through greater fiscal autonomy and decision-making powers (Chapter 5). While LAOs levy local taxes and duties, they rely on central government transfers for around 90% of their income.

In 1999, the government introduced laws to guarantee the level of revenue transferred from the central government to LAOs. In 2007, it was mandated that the central government would distribute no less than 25% of net revenues. As a result, the proportion of central government net revenue distributed to LAOs has increased from 13% in 2000 to an estimated 29% for the financial year 2018. Central government revenues are distributed through three types of intergovernmental grants:

(i) *General grants* are allocated to equalise fiscal capacity across LAOs, based on a formula whereby the amount is inversely related to each local jurisdiction's revenue-generating capacity. Local governments enjoy broad discretion concerning their use. Unspent funds at the end of the fiscal year do not have to be returned to the Ministry of Finance.

(ii) *General purposive grants* are allocated on a per-recipient basis to implement government programmes transferred to local authorities under to the National Decentralisation Plan (e.g. school lunch programmes, student achievement programmes, HIV-infected patients' stipends). Unspent funds at the end of the fiscal year do not have to be returned to the Ministry of Finance.

(iii) *Specific grants* are the instrument used to implement the central government's policy agenda at the local level. Allocation is not based on a formula and is determined by the specific aspects of the projects local governments must implement. Unspent funds at the end of the fiscal year must be returned to the Ministry of Finance.

Although the fiscal autonomy of the regions has increased, local experience suggests that further improvements can be made regarding the distribution of funds. For instance, a review of the distribution of general (non-earmarked) grants in Khon Kaen province revealed that grants were made available to local governments with higher revenue-generating capacity and higher per capita income, contrary to the intended purpose of the grant scheme. Instead of promoting horizontal fiscal equalisation, this practice risks fuelling imbalances in fiscal capacity, hampering inclusiveness and government effectiveness across municipalities (Chapter 5).

As part of the 12th Plan, the government seeks to further improve the capacity of LAOs, by increasing their financial independence over the longer term. To this end, the government aims to increase local revenue streams by providing subsidies to LAOs to undertake local tax reform, undertaking further decentralisation of government taxes, revising laws to increase LAOs' non-tax revenue base and strengthening local fiscal management capacity.

Source: BoB (2017); FPO (2017b); Marks and Lebel (2016); Sudhipongpracha and Wongpredee (2015); and Wongpredee and Sudhipongprac (2014).

Direct taxes were cut to boost competitiveness

Between 2011 and 2013, the corporate income tax rate for large firms was cut by one-third to 20%, down to the lower end of the international range, leading to a fall in corporate tax collection (Figure 3.6). The lower rate applied to small and medium enterprises (SMEs) remained unchanged at 15% over this period. Moving forward, Thailand should avoid further corporate tax cuts and look to other areas to improve competitiveness. Indeed, OECD experience indicates that when institutional efficiency and macroeconomic stability are not in doubt, the corporate tax rate has a limited impact on overall attractiveness as an investment destination (Matthews, 2011).

Figure 3.6. **Thailand's corporate tax rate is now at the lower end of the international range**

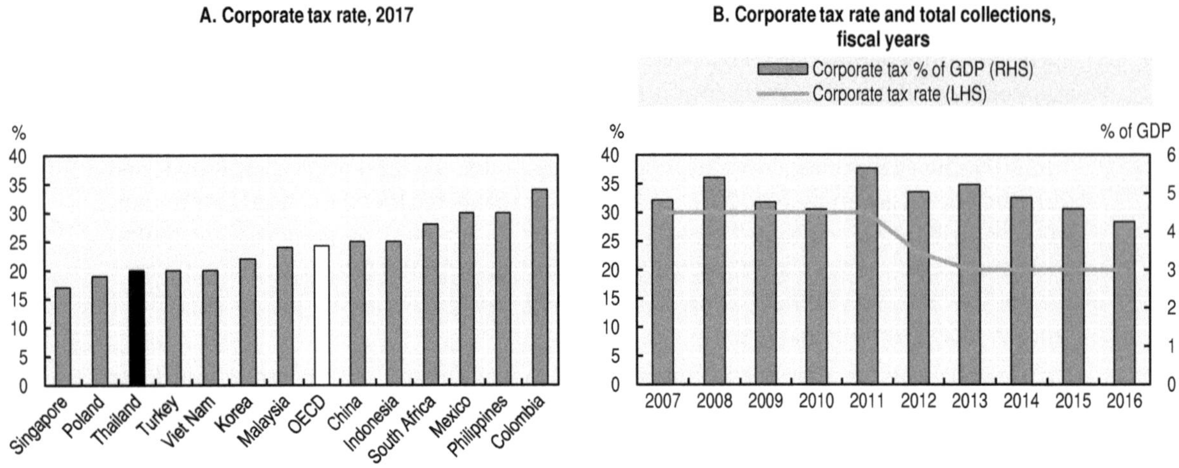

Source: KPMG (2017a); Thailand Ministry of Finance, Government Finance Statistics (2017).

StatLink http://dx.doi.org/10.1787/888933692275

Thailand has also adjusted personal income tax settings, but high labour force informality – estimated at 56% (Chapter 1) – combined with a generous tax-free threshold mean that only one-fifth of the working-age population (15-64) pay any income tax. In 2013, the top rate was cut from 37% to 35%, and in 2017, thresholds and deductibles were raised substantially. Personal income tax is levied at a progressive rate ranging between 5% and 35%. It includes a tax-free threshold of up to THB 150 000 (around USD 4 500), only slightly below the average wage of around THB 165 000 per year. Continuing efforts to reduce the high levels of informality are also key to improving revenue collection and ensuring more people benefit from appropriate safeguards under labour laws and are easily identified for social security purposes.

Increasing indirect taxes can raise additional revenue

Net VAT collections account for over a third of indirect tax collection. As noted, individual excises are also major contributors, accounting for just under 40% of indirect taxes. Their share has grown substantially in recent years following reforms to reduce fuel subsidies and reinstate excises on diesel, gasoline and oil (intake from oil excises tripled between 2014 and 2016). Such reforms reduce price distortions, rationalise public expenditures and improve environmental outcomes. Thailand is also raising excises on other goods and services deemed harmful including alcohol, tobacco and gambling.

The statutory rate of VAT is 10%, but in practice it has been set at 7% since 1999 through royal decrees, making it one of the lowest rates in the world (Figure 3.7). Thailand's VAT has a single rate and is relatively simple. However, its contribution to revenue is undermined by non-compliance and a range of exemptions (e.g. businesses with an annual turnover below THB 1.8 million, sales of agricultural products, and transportation, healthcare, educational and cultural services). As a result, the VAT revenue ratio (actual VAT revenues divided by potential revenues, assuming the standard rate applies to all consumption) is only 38%, against a 56% OECD average (Figure 3.8) (OECD, 2016). Raising the VAT revenue ratio to the OECD average by abolishing VAT exemptions and/or improving compliance would increase revenues by up to 1.5% of GDP.

Thailand should consider gradually broadening the scope of the VAT and raising its rate, using additional revenues to fund increases in targeted social protection to ensure that the most vulnerable remain supported. Indeed, recent analysis suggests that increasing the VAT rate by one percentage point could yield as much as 0.6% of GDP in additional revenue, although around a quarter thereof would be required to compensate for the ensuing consumption loss borne by the bottom quintile (IMF, 2017).

Figure 3.7. **The VAT rate is low by international standards**

VAT rate in 2017, %

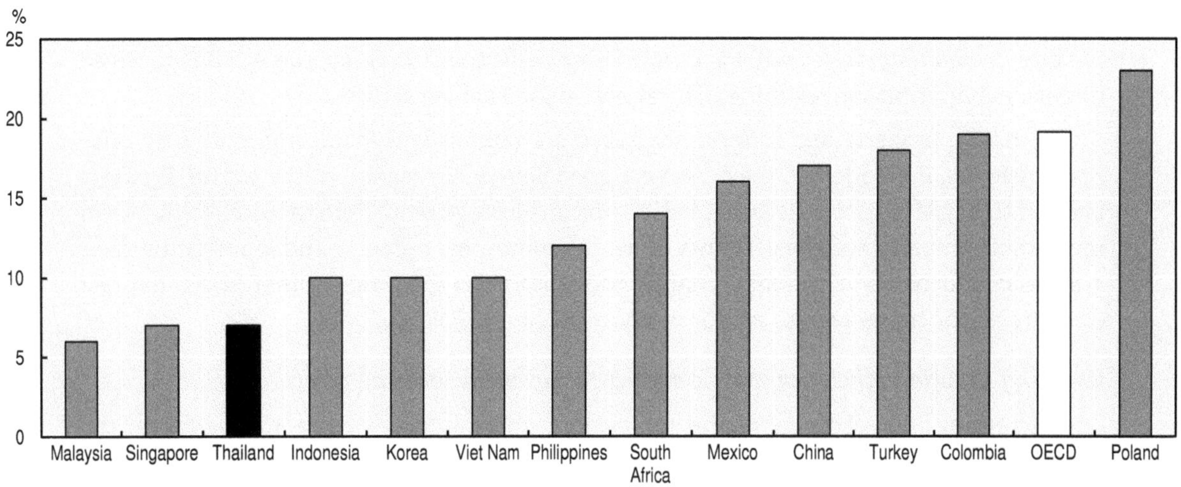

Source: KPMG (2017b).

StatLink http://dx.doi.org/10.1787/888933692294

Figure 3.8. **Thailand's VAT revenue ratio remains below some comparator countries**

VAT revenue ratio in 2014, %

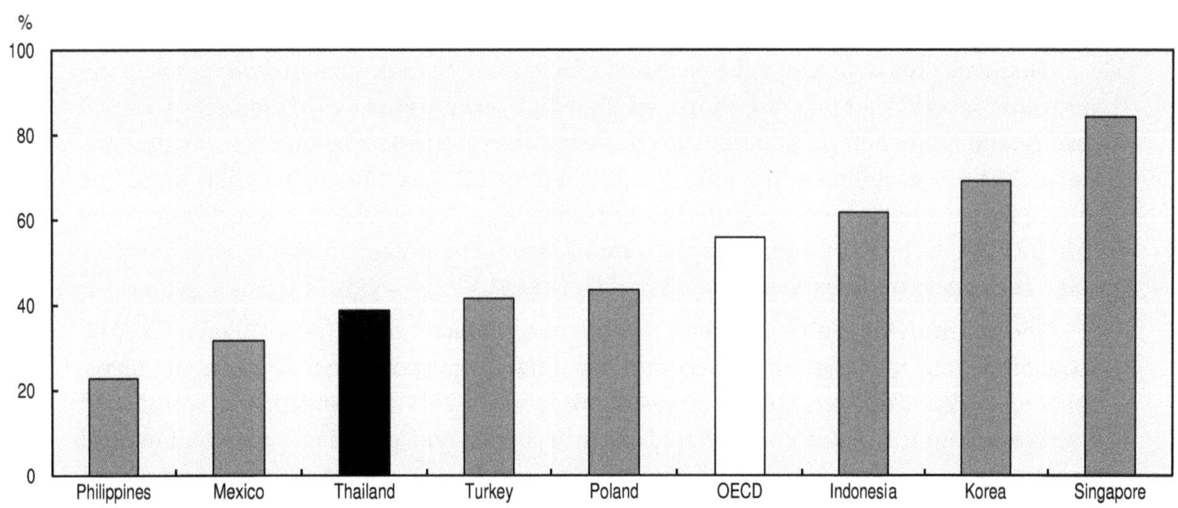

Note: The VAT revenue ratio is defined as the ratio between actual VAT revenue collected on a net basis and the revenue that would theoretically be raised if VAT was applied at the standard rate to all final consumption.

Source: OECD (2016), *Consumption Tax Trends*; OECD (2017c), *Revenue Statistics in Asian Countries: Trends in Indonesia, Japan, Kazakhstan, Korea, Malaysia, the Philippines and Singapore*; and OECD calculations based on data from Thailand Revenue Department.

StatLink http://dx.doi.org/10.1787/888933692313

Thailand is introducing other forms of taxation that should, over time, increase progressivity and the revenue base. In 2016, Thailand instituted an inheritance tax that requires inheritors of assets valued over THB 100 million (around USD 3 million) to pay a tax of 5% for lineal descendants or 10% for others (RD, 2015). In addition, a draft Land and Building Tax Act, if passed, will apply progressive taxation to unused properties, first properties over THB 50 million and additional properties over THB 5 million. It also includes provisions that allow local authorities to raise immovable property taxes, encouraging further policy and fiscal decentralisation. However, in its current form, it is estimated that the land and immovable property tax will collect less than 1% of total tax revenue. Only around 100 residencies worth more than THB 50 million are sold each year and it is estimated that only 10% of homeowners who own more than one house or own houses valued above THB 50 million will actually be taxed (World Bank, 2017a). Moreover, exemptions provided to state-owned enterprises will also undermine collections. Even so, the Act has received intense public criticism, resulting in a review by the Thai legislature.

Although property and inheritance taxes are politically difficult and currently raise scant revenue, if broadened, they can be a good source of revenue in the future. Property taxes of this type tend to be less distortive and can be progressive. Due to the fixed nature of immovable property and the certainty of death, immovable property and inheritance taxes are less conducive to behavioural change and distortions than many other taxes that rest on more elastic bases such as labour or financial capital (OECD, 2012b).

Boosting taxation efficiency and compliance can yield revenue gains

Increasing the efficiency of the tax system and inducing people to operate in the formal economy would also help increase revenue. In relation to VAT alone, the Revenue Department estimates that tax collections are currently 15% lower than they would be under full compliance with the law. Addressing compliance and efficiency is a priority of the government in its efforts to boost tax collection towards 20% of GDP by 2020. To achieve this, the government is adopting a multipronged approach that consists of improving ease of compliance through technological innovation, providing financial incentives to stimulate tax compliance and strengthening tax enforcement.

Thailand aims to improve the ease and efficiency of the tax system by increasing the electronic processing of all tax filings, refunds and social transfers. To facilitate this, the government is amending regulations to enable the electronic submission of tax documents. Meanwhile, the government has already launched the RD Smart Tax application, an online service for personal income tax, with the aim of having all tax returns filed electronically by 2020 (RD, 2014). The VAT system has also already been modernised to enable e-tax invoices and e-receipts to replace paper documents (MoF, 2017).

The government is also providing incentives to induce tax compliance. Prior to 2016, SMEs often kept multiple sets of accounts for different purposes including paying taxes, applying for loans and for internal business purposes. In 2015, the government introduced a single account. If SMEs consolidated their accounts and provided accurate financial statements to the Revenue Department, they received a full company tax exemption in 2016, and SMEs with a net profit greater than THB 300 000 were taxed at a discounted rate of 10% in 2017. Participating SMEs also received immunity from the Revenue Department and were not subject to tax audits for previous unpaid back taxes. In 2016, around 465 000 SMEs registered, far exceeding the government's initial expectation of around 100 000. As a result, more accurate reporting of business sales is already contributing to an increase in VAT collection. To support the plan, the government offered free and easy-to-use accounting software for SMEs that is compatible with smartphones, tablets and PCs. The software helps SMEs develop budgets and record and process accounting transactions. SMEs can also submit their electronic financial reports to the Department of Business Development via the software.

To reduce informality, the government has also encouraged small businesses to incorporate. Those who registered before the end of 2017 are eligible for exemptions for real estate transfers and double deductions for all registration fees including accounting and auditing fees. Moreover, fees for the transfer of registration of immovable property and condominiums were cut from 2% to 0.01% (RD, 2016).

Thailand is also strengthening some enforcement procedures. Through back-office investment in digital infrastructure, the government is seeking to enhance communication between agencies to better identify fraudulent cases. Moreover, from January 2019, commercial banks will only be allowed to provide credit to SMEs on the basis of the single account submitted and accepted by the Revenue Department. This means that should SMEs under-report revenue to the government, they will undermine their access to credit (Suteerapongpun, 2016). Thailand is also working to address issues of international tax avoidance. In 2017, Thailand joined the Inclusive Framework on Base Erosion and Profit Shifting (BEPS). Thailand will collaborate with other countries and implement the OECD/G20 BEPS package (OECD, 2017b).

Government outlays will need to rise to foster development

At around 21% of GDP, general government expenditure is similar to regional comparator countries (Figure 3.9). However, it is expected to increase in line with growing infrastructure requirements and expanded social welfare outlays associated with an ageing population. Ensuring Thailand maintains prudent expenditure practices will be important, including by undertaking cost-benefit analysis where appropriate and giving consideration to institutional capacity to spend efficiently. Moreover, it is crucial that budget allocation aligns with the priorities identified in the National Economic and Social Development Plan.

Figure 3.9. **General government expenditure is similar to regional comparators**

General government expenditure by economic transaction, latest available year

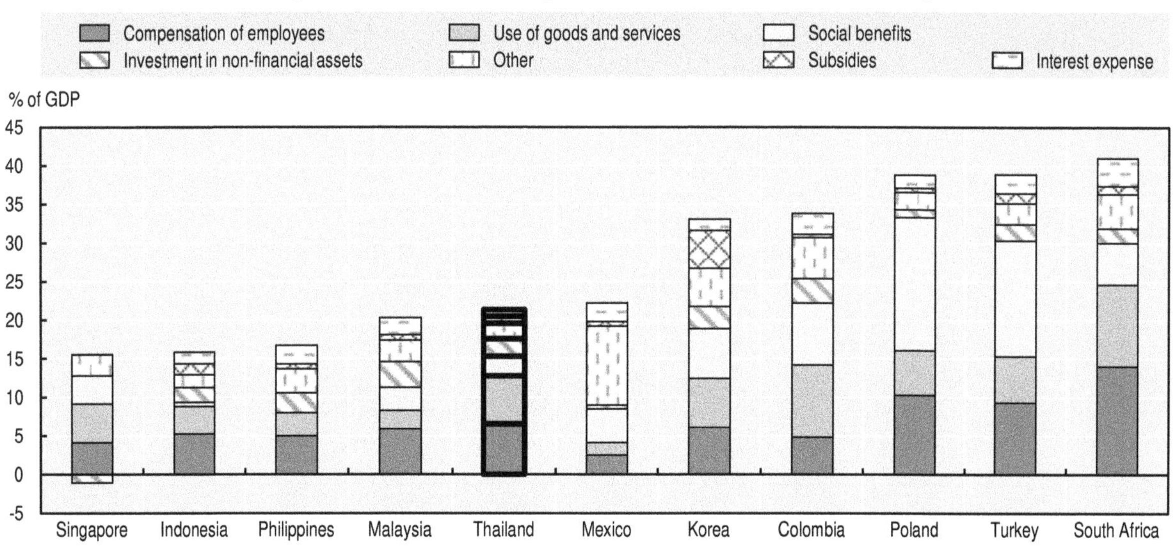

Note: Other categories include consumption of fixed capital, grants expenses and other expenses. Data for Malaysia, Mexico and the Philippines refer to central government expenditure.

Source: IMF Government Finance Statistics (2017).

StatLink http://dx.doi.org/10.1787/888933692332

More efficient infrastructure financing

To boost the productive capacity of the economy and foster inclusive and sustainable growth, the government is undertaking an ambitious infrastructure investment programme, spearheaded by the Eastern Economic Corridor (Chapter 2). However, to ensure value for money and optimal risk allocation, consideration needs to be given to the best means of financing the investment.

To date, there has been limited use of securities financing for infrastructure projects. As a result, project financing has ended up being more expensive than necessary. Thailand is seeking to make greater use of diversified funding sources, notably through the establishment of a Thai Future Fund, but has had limited success so far. This has affected the disbursement schedule and commencement of projects. For instance, the planned Thai Future Fund, first announced in 2015, seeks to raise THB 100 billion (around USD 3 billion) with the initial aim of financing several tolled road expressway projects, which are deemed commercially viable with the potential for high returns. However, its launch as an initial public offering has been delayed due to concerns over issuance and servicing costs. This continued uncertainty tends to delay further investment decisions.

Moving forward, additional sources of financing for infrastructure could be considered, in particular infrastructure bonds priced in Thai baht that can be less costly than bank financing and better match the long-term nature of such investments. Such bonds have long been used in neighbouring Malaysia and Indonesia, both in the form of conventional and Islamic securities, to finance road, airport, mass rail and seaport projects over the past two decades. This has also helped Malaysia develop a vibrant and sizable private domestic debt securities market. The current low yields on Thai government debt (Figure 3.10) make infrastructure bonds particularly attractive.

Figure 3.10. **Thailand should take advantage of low yields to step up infrastructure investment**

Thai government bond yields, %

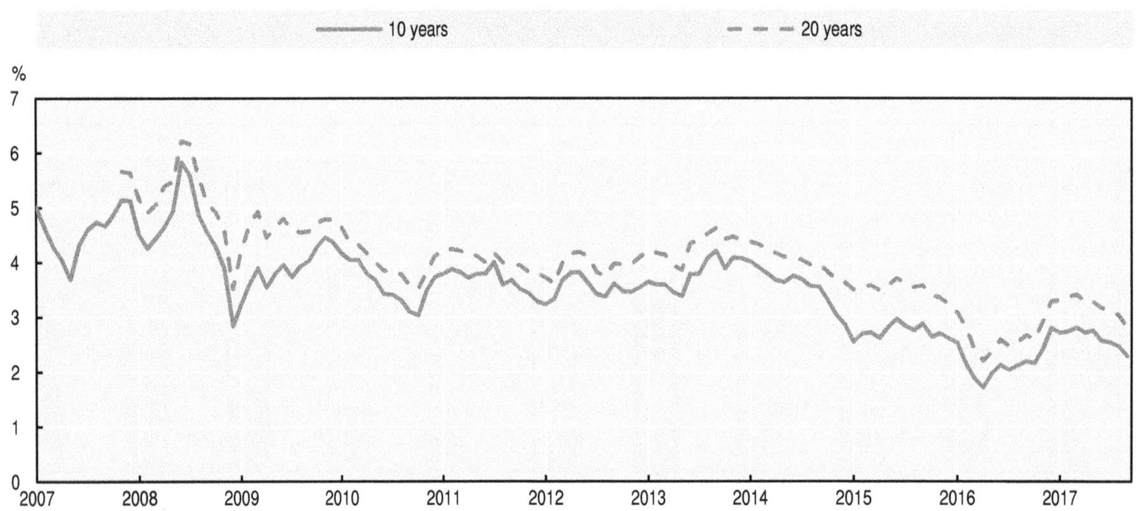

Source: Bank of Thailand and Asian Development Bank.

StatLink http://dx.doi.org/10.1787/888933692351

Another way forward is the broader use of public-private partnerships (PPPs) – a useful tool to boost private participation in infrastructure investment, delivery and management. Thailand has longstanding experience in this area, having established many large PPPs in the 1980s and 1990s, as reflected in the high ratio of the PPP capital stock to GDP (5.9% in 2015), which is more than twice the OECD average (Figure 3.11). However, success on this front has been limited in subsequent years.

Figure 3.11. **Public-private partnership capital stock**

In % of GDP, as of 2015

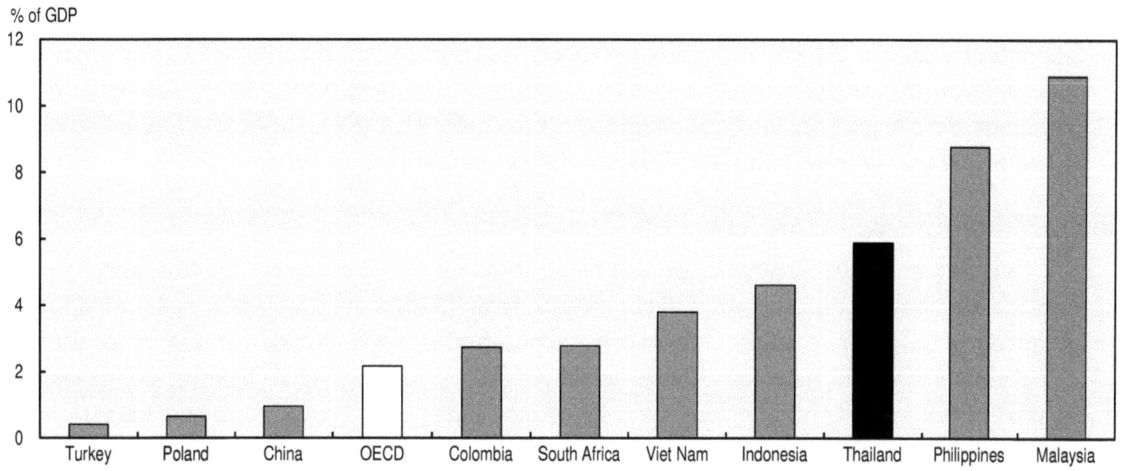

Source: IMF, Investment and capital stock dataset, January 2017, *www.imf.org/external/np/fad/publicinvestment/#5.*

StatLink http://dx.doi.org/10.1787/888933692370

In an effort to reinvigorate PPPs, the government has sought to reduce red tape and improve bureaucratic efficiency, reforming PPP legislation in 2013 with the introduction of time limits and standardised contracts. Moreover, the Cabinet issued a resolution in 2015 approving a means to fast-track PPPs that expedites the project introduction phase from two years to nine months. The new legislation also requires governments to establish five-year strategic plans, with the current plan (2015-19) prioritising investment in the transport sector (Chittmittrapap and Thammavaranucupt, 2017). The plan foresees total investment of THB 1.41 trillion (i.e. over 10% of 2015 GDP) (SEPO, 2015). However, it remains to be seen whether this target will be met without further institutional improvements. Indeed, Thailand's assessed capability to prepare, procure and manage contracts remains below most comparator countries (Figure 3.12).

Figure 3.12. **Thailand can improve the preparation, procurement and management of PPPs**

Benchmark score, 2017

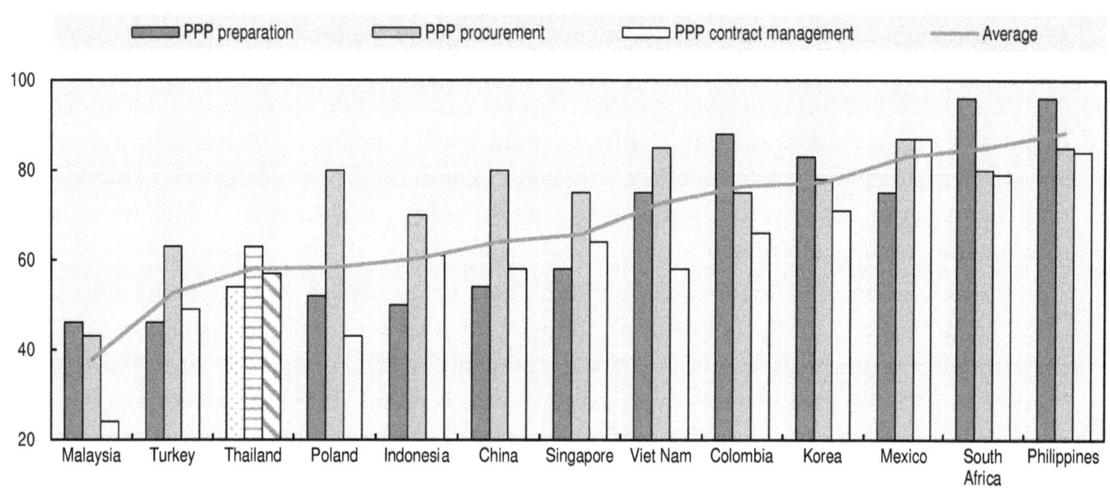

Note: The higher the score, the more aligned with international best practice. Scores for unsolicited proposals are not considered in the above analysis as Thailand, Malaysia, Turkey, Poland and Singapore do not have any regulatory procedures.

Source: World Bank Group/PPIAF (2017), *Benchmarking Public-Private Partnerships Procurement 2017.*

StatLink http://dx.doi.org/10.1787/888933692389

Thailand should seek to make greater use of PPPs as urbanisation and infrastructure demands grow. However, it will be critical to put in place processes that ensure risks are allocated fairly and public liabilities are minimised. Further reform would help, especially to promote alignment with the OECD's Principles for Public Governance of Public-Private Partnerships (OECD, 2012a). In particular, there is a need for: (i) clear mandates and sufficient resources among key institutions engaged in PPP projects, prudent procurement and clear lines of accountability; (ii) sufficient market competition realised through a competitive tender process.

More sustainable healthcare and pension systems

With a rapidly ageing population and rising standards, the burden on public finances to provide healthcare and pensions will continue to grow. Healthcare and pensions are mostly financed by tax revenue, so the reform options outlined above to broaden and increase the tax revenue base will help fund these needs. At the same time, OECD experience shows that well-designed health and pension policies can deliver cost containment and efficiency gains (OECD, 2015a). The effectiveness and coverage of Thailand's healthcare and pension systems are assessed in Chapter 1.

Paying for universal healthcare

In 2002, the government launched the public Universal Coverage Scheme (UCS), which provides free healthcare for previously uninsured people. As a result, Thailand achieved universal health coverage, considerably boosting health outcomes. The UCS led to a significant decline in out-of-pocket expenditure and the rich–poor gap in out-of-pocket expenditure was eliminated (HISRO, 2012).

Total healthcare expenditure has grown from 3.3% of GDP in 2001 to 4.1% in 2014, but remains low. Among comparator countries, only Indonesia spends less (Figure 3.13A). However, as the UCS covers around three-quarters of the population and is entirely government funded (Chapter 1), the share of public expenditure has increased more dramatically, from 56% in 2001 to 78% in 2014, above all comparator countries and the OECD average (Figure 3.13B). Government outlays on health thus rose from 1.9% to 3.2% of GDP over the same period.

Although healthcare costs are relatively low, they are bound to rise in line with a rapidly ageing population, and public finances will bear the brunt of the increase. According to one estimate, public healthcare costs are set to increase to over 5% of GDP over the next 30 years (Figure 3.13C). While this is below most OECD countries, it exceeds the costs of comparable economies within the region. Given Thailand's sound fiscal position, it can and should avoid near-term regressive and often ineffective blanket cuts to the health budget and, instead, implement targeted supply-side measures to yield efficiency gains (Chapter 1) and financing reforms that improve affordability.

Efforts to reform the financing of Thailand's healthcare system by introducing greater private contributions, for those able to afford them, can also improve sustainability. In 2006, the mandatory co-payment under the UCS was abandoned, raising the government's financial burden. In 2012, the government reintroduced the co-payment, but with exemptions for a range of different groups. Around 80% of UCS members continued to receive free services, even as high degrees of non-compliance undermined collections from those required to pay (Feige and Tiavongsuvon, 2015; Paek et al., 2016). One option is to streamline exemptions by better targeting those most in need, while improving the enforcement of co-payments for those required to pay. In addition, the co-payment amount could be linked to income.

Figure 3.13. **Healthcare expenditure is bound to grow**

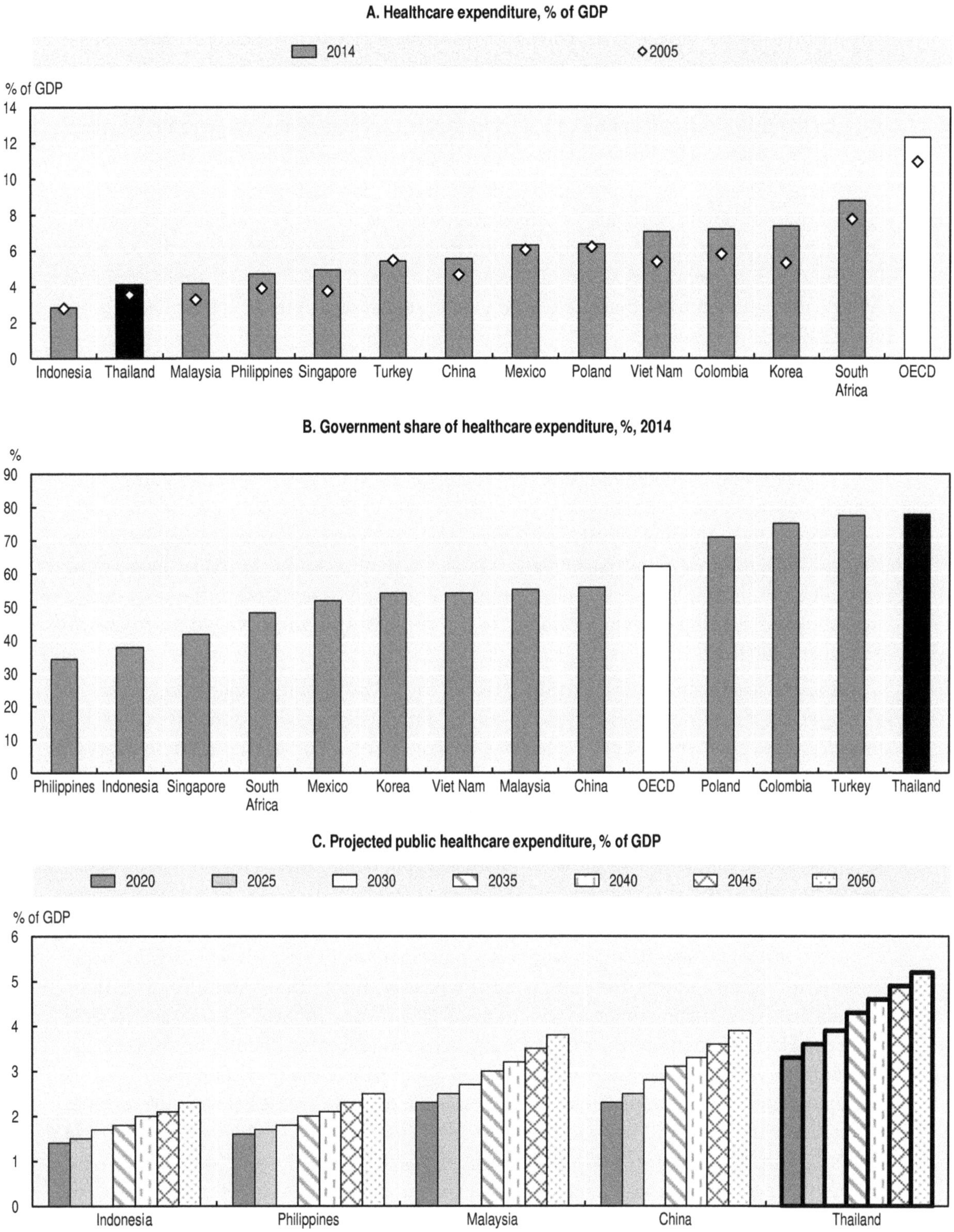

Source: World Bank (2017), *World Development Indicators* (database); Clements, Coady and Gupta, (2012), *The Economics of Public Health Care Reform in Advanced and Emerging Economies*.

StatLink http://dx.doi.org/10.1787/888933692408

The publicly funded Civil Servant Medical Benefit Scheme, which covers around 9% of the population, also needs reform. Unlike the UCS, it pays healthcare providers on a retrospective fee-for-service basis. This provides adverse incentives and contributes to cost inflation, notably through overuse of diagnostics and non-essential drugs (HISRO, 2012). Thailand could consider moving the scheme towards the UCS close-ended capitation model, whereby medical practitioners receive a fixed per person payment to cover all healthcare services. The payment is then adjusted depending on the patient's expected needs.

Greater participation in private health insurance can also serve to address rising healthcare costs. Uptake of private health insurance in Thailand is low and has not materially increased over the past decade despite an increase in real incomes (APO, 2015). As such, it covers only a modest share of overall healthcare costs. Given the small share of people paying personal income tax, the tax relief provided to encourage uptake of private healthcare has had limited success.

Reforming the pension system to ensure sustainability

As outlined in Chapter 1, Thailand has a fragmented pension system with low replacement rates, particularly for non-government employees and informal workers. In 2015, Thailand's pension expenditure accounted for 2.2% of GDP, lower than comparator countries in the region including Viet Nam (2.5%), the Philippines (2.9%), Malaysia (3.8%) and China (3.6%). Although Thailand spends less than comparator countries, its future liability is likely to grow faster, particularly if the government seeks to increase the very low replacement ratios for social pension recipients. Therefore, in addition to the tax reforms suggested above, complementary reforms to the pension system are called for to ensure fiscal sustainability.

Thailand is already facing a shrinking labour force. The total number of working years is being squeezed as more people spend time obtaining a higher education before entering the workforce (Chapter 1). Thai people are also living longer and spending more years in retirement than most countries in the region (Figure 3.14). As a result, there are fewer work years available to support the burgeoning number of retirees. Moreover, with declining family sizes adult children will shoulder greater financial and caregiving responsibility. Although the universal old-age allowance provides financial support, almost 80% of older persons still receive income from their children and 37% of elderly rely on this as their primary source of income (Knodel et al., 2015).

OECD research suggests that postponing retirement is an efficient way to both boost retirement income and improve the financial sustainability of the system (OECD, 2017a). Thailand's private pension scheme (which covers 30% of the population) has a pensionable age of 55, while Thailand's public sector scheme (covering 6% of the population) and old-age allowance (covering the informal workforce and about 64% of the population) both have a pensionable age of 60 (Chapter 1 discusses coverage adequacy). This is below many regional comparators and the OECD average. As a first step, Thailand should align the pensionable age of the private pension scheme with the public sector and the social pension scheme, and put in place transitional arrangements for current or imminent retirees. Moreover, the government should consider progressively raising the official retirement age in line with life expectancy.

Thailand should also gradually increase the mandated private sector contribution rate (i.e. the share of wages mandatorily contributed to a pension fund). Under the national private pension fund, employers and employees combined contribute 6% of wages. This is below the contribution rates for comparator countries and the OECD average (Figure 3.15). In this regard, the government is considering a proposal to phase in increased contribution rates. Businesses with over 100 employees would have to match mandated employee contribution rates, starting from 3% of wages (capped at THB 1 800 per month) in the first year to 10% by the tenth year (capped at THB 60 000 per month). The scheme would be expanded to smaller businesses within five years (TBS, 2017).

Figure 3.14. **Thai citizens can expect a lengthy retirement**

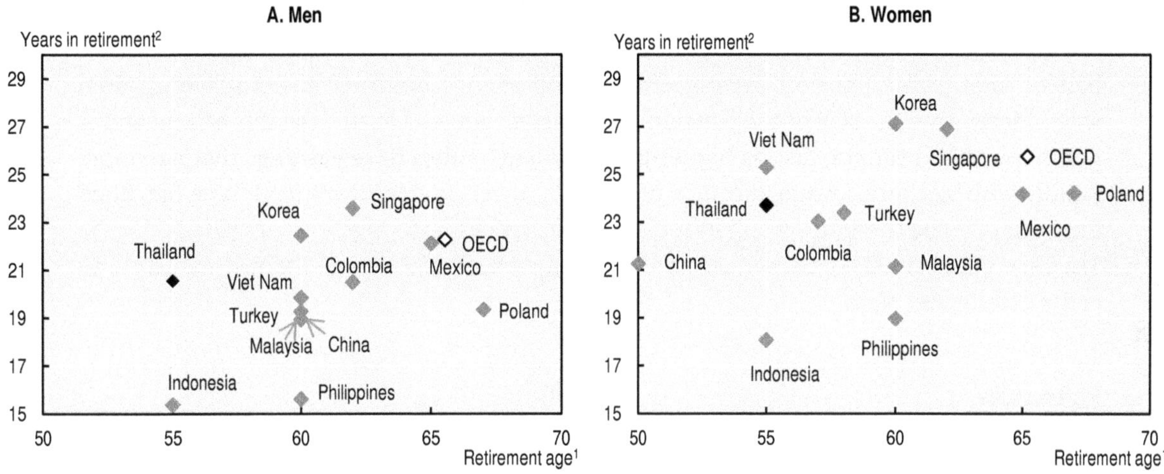

1. The age at which a man/woman can retire and receive full benefits.
2. Gap between the retirement age and life expectancy at age 60 (2015-20). The retirement age for Thailand refers to the private pension scheme, given the very low replacement rates under the old-age allowance (Chapter 1). The retirement age for Chinese women refers to those in blue-collar jobs. The retirement age for Chinese women in white-collar jobs is 55.

Source: World Bank, Women, Business and Law (database); UN Population projections, 2017 revision.

StatLink http://dx.doi.org/10.1787/888933692427

Figure 3.15. **Thailand can boost mandatory contributions to pensions**

Employer and employee contribution % of wages, 2014

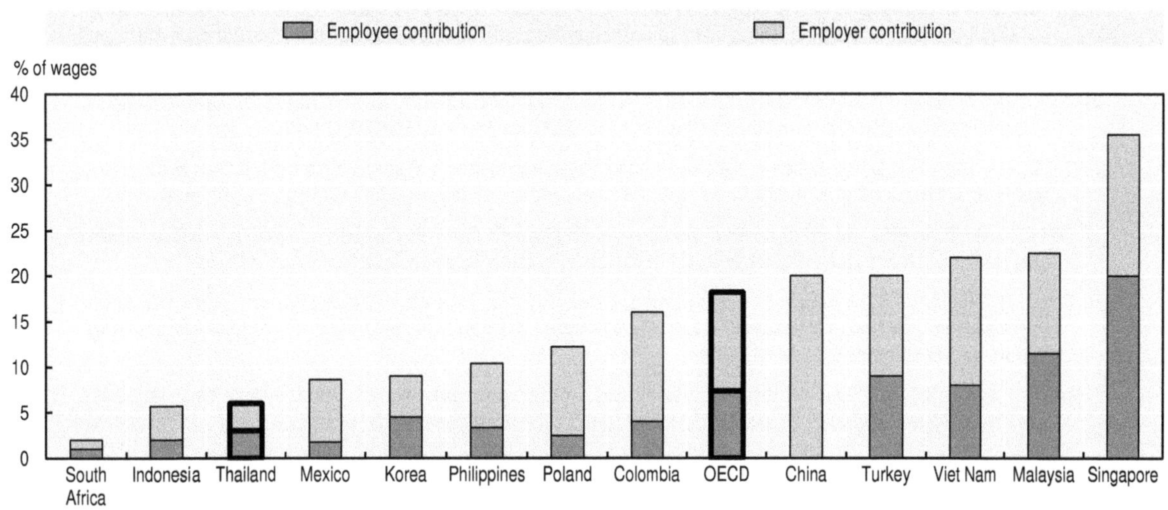

Note: South Africa includes contributions for all social spending. In China, the employer contribution rate is 20% for the basic pension, but in the case of the Provident Fund the contribution rates vary by province. The OECD average only includes countries that have isolated contribution rates for pensions and excludes countries that have larger contribution rates for broader social security measures.

Source: OECD calculation based on World Bank Pension Data; and OECD (2015b), *Pensions at a Glance*.

StatLink http://dx.doi.org/10.1787/888933692446

The government is also seeking to boost retirement savings for the informal workforce through the launch of the National Savings Fund (NSF) in 2015, and by providing grants under Section 40 of the Social Security Fund (Chapter 1). The NSF provides a matching grant of 50% for people aged under 30, 80% for people aged between 30 and 50, and 100% for those aged over 50, capped at THB 100 per month. Although uptake for both schemes remains relatively low, they should remain in place, but perhaps be adjusted administratively or financially to encourage participation. Indeed, OECD experience indicates that matching contributions are generally much more progressive and effective than tax incentives for workers on low-to-median incomes (OECD, 2013a).

Although relatively small in headcount coverage, civil servant pensions account for half of total public pension expenditure. In civil service defined-benefit schemes, final wages determine the size of the pension. This design can lead to undesirable effects and is not in line with best practice, as higher-paid workers tend to have earnings that rise more rapidly with age, while wage-earnings profiles for lower-paid workers tend to be flat. Such final salary plans therefore result in redistribution from low to high earners (OECD, 2013b). Thailand could consider transitioning to a scheme based on average lifetime earnings, as is the case in Viet Nam.

References

APO (2015), *The Kingdom of Thailand Health System Review*, Health Systems in Transition, Vol. 5/5, Asia Pacific Observatory on Health Systems and Policies/World Health Organization, Geneva, *http://iris.wpro.who.int/bitstream/handle/10665.1/11359/9789290617136_eng.pdf*.

BoB (2017), *Thailand's Budget, In Brief Fiscal Year 2018*, Bureau of the Budget, Bangkok.

Chittmittrapap, W. and J. Thammavaranucupt (2017), "Thailand", in *The Public-Private Partnership Law Review – Edition 3*, The Law Reviews, London, *http://thelawreviews.co.uk/edition/the-public-private-partnership-law-review-edition-3/1141279/thailand*.

Clements, B., D. Coady and S. Gupta (2012), *The Economics of Public Health Care Reform in Advanced and Emerging Economies*, International Monetary Fund, Washington, DC, *http://dx.doi.org/10.5089/9781616352448.071*.

Feige, M., and W. Tiavongsuvon (2015), *The Future of Thailand's Healthcare Industries in Tier 2 Cities. Outlook for 2015-2020*, Solidiance, Bangkok, *www.solidiance.com/whitepaper/future-of-thailands-healthcare-industry-in-tier-2-cities.pdf*.

FPO (2017a), *Monthly Fiscal Report (October 2016 – July 2017)*, Fiscal Policy Office, Bangkok, *www.fpo.go.th/FPO/member_profile/it-admin/upload/file/Executive%20summary_0760%20(1).pdf*.

FPO (2017b), *Table FIT_D108: Revenue Local Administrative Organisation*, Fiscal Policy Office, Bangkok, *www.fpo.go.th/FPO/index2.php?mod=Category&file=categoryview&categoryID=CAT0001203* (in Thai).

HISRO (2012), *Thailand's Universal Coverage Scheme: Achievements and Challenges. An Independent Assessment of the First 10 Years (2001-2010)*, Health Insurance System Research Office, Nonthaburi.

IMF (2017), *Thailand: 2017 Article IV Consultation*, International Monetary Fund, Washington, DC. *www.imf.org/en/Publications/CR/Issues/2017/05/31/Thailand-2017-Article-IV-Consultation-Press-Release-Staff-Report-and-Statement-by-the-44948*.

Knodel, J. et al. (2015), "The situation of Thailand's older population: An update based on the 2014 Survey of Older Persons in Thailand", *Population Studies Center Research Reports*, 15-847, University of Michigan Institute for Social Research, Ann Arbor, MI, *www.psc.isr.umich.edu/pubs/pdf/rr15-847.pdf*.

KPMG (2017a), "Corporate Tax Rates Table" (database), *https://home.kpmg.com/xx/en/home/services/tax/tax-tools-and-resources/tax-rates-online/corporate-tax-rates-table.html*.

KPMG (2017b), "Indirect Tax Rates Table" (database), *https://home.kpmg.com/xx/en/home/services/tax/tax-tools-and-resources/tax-rates-online/indirect-tax-rates-table.html*.

Matthews, S. (2011), "What is a 'competitive' tax system", *OECD Taxation Working Papers*, No. 2, OECD Publishing, Paris, *http://dx.doi.org/10.1787/5kg3h0vmd4kj-en*.

Marks, D., and L. Lebel (2016), "Disaster governance and the scalar politics of incomplete decentralization: Fragmented and contested responses to the 2011 floods in Central Thailand", *Habitat International*, Vol. 52, pp. 57-66.

MoF (2017), *Project 3: Taxation and Electronic Transaction Documents*, Ministry of Finance, Bangkok, *www.epayment.go.th/home/app/project-3* (in Thai).

OECD (2017a), *Pensions at a Glance 2017: OECD and G20 Indicators*, OECD Publishing, Paris, *http://dx.doi.org/10.1787/pension_glance-2017-en.*

OECD (2017b), "Thailand joins the Inclusive Framework on BEPS and participates in first joint programme for the implementation of international tax standards", OECD, Paris, *www.oecd.org/ctp/beps/thailand-joins-the-inclusive-framework-on-beps-and-participates-in-first-joint-programme-for-the-implementation-of-international-tax-standards.htm.*

OECD (2017c), *Revenue Statistics in Asian Countries 2017: Trends in Indonesia, Japan, Kazakhstan, Korea, Malaysia, the Philippines and Singapore*, OECD Publishing, Paris, *http://dx.doi.org/10.1787/9789264278943-en.*

OECD (2016), *Consumption Tax Trends 2016: VAT/GST and Excise Rates, Trends and Policy Issues*, OECD Publishing, Paris, *http://dx.doi.org/10.1787/ctt-2016-en.*

OECD (2015a), *Fiscal Sustainability of Health Systems: Bridging Health and Financing Perspectives*, OECD Publishing, Paris, *http://dx.doi.org/10.1787/9789264233386-en.*

OECD (2015b), *Pensions at a Glance 2015: OECD and G20 Indicators*, OECD Publishing, Paris, *http://dx.doi.org/10.1787/pension_glance-2015-en.*

OECD (2013a), *Design and Delivery of Defined Contribution (DC) Pension Schemes. Policy Challenges and Recommendations*, Cass Business School, London, *www.oecd.org/daf/fin/private-pensions/DCPensionDesignHighlights.pdf.*

OECD (2013b), *Pensions at a Glance Asia/Pacific 2013*, OECD Publishing, Paris, *http://dx.doi.org/10.1787/pension_asia-2013-en.*

OECD (2012a), *Recommendation of the Council on Principles for Public Governance of Public-Private Partnerships*, OECD Publishing, Paris, *www.oecd.org/governance/budgeting/PPP-Recommendation.pdf.*

OECD (2012b), "What are the best policy instruments for fiscal consolidation?", *OECD Economics Department Policy Notes*, No. 12, April, *www.oecd.org/eco/public-finance/50100775.pdf.*

Paek, S., N. Meemon and T. Wan (2016), "Thailand's universal coverage scheme and its impact on health-seeking behaviour", *SpringerPlus*, Vol. 5/1, p. 1952, *www.ncbi.nlm.nih.gov/pmc/articles/PMC5104696.*

RD (2016), *Roadmap Digital RD 2020: 2016-2020*, Revenue Department, Bangkok, *http://download.rd.go.th/fileadmin/download/plan/RD2020.pdf* (in Thai).

RD (2015), *The Revenue Department Annual Report: 2015*, Revenue Department, Bangkok, *http://download.rd.go.th/fileadmin/download/annual_report/annual_report58.pdf.*

RD (15 December 2014), "The Revenue Department announced the "RD Smart Tax" application", *Revenue Department news: 8/2015*, Revenue Department, Bangkok, *www.rd.go.th/publish/fileadmin/images/image_eng/englishnews08_2558.pdf.*

SEPO (2015), "Public Private Partnership (PPP) in Thailand", State Enterprise Policy Office, Ministry of Finance, Bangkok, *www.unescap.org/sites/default/files/PPP%20Thailand-sent.pdf.*

Siksamat, S., and J. Wanitthanankun (2015), "Government finance statistics for fiscal transparency and sustainability: A case study of Thailand, Bank of International Settlements", *IFC Bulletin*, No. 39, *www.bis.org/ifc/publ/ifcb39zk.pdf.*

Sudhipongpracha, T., and A. Wongpredee (2015), "Disequalizing equalization grant: an assessment of the relationship between equalization grant and local fiscal capacity in Northeast Thailand", *Asian Affairs: An American Review*, Vol. 42/1, pp. 1-21.

Suteerapongpun, C. (2 February 2016), "2-year tax breaks for SMEs in Thailand: What you need to know", *PKF Thailand, www.pkfthailand.asia/news/news/2-year-tax-breaks-for-smes-in-thailand-what-you-need-to-know.*

TBS (30 September 2017), "Mandatory provident fund options to be widened", *Thailand Business Supplement, https://thailand-business-supplement.com/2017/05/09/mandatory-provident-fund-options-to-be-widened.*

UNFPA and NESDB (2015), *The State of Thailand's Population 2015*, the United Nations Population Fund Thailand and the Office of the National Economic and Social Development Board, Bangkok, *http://thailand.unfpa.org/sites/default/files/pub-pdf/State%20of%20Thailand%20Population%20report%202015-Thai%20Family_en.pdf*

Wongpredee, A., and T. Sudhipongprac (2014), "The politics of intergovernmental transfers in Northeast Thailand", *Journal of Developing Societies*, Vol. 30/3, pp. 343-363.

World Bank (2017a), *Thailand Economic Monitor 2017: Digital Transformation*, World Bank, Bangkok, *http://pubdocs.worldbank.org/en/823661503543356520/Thailand-Economic-Monitor-August-2017.pdf.*

World Bank (2017b), "World Development Indicators" (database), Washington, DC, *https://data.worldbank.org/data-catalog/world-development-indicators.*

World Bank and PPIAF (2017), *Benchmarking Public-Private Partnerships Procurement: Assessing Government Capability to Prepare, Procure, and Manage PPPs*, World Bank/Public-Private Infrastructure Advisory Facility, Washington, DC, *http://bpp.worldbank.org/~/media/WBG/BPP/Documents/Reports/Benchmarking PPP2017Fullreport.pdf?la=en.*

Chapter 4

Planet: Conserving nature

The Planet pillar of the 2030 Agenda for Sustainable Development covers six environmental areas including water, clean energy, responsible production and consumption, climate action, life below water and life on land. Rapid industrialisation, urbanisation and the expansion of intensive agriculture in Thailand placed a heavy strain on the environment. In the past two decades, the country has made improvements with respect to environmental performance and has set ambitious targets in areas such as greenhouse gas emissions. Remaining challenges include: managing water resources to mitigate floods and droughts, designing strategies for resilient and sustainable development of urban areas, increasing forest area and enhancing land-ownership opportunities, conserving and sustainably using biodiversity, improving air and water quality (especially in major urban centres and industrial zones), dealing with growing volumes of solid waste, and addressing climate change.

As in other emerging market economies, Thailand's economic development has come with intense use of natural resources and a heavy environmental toll. Large swaths of the country's forests were converted to agricultural land after the 1950s, as Thailand established itself on the global stage as a major agricultural producer and exporter. Rapid industrialisation and urbanisation were accompanied by increasing pollution levels and rising carbon emissions. Recently, however, Thailand has made improvements with respect to environmental performance and has set ambitious targets in areas such as greenhouse gas emissions. Nevertheless, a number of challenges remain if it is to meet the Sustainable Development Goals set by the 2030 Agenda on water, clean energy, responsible production and consumption, climate action, life below water and life on land.

This chapter discusses a number of major environmental challenges facing Thailand including: managing natural resources, especially water and biodiversity; enhancing the environmental quality of life, notably with respect to pollution and waste; and tackling climate change through mitigation and adaptation measures. It also reviews the legislative framework, institutional arrangements and policy instrument mix for the environment, as well as the system for environmental impact assessment.

Thailand can improve its management of natural resources

Thailand's sustainable development rests on astute management of natural resources that underpin vital economic sectors and millions of livelihoods. In particular, Thailand needs to focus on the management of water resources and biodiversity.

Water management in the face of droughts and floods

Thailand is exposed to cycles of drought and flooding that cause loss of life and economic disruption. In particular, drought and flooding have negatively affected agricultural production, especially in the rural provinces in the North, the Northeast and the South regions, where the share of agriculture in GDP exceeded 20% in 2015, compared to the national average of 9% (Figure 4.1).

Droughts affect more people than flooding in Thailand, although the resulting economic damage tends to be less. In 2016, at the end of the dry season, Thailand faced its worst water shortages in two decades: drought was declared in 14 provinces and water rationing was imposed as major dams dropped to their lowest levels since 1994 (Thepgumpanat and Tanakasempipat, 2016). In addition to the direct impacts and economic disruption caused by limited access to water for people, farms and businesses, droughts also damage infrastructure. For example, roads in eastern Bangkok were damaged when the water in the adjacent canals dropped during the 2015 droughts.

Droughts are driven in part by natural climatic patterns. The absolute quantity of rainfall that Thailand receives should be enough to meet demand. Water availability per capita is high, although on a declining trend. However, despite reassuring annual averages, seasonal variation in precipitation due to the monsoon-dry season pattern creates challenges for water management. Moreover, the geographical distribution of water resources is uneven, with the major demand centres of Bangkok and the Central Plain relying on supplies from other regions in the absence of their own large water reservoirs. Risk of drought is higher in the North and the Northeast regions, where annual rainfall is below the national average (Figure 4.2). Finally, the El Niño climate phenomenon, which occurs at irregular intervals every two to seven years, brings drier rainfall conditions during the typical monsoon months, inducing drought conditions.

Figure 4.1. **Droughts and floods affect many areas**

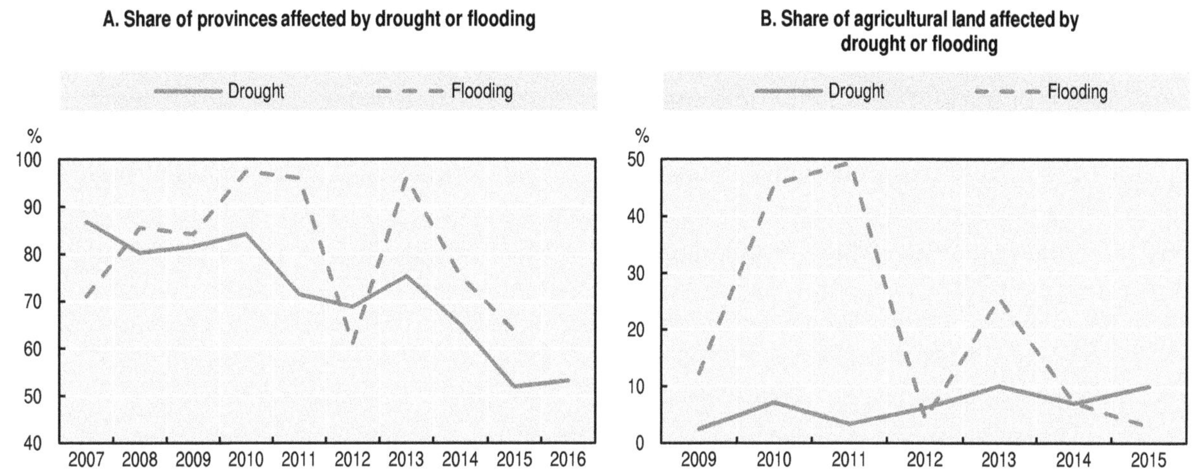

Source: NESDB (2017), Social and Quality of Life Database System, *http://social.nesdb.go.th/social/Default.aspx?tabid=40*; OAE (2017), Agricultural Statistics of Thailand 2016.

StatLink *http://dx.doi.org/10.1787/888933692465*

Figure 4.2. **Erratic rainfalls in recent years have amplified natural disasters**

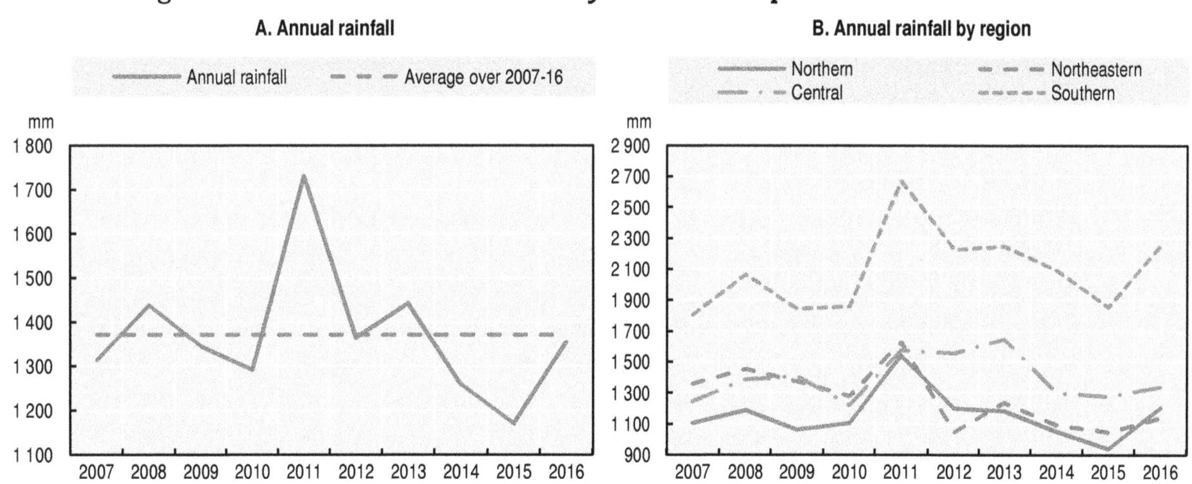

Source: OAE (2017), *Agricultural Statistics of Thailand 2016.*

StatLink *http://dx.doi.org/10.1787/888933692484*

Thailand has experienced drought conditions even in years when rainfall has exceeded the long-term average, pointing to drivers beyond climatic variables. This reflects patterns in water consumption behaviour, agricultural and industrial land development, urbanisation and population growth (Thaiturapaisan, 2016). Over 90% of water withdrawal is used for agricultural purposes, 5% for domestic usage and 5% for industry (FAO, 2016).

Excessive groundwater abstraction is another consequence of poorly managed water resources. Groundwater supplies 6% of water demand in the country. However, for many years groundwater has been extracted at rates surpassing its natural recharge capacity. This has led to a decline in groundwater levels, land subsidence and seawater intrusion, especially in the Greater Bangkok Region (Fornes and Pirarai, 2014). The government recognises that water shortage problems are likely to increase as projected future water demand outstrips current water storage capacity (VNR Taskforce, 2017).

Flooding has caused major economic damage in Thailand, sometimes resulting in broader international impacts. The cost of floods averaged over THB 6 billion (nearly USD 190 million) per year between 1989 and 2013. The 2011 floods were among the most devastating, claiming over 1 000 lives, affecting 16 million people and accounting for over THB 23 billion (USD 690 million) in damage (MOI, 2013). They also affected global supplies of electronics and automobiles as production was forced to shut down, highlighting Thailand's role as a key manufacturing hub in Southeast Asia and a vital cog in global supply chains (GVCs) (Chapter 2).

Heavy monsoon rains are the immediate cause of flooding, but several other factors contribute. Poorly planned urban expansion, intensification of agriculture, and the deterioration or loss of watershed forests have led to the decline of flood retention areas and flood plains (MFA Netherlands, 2016). Subsidence linked to the excessive and uncontrolled pumping of groundwater – a particular problem in Bangkok – also increases flood risks.

Climate change is expected to exacerbate the challenge even further. National projections indicate that heavier rainfalls are expected in areas with already high precipitation, such as the southern peninsula, leading to increased potential for flooding. Precipitation is expected to decline even further in the arid, inland Northeast region, making drought more likely (ONEP, 2015).

A lack of integrated water management hinders an effective response to these challenges. Water management in Thailand is characterised by a highly fragmented institutional framework consisting of least 31 ministerial departments under 10 ministries, one national unit under the Prime Minister's Office, one agency and six national committees (Box 4.1). Overlapping responsibilities can lead to conflicts of interest and impede the development of integrated water management.

Unlike many countries, Thailand has no single law governing water management. Currently, there are 36 primary laws and 2 000 secondary legal frameworks relating to water resource management. For this reason, the Department of Water Resources has been working since 1992 to draft the Water Act. This Act aims to rationalise the legal framework, strengthen existing legal instruments and ensure the effectiveness of policies. By providing policy guidance and setting homogeneous national priorities, it is intended to allow different entities and stakeholders develop and implement their respective water management plans in accordance with the overarching national framework. Budget allocation will also be compliant with agreed national priorities. Good practice of unified management will be drawn from the Ministry of Energy's experience.

In the absence of a comprehensive law, Thailand has launched a number of water management plans and strategies. For example, the Water Resources Management Strategy 2015-2026 covers water source management, water usage and wastewater management; and the Strategy for Green Growth under the 20-Year National Strategy Framework 2017-2036 and the Strategy for Green Growth toward Sustainable Development under the 12th National

Economic and Social Development Plan (NESDP) 2017-2021 (12th Plan) foresee numerous activities related to water management (VNR Taskforce, 2017). However, implementation is hampered by institutional complexity and political issues. Furthermore, Thailand's water management plans cover a relatively short time span. Longer-term projections and planning are needed which incorporate factors that influence the probability of future floods such as rising sea levels and land subsidence.

Box 4.1. **Government bodies and departments involved in water management in Thailand**

A significant number of ministerial departments and national and sub-national bodies are involved in water management in Thailand:

- The National Water Resource Committee (NWRC), established in 1988, is the most important formal body with responsibility for supervising and monitoring projects and advising the Cabinet on policies and regulations.
- The National Water Management Unit was established in August 2017 under the Prime Minister's Office. It has a mandate to oversee the government's efforts to tackle flooding and droughts across relevant ministries and government agencies.
- The National Water Resources and Flood Policy Committee (NWFPC) and the Water Flood Management Commission (WFMC) formulate policy, approve investment projects, and monitor the implementation and impact of these projects.
- Twenty-five River Basin Committees (RBCs) composed of government officials, user groups and experts are responsible for preparing river basin water resource management frameworks and plans.
- The Department of Water Resources under the Ministry of Natural Resources and Environment manages surface water in non-irrigated areas and monitors flood mitigation.
- The Royal Irrigation Department (RID) under the Ministry of Agriculture and Cooperatives is responsible for overseeing the supply of water for the agricultural sector, improving reservoirs and managing surface water in irrigated areas. It also plays a role in constructing and maintaining waterways and flood protection systems.
- The Department of Groundwater Resources (DGR) under the Ministry of Natural Resources and Environment regulates groundwater use.
- The Department of Disaster Prevention and Mitigation under the Ministry of Interior ensures the integration of disaster risk mitigation strategies into sectoral plans for risk sensitive investment, including those in the water management sector. The Department moreover promotes co-ordination in emergency responses as well as in recovery efforts.

A number of other ministerial departments are involved in different aspects of water management, including the construction of small-scale irrigation-related projects and/or flood prevention, oversight and management.

Source: Fornés and Pirarai (2014) and MFA Netherlands (2016).

The government has tended to focus on hard infrastructure, supply-side solutions to water management (PRD, 2015), while demand-side measures have received less attention. Experience from countries such as the Netherlands could provide useful examples of the benefits of a more holistic approach to water management and flood defence (Box 4.2).

Box 4.2. **Water governance in the Netherlands: The Delta Programme**

Without a flood defence system, approximately 60% of land in the Netherlands would be at risk of flooding. It is estimated that 9 million people live in flood risk areas, which account for an estimated 70% of GDP. To protect against flooding and in turn secure freshwater supplies, the Delta Programme adopts demand-side management measures combined with «soft» infrastructure. It is widely recognised as the global reference for water management and flood protection (OECD, 2014a). The first Delta Programme was presented to the House of Representatives in 2010, introducing a new flexible approach to water management. Its effectiveness is based on a combination of three features: multi-level public responsibility, the use of cutting-edge delta technologies and public awareness campaigns.

Demand-side water management measures are a prominent feature of the Delta Programme and include the adoption of cutting-edge delta technologies and knowledge development across four areas:

1. *Eco-engineering:* This approach targets flood prevention and aims to achieve natural and environmental goals. For example, the Netherlands conducts marsh restoration projects to transform open freshwater into land, thereby generating stronger flood protection and encouraging biodiversity.
2. *Water safety:* These programmes encompass «multi-layer safety» measures and use integrated, sensible and risk-based protection systems to tackle high water levels. The new Flood Control 2100 innovation programme plays an important role in meeting this challenge.
3. *Smart dikes:* The Digital Delta and Energy Dikes innovation programmes deal with smart dikes. The former involves integrating and linking data, models, algorithms, tools and applications. The combined information is made available to the entire sector and offers innovations to stakeholders at a limited cost. The Energy Dikes programme focuses on ways of generating energy, including freshwater-saltwater transition and tidal power, thereby helping to make energy provision becomes more sustainable.
4. *Liveable deltas:* Work is being performed on a cohesive portfolio of knowledge, technology and services to ensure living in deltas is sustainable. The three main approaches are mapping and monitoring delta cities, designing and planning resilient delta cities, and climate-adaptive construction and (re)development. Water awareness campaigns play an important role in implementing the Delta Programme. The government is working with partners under the Administrative Agreement of Water (including provinces, water boards, municipalities, drinking water companies and the Rijkswaterstaat), to launch the "Our Water" public awareness campaign (*www.onswater.nl*), which aims to help the population anticipate and respond to extreme drought and flood situations.

The 2018 Delta Programme will be the first to include spatial adaptation strategies. The Delta Plan on Spatial Adaptation features multi-level public responsibility structures at local and regional levels. By 2019, all municipalities will conduct water assessments and stress tests in collaboration with the provinces, district water boards and national government. Water assessments allow municipalities to factor in water-related risks and costs in spatial planning decisions, while stress tests will provide insights into vulnerabilities to water extremes, enabling authorities to take appropriate measures to tackle them.

Source: Netherlands Ministry of Infrastructure and the Environment (2016), *Netherlands National Water Plan 2016-2021*; and OECD (2014b), *OECD Studies of Water: Water Governance in the Netherlands, Fit for the Future?*

The recent establishment of the National Water Management Unit reflects the government's growing attention to this issue. Following the floods in the Northeast region in August 2017, the Prime Minister established the unit under his office with a mandate to oversee government efforts to tackle flooding and droughts across relevant ministries and government agencies. The operational success of the unit, its relationship with existing bodies and its effectiveness in addressing the challenges outlined above remain to be seen.

The response to disasters such as flooding also falls under Thailand's disaster risk governance frameworks. Taking the Sendai Framework for Disaster Risk Reduction 2015-2030 as a set of guiding principles, the government adopted the National Disaster Risk Management Plan in 2015, supplementing the Disaster Prevention and Mitigation Act 2007. One of the goals of the plan is to improve co-ordination between the different parts and levels of government responsible for disaster management – an identified weakness of previous approaches. The plan also makes reference to non-structural mitigation measures such as land-use planning, zoning, building codes and other incentive measures, which were also lacking in previous approaches, but play a vital role in moving from a "reactive" disaster response and recovery mode to a proactive approach that encompasses disaster risk reduction. Combining disaster risk management with plans for climate change adaptation (see below) would further contribute to increasing Thailand's resilience to disasters.

Sufficient funding and increased capacity at the local level will be needed if plans are to be effective. Currently, a lack of oversight means that funds transferred to the local level can be diverted for other purposes. Effective response to disasters is also hampered by the incomplete decentralisation of disaster governance (Marks and Lebel, 2016). Local authority organisations (with the exception of the Bangkok Metropolitan Area) lack the capacity to respond effectively to disasters and receive insufficient assistance from the central government (Chapter 5).

Thailand's rich biodiversity needs to be conserved and managed sustainably

Thailand is one of the most biodiverse countries in the world, thanks to its location between two major biogeographical regions: the Indochinese region in the north and the Sundiac region in the south. Its varied climate and topography of mountain ranges, major river basins and coastline supports a wide range of ecosystems, including 15 categories of forest varying from rainforest, evergreen and deciduous to mangroves found along the coastline. Thailand is also home to 15 000 plant species, representing 8% of the world's total (CBD, 2017). Coastal and marine areas cover 316 000 km^2 stretch along the Pacific Coast and the Indian Ocean and host coral reefs containing over 400 coral species – 10% of the world's total (ONEP, 2014).

Thailand derives many benefits from its rich biodiversity. Its forests provide important ecosystem services such as watershed functions that help mitigate floods and carbon sequestration for climate change mitigation. Its ecosystems underpin important sectors of the economy and millions of jobs, including in agriculture, the seafood industry and tourism.

Thailand has six types of protected areas: national parks, forest parks, wildlife sanctuaries, non-hunting areas, botanical gardens and arboretums. Nearly 19% of the country's total land is classified as territorial protected area (World Bank, 2017b) and at least 20% of the marine and coastal areas in Thai waters have been designated as protected areas (CBD, 2017). In addition, 16% of total marine areas are subject to ecosystem management measures.

However, biodiversity remains under threat. Compared to other middle-income countries, Thailand performs poorly on several indicators of biodiversity (Figure 4.3). Numerous species are at risk of extinction, including 118 mammals (35% of known mammal species in Thailand), 168 birds (17%), 49 reptiles (12%), 18 amphibians (11%), 202 fish (7%) and 1 131 plants. Ecosystem loss due to land use change is also a concern. For example, the country's wetlands are decreasing due to irrigation and farmland encroachment, especially in the North and Northeast regions (ONEP, 2014). Other threats include invasion of alien species (especially in wetlands), trafficking of wild animals and plants, and climate change and pollution, which affects freshwater, marine and coral reef ecosystems. Parts of the country's forests are also being degraded or destroyed.

Figure 4.3. **Thailand performs poorly on several indicators of biodiversity**

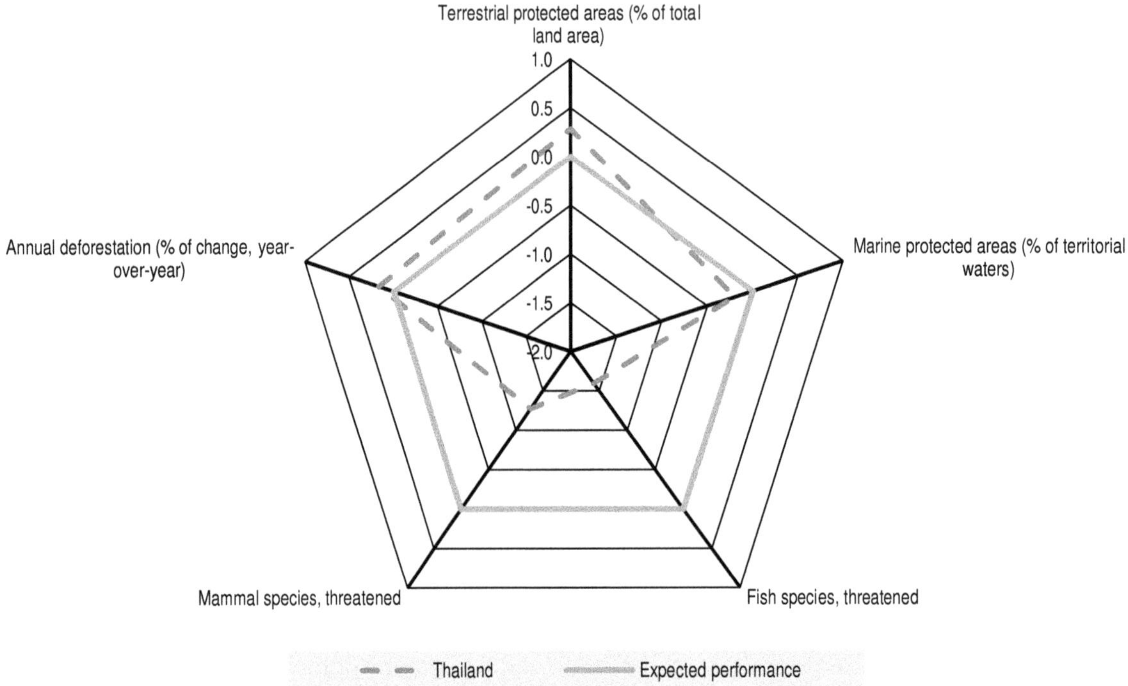

Note: The blue line represents Thailand's performance when benchmarked against other middle-income countries. The grey line represents the performance that might be expected given the country's level of income per capita. Places where the blue line lies inside the grey line represent poorer than expected performance on a given indicator.

Source: Author calculations based on World Bank (2017a), *World Development Indicators* (database); and World Bank (2017b), *Deforestation and Biodiversity*.

StatLink http://dx.doi.org/10.1787/888933692503

At the national level, forest cover has been improving in recent years thanks to reforestation and forest rehabilitation programmes combined with increased conservation efforts, including the creation of protected areas and public awareness raising (ONEP, 2014). These programmes have reversed a decades-long deforestation trend. In the 1960s, over half the country was forested, however much of this forest cover was lost due to the massive expansion of agricultural land associated with the promotion of cash crops. Thailand's forest cover has since recovered from a low of 25% in 1998 to nearly 32% in 2016.

However, deforestation continues to be a problem in the Northeastern and Northern regions. Today, under 15% of land in the Northeast region is forested, with over 1.5 million rai (240 000 hectares) lost since 2008. The Northern region has experienced an even faster rate of deforestation since 2008, although the region still has much higher levels of forest cover at nearly 53% (RFD, 2017).

Several factors drive deforestation. Thailand's national report to the Convention on Biological Diversity (CBD, 2014) states that forest area has been lost through the expansion of agricultural land, especially due to the promotion of cash crops such as rubber and oil palm planting. Price subsidies incentivised farmers to expand production, which was sometimes achieved by encroaching into forest land. These subsidies have since been removed. Illegal rosewood logging in the Northeast region, even in protected national parks (CBD, 2014), and the development of resorts for tourism, have also led to deforestation.

Land has also become degraded through intensive agriculture. Levels of vital nutrients such as nitrogen are five times below the accepted global standard, and 54% of land is considered low grade. Intensive agriculture and mono-cropping since the 1970s has led to nitrogen and nutrient leaching; misuse of chemical fertilisers has led to acid soils.

Biodiversity in marine and coastal areas has also deteriorated markedly with Thailand falling short of international targets for marine conservation. The fishing industry has caused coastal and marine ecosystem destruction and overfishing has resulted in a dramatic reduction in fish stocks. Fishing yields in Thai seas have declined from 300 kg/hour in 1961 to 25 kg/hour in 2011 (ONEP, 2014). As a result, the domestic fish processing industry must now rely on fish from other sources. Even in protected areas such as national marine parks, biomass has declined due to illegal fishing and tourism (Hockings et al., 2012). Other pressures on marine biodiversity include ocean acidification and the deteriorating quality of coastal waters from tourism and industrial activity along the coastline such as oil production. Thailand thus failed to meet the Millennium Development Goal target to reduce biodiversity loss and has not yet met several of the targets set by the Convention on Biological Diversity (CBD) (ONEP, 2014; VNR Taskforce, 2017).

Nevertheless, Thailand has made some notable gains in reversing or slowing biodiversity loss. For example, it has met targets set out in its National Policies, Strategies and Action Plan on the Conservation and Sustainable Use of Biodiversity (NBSAP) 2008-2012 to increase forest cover to 33% of total land area (reached in 2008, although cover has since dropped to below 32%), at least 18% of which comprises conserved forests, and to increase mangrove areas (ONEP, 2014).

The issue of biodiversity has been integrated into NESDPs with details laid out in the Master Plan for Integrated Biodiversity Management 2015-2021 and associated action plans. The 12th Plan lays out Thailand's ambition to increase forest cover to 40% of total land area by 2030, a target that should contribute to biodiversity, as well as to water management and climate change mitigation. In addition, the National Biodiversity Action Plan 2015-2021 aims to reduce the rate of habitat loss by 50%. Within this framework, in 2015, the government enacted the Marine and Coastal Resources Management Act. Thailand's Sustainable Consumption and Production Roadmap 2017-2036 also aims to restore biodiversity in agricultural areas to 2016 levels by 2025, and includes targets such as reducing the use of pesticides by 30% by 2026, and increasing sustainable and organic farming practices.

Challenges remain in securing environmental quality of life

The quality of the local living environment has a direct impact on people's health and well-being, as well as repercussions for ecosystems. Thailand has been grappling with the environmental impacts of rapid industrialisation and urbanisation, and while there have been improvements, challenges remain in three major areas: air pollution, water pollution and waste generation.

Air pollution has tended to worsen

While some measures of air pollution have shown improvement over the past 20 years, emissions of other pollutants continue to increase. PM2.5 pollution (atmospheric particulate matter pollution under 2.5 µm in diameter) has been creeping up in Thailand since 2010, after modest improvement between 1990 and 2010 (Figure 4.4). Other measures of pollution exhibit mixed performance over time and between regions (PCD, 2017a). On the positive side, levels of PM10 (particles 10 µm in diameter or under) have generally declined in Bangkok and across all regions since the late 1990s (a notable exception being Rayong in the East). Similarly, SO_2 emissions in Bangkok and some regions have also declined. However, NO_2 emissions and ozone pollution have worsened over the same period. NO_2 emissions have been roughly stable in Bangkok, but have increased significantly in some regions, for example, Chiang Mai in the North and Rayong in the East. Ozone levels have been increasing in Bangkok and nearly every region, even doubling in some areas of the East and South.

Figure 4.4. **Air pollution in Thailand has been increasing**

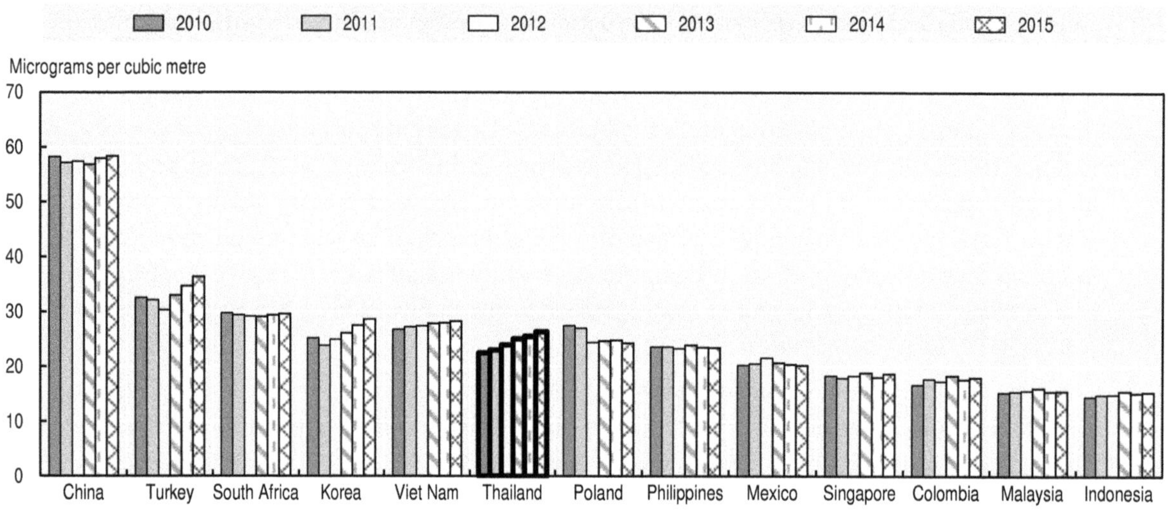

Source: World Bank (2017a), *World Development Indicators* (database).

StatLink http://dx.doi.org/10.1787/888933692522

Four major sources of air pollution in Thailand include:

- *Industrial activity*: Pollution limits are regularly exceeded in Thailand's major industrial zones (PCD, 2015). For example, dust pollution from cement factories and industrial plants is a concern in Na Phra Lan in Saraburi, and volatile organic compounds (VOCs) exceed safety standards in Map Ta Phut, the country's largest industrial estate.
- *Vehicle traffic in urban areas*: Rising populations combined with increasing car ownership is leading to deteriorating air quality in urban areas. The number of vehicles in Bangkok more than doubled between 2000 and 2016, from 4.5 million to 9.4 million. Their number increased by almost 17 million in the country as a whole (DLT, 2017).
- *Smoke and haze from burning in the North*: A combination of agricultural burning and forest fires during the dry season creates smoke and haze across Northern Thailand from February to April. Land and vegetation may be slashed and burnt to clear and fertilize plots for agricultural use. Other contributors to the haze include forest clearance for crop land expansion, burning of agricultural waste and accidental forest fires.

- *Transboundary air pollution*: Poor air quality in Thailand can sometimes be attributed to pollution from sources beyond its borders, including forest fires and agricultural burning in neighbouring Indonesia, Laos, Malaysia and Myanmar.

The authorities have taken steps to alleviate some of these pressures. Stricter emissions standards, fuel reformulation and inspection processes have been progressively introduced to tackle urban air pollution. Other measures have included public campaigns for carpooling and car-free days. The expansion of public transport systems has also helped tackle urban air pollution, although efforts have been concentrated in Bangkok. Cities such as Chiang Mai have no public transport systems and have seen traffic congestion and air pollution rise over the years. Moreover, even in Bangkok, public transport remains underdeveloped, although the Bangkok Mass Transit Master Plan foresees a massive expansion of the rail network.

In 2013, the government introduced the Northern Haze Prevention and Mitigation Plan, putting in place monitoring systems and co-ordination mechanisms to ensure that farmers do not carry out burning at the same time. Results from monitoring stations reportedly show that the situation is improving. Thailand is also party to the ASEAN Agreement on Transboundary Haze Pollution, a legally binding environmental agreement signed in 2002, and in 2015 it adopted a regional roadmap to achieve a transboundary haze-free ASEAN by 2020. In response to industrial pollution, Thailand's Sustainable Consumption and Production Roadmap 2017-2036 is aiming to achieve a 30% reduction in pollution from industrial sources by 2030.

However, sometimes policy measures are contradictory and work against improving air quality. For example, in 2012 a new fuel quality law was introduced to cut SO_2 and vehicle emissions, yet in the same year the government announced a first-car buyer scheme whereby people would receive a tax refund upon the purchase of a car. As a result, 2.3 million additional vehicles were registered in 2012 compared to 2011, a much higher increase than typical year-on-year growth, which ranged between 700 000 and 1.3 million before 2011 (DLT, 2017).

Water quality needs to improve

According to estimates, 23% of surface water was of poor quality in 2016 (PCD, 2017b), although this represents a slight improvement on 2007. Groundwater pollution includes nitrates from agricultural sources in shallow aquifers, organic compounds from the petrochemical industry in coastal aquifers southeast of Bangkok, cadmium and fluoride in the Northwest, sodium chloride in the East and Northeast, arsenic in the South, and problems of seawater intrusion along the coastline (Fornés and Pirarai, 2014).

The agricultural sector is the largest polluter, discharging up to 39 million m^3 of wastewater per day last year, followed by the industrial sector (17.8 million m^3 per day) and the municipal sector (9.6 million m^3 per day) (PCD, 2017b).

Inadequate capacity for wastewater treatment and a lack of compliance with regulations results in poor water quality. Only 15% of municipal wastewater from over 24 million households is treated (PCD, 2017b) and many communities located along watercourses release wastewater directly into rivers (ONEP, 2014). Furthermore, not all of the wastewater treatment plants that exist are operational. In 2016, 13 out of the 101 plants were not functional, a situation which the Pollution Control Department attributed to limited budget allocation for investment and maintenance of plants by local administration organisations (PCD, 2017b).

Monitoring and enforcement systems are falling short. The Industrial Works Department monitors the wastewater quality of 291 big factories in real time and regularly carries out surprise inspections on others. Nevertheless, river basins located in the main industrial bases of the country, including the Chao Phraya, Tha Chin and Rayong River basins, have severe water pollution problems. Over half of pollution point sources near the San Saab canal (Bangkok) and 16% of the sources near the Tha Chin River Basin did not treat their wastewater according to regulations (PCD, 2017b). Furthermore, only a few water pollution indicators are monitored, leaving dangerous substances such as heavy metals potentially undetected.

Finally, there are no financial disincentives to pollute, as users do not pay for the cost of treating wastewater. Introducing wastewater tariffs could address this issue. Such tariffs should factor in distributional effects on the poor, and be based on per unit costs of water usage amounts to discourage over-consumption through marginal pricing structures (OECD, 2015).

Managing solid waste is a growing challenge

As in many countries in Asia, solid waste generation is growing rapidly in Thailand. In 2016, 27 million tonnes or 74 000 tonnes per day of municipal solid waste were generated nationwide, representing an 80% increase since 2010 (PCD, 2017b, 2010). This amounts to 416 kg per person per year, which is relatively high among comparator countries (Figure 4.5). In addition, an estimated 3.5 million tonnes of hazardous waste were generated in 2016.

Figure 4.5. **Thailand's municipal waste per capita is higher than in many comparator countries**

Municipal waste, latest available year

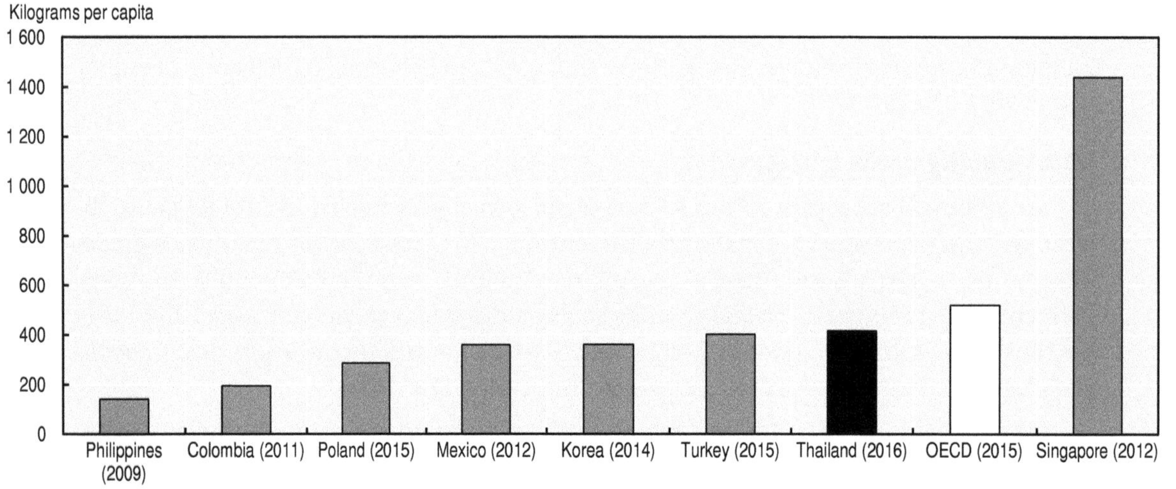

Source: Data for OECD countries are from OECD (2017). Data for Thailand are from PCD (2017b), Thailand State of Pollution 2016. Data for the Philippines and Singapore are from *http://unstats.un.org/unsd/ENVIRONMENT/qindicators.htm.*

StatLink *http://dx.doi.org/10.1787/888933692541*

Much of Thailand's solid waste is not collected and treated correctly, in particular outside of major urban areas. Only 58% of the country's municipalities provide refuse collection and disposal services (PCD, 2017b). As a result, just 50% of the total waste generated in the country is collected. Moreover, 43% of total waste is disposed of through open burning or illegal dumping, while just 36% is disposed of correctly, most of which is sent to sanitary landfills. Out of Thailand's 2 500 open rubbish pits, only around one-fifth are properly managed. The rest entail risks of illegal dumping including of hazardous waste. In 2016, 1.9 million tonnes of hazardous industrial waste went unaccounted for after leaving factory gates (PCD, 2017b).

Numerous environmental problems result from the increasing quantity of waste and its inappropriate disposal. Seepage into nearby land and water systems and air pollution from waste fires can threaten public health. Methane, a more potent greenhouse gas than CO_2, is also released from waste, which contributes to climate change. Rising waste is also a reflection of poor resource productivity, which works against the transition to more sustainable consumption and production patterns.

The composition of collected waste shows a high potential for composting, recycling and waste-to-energy. Currently, only 21% of waste is recovered in this way, against a potential 60% or more. Half of all waste collected in Bangkok (national data are not available) is organic material that could be composted (Table 3.1). This would reduce the demand for incineration and enable authorities to incinerate only non-recyclable waste. The rate of recycling could also be increased. Finally, introducing waste-to-energy is a good option as such plants can divert waste from landfill and recover heat and electricity from waste incineration. Thailand has recently started installing waste-to-energy plants, and there is potential for expansion (OECD, 2015). To realise this potential, there is a need to provide facilities for better sorting at source combined with public awareness building and education programmes.

Table 4.1. **Composition of waste at transfer stations in the city of Bangkok, 2013**

	%
Compostable	**49.8**
Food waste	*43.3*
Wood and leaves	*6.4*
Recyclable	**11.3**
Recycled paper	*1.9*
Recycled plastic	*3.6*
Foam	*1.6*
Glass	*3.1*
Metal	*1.2*
Others	**38.9**
Non-recycled paper	*9.7*
Non-recycled plastic	*21.5*
Leather and rubber	*1.5*
Textiles and textile waste	*3.9*
Rock and ceramic	*0.7*
Bone and shells	*1.6*
Total	**100.0**

Source: OECD (2015), *Green Growth in Bangkok, Thailand.*

Governance arrangements and associated financing issues are hampering progress in addressing waste management challenges. The Ministry of Natural Resources and Environment regulates solid waste management, while implementation is the responsibility of local authorities. The Ministry of Public Health sets the collection fee ceiling and the local government then sets the actual fee at or below this ceiling, with the fee going to the municipality. In general, municipalities pay private companies to provide waste collection and disposal services (and sometimes the facilities as well), which are established under public-private partnerships (PPPs) and fall under the oversight of the Ministry of Finance. One barrier to greater private sector participation could be the long timeframe needed to establish PPPs (Chapter 3).

Collection fees vary by municipality but are currently about THB 20/household/month (USD 0.60), and suffer from two main problems. First, pricing is far below the real cost of waste collection and disposal and, as such, does not contribute substantially to the sustainable financing of solid waste management. When local authorities are elected they tend to avoid raising fees, fearing that such a move will be politically unpopular. Second, this pricing mechanism does not provide incentives to reduce the absolute quantity of waste, as the fees are not set by volume, but per household.

A stronger commitment to reducing the overall amount of waste produced, in addition to the current focus on proper treatment, is essential. In 2015, the government has adopted a Waste Management Roadmap which aims to promote efficient and sustainable waste management and power generation from waste-to-energy technologies. By 2021, 75% of municipal solid waste and 100% of hazardous industrial and infectious waste should be properly managed, according to the Roadmap's targets. There are also discussions about introducing a Solid Waste Act. These measures could be complemented by a strategy to reduce, reuse and recycle (the "3Rs") to address the challenge of rising quantities of waste, in addition to the issue of how to collect and treat waste. This would put Thailand on the path to a more resource-efficient economy, in line with the sufficiency philosophy. Specific recommendations for the solid waste sector in the Bangkok Metropolitan Area (which accounts for around 16% of municipal solid waste generated in the country) can be found in the OECD report *Green Growth in Bangkok, Thailand* (OECD, 2015).

Addressing climate change requires both mitigation and adaptation

Climate change poses serious risks to economies, societies and ecosystems. Reductions in greenhouse gas emissions need to be complemented by adaptation policies. Transitioning to a low-carbon economy and adapting to the impacts of climate change are key medium to long-term challenges facing Thailand.

Climate change mitigation efforts need to be stepped up

Thailand's carbon dioxide (CO_2) emissions have risen rapidly in line with economic growth. Between 1990 and 2015, absolute CO_2 emissions increased from 80 million to 244 million tonnes per year (Figure 4.6A). Emissions have also more than doubled in per capita terms, although levels remain well below OECD country levels (Figure 4.6B). The overall carbon intensity of the economy has grown marginally since 1990, in contrast with most comparator countries (Figure 4.6C), but has been on a declining trend since 1997. Thailand's growing GDP per capita explains the trend of rising emissions, rather than energy intensity, population growth or the carbon intensity of the country's fuel mix.

Thailand has set ambitious greenhouse gas emission targets. The Nationally Determined Contribution Roadmap on Mitigation 2021-2030 identifies the energy and transport sectors as possessing the greatest potential for emission reductions. Thailand intends to reduce its greenhouse gas emissions by 20-25% from the projected business-as-usual level by 2030 (ONEP, 2015). The country's energy plans, consolidated in the Integrated Energy Blueprint (MOE, 2016), define several targets to contribute to this goal. The Power Development Plan (PDP) 2015 set an objective of 20% of electric power generation from renewables (including hydropower) by 2036. The Alternative Energy Development Plan 2015 aims to achieve a 30% share of renewable energy in total final energy consumption in 2036, up from nearly 12% in 2014, by prioritising power generation from waste, biomass and biogas. It also foresees greater use of biofuels for transport. Finally, the Energy Efficiency Plan has set a goal of reducing energy intensity by 30% in 2036, compared to 2010, and introduces measures to increase the energy efficiency of transport.

Figure 4.6. **Carbon emissions continue to rise**

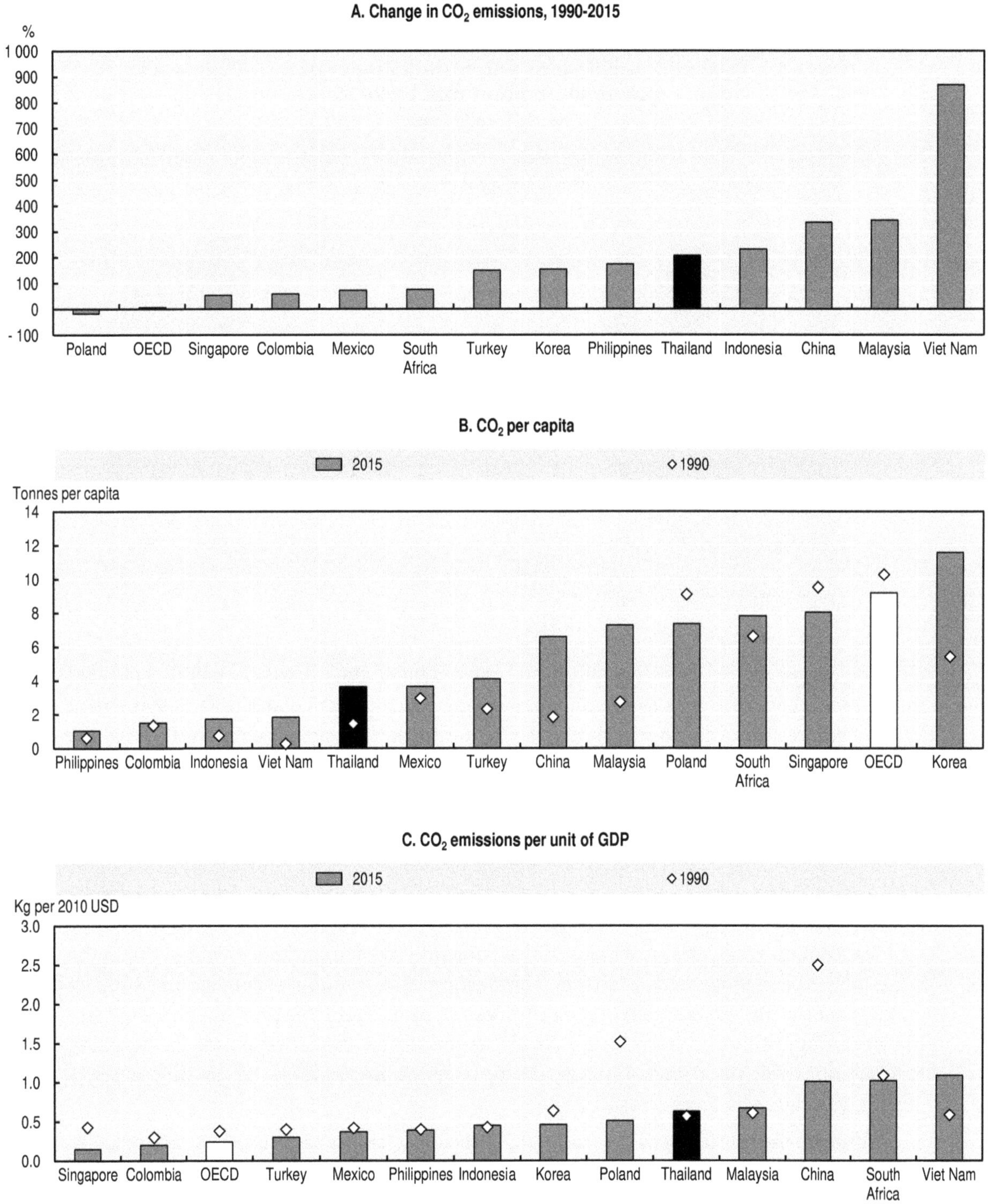

Source: IEA (2017a), *CO2 Emissions from Fuel Combustion 2017 Edition*; OECD stat.

StatLink http://dx.doi.org/10.1787/888933692560

However, the PDP also foresees an increase in the share of coal in the energy mix, which will push up the absolute level of carbon emissions. Coal currently represents 10-15% of power generation, and its share is projected to rise to 17% by 2036 (Figure 4.7). While the overall carbon intensity of Thailand's energy mix is set to be lower under the PDP, thanks to the increasing share of renewables and hydro, increasing the share of coal to 17% represents more than a doubling in absolute terms (IEA, 2016a).

Figure 4.7. **Coal and renewables will form a bigger part of Thailand's power generation mix by 2036**

Power generation mix

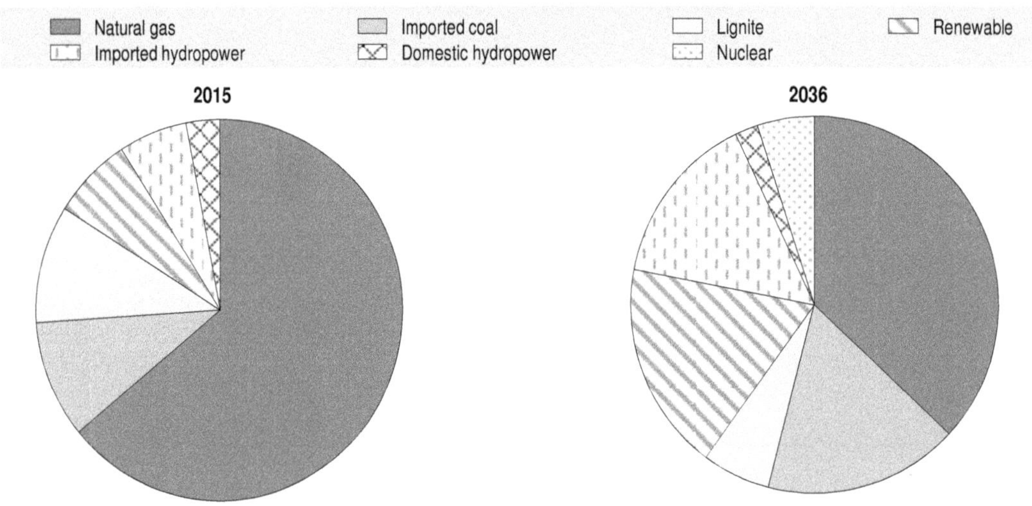

Source: MOE (2016), Thailand Integrated Energy Blueprint.

StatLink http://dx.doi.org/10.1787/888933692579

The plans to increase the share of coal may not be consistent with Thailand's international commitments to greenhouse gas reduction. In particular, the Paris Agreement in 2016 requires countries to submit increasingly stringent intended nationally determined contributions. Future PDPs will therefore need to aim for a greater reduction in emissions intensity that may require a reduction in the absolute level of coal generation. As such, investment decisions being taken today risk locking Thailand into a higher emissions path.

As well as being a carbon-intensive energy source, coal-fired power plants can cause local environmental stress. Smog, acid rain and air pollution may result from emissions of sulphur dioxide, nitrogen oxides and particulate matter, which can have health impacts for local communities. Coal-fired plants also consume large quantities of water. Given the water resource management challenges highlighted above, the government will need to ensure that the implementation of the PDP does not exacerbate this problem further. There has been domestic opposition to the development of new coal-fired plants in the south of Thailand, leading to delays in the finalisation and implementation of the PDP, which is currently under revision as a result.

Although the PDP foresees the use of high-efficiency, low-emissions (HELE) technologies for coal plants, this will not guarantee a low-carbon path for Thailand. HELE technologies do reduce the environmental impact of power plants, but will not be sufficient on their own to achieve a low-carbon energy mix. To be consistent with a low-carbon future, coal-fired power plants will eventually need to be fitted with carbon capture and storage technology in order to make the deep cuts in emissions required. Deployment will take time, resources and policy commitment, particularly for the development of a geological CO_2 storage resource in Southeast Asia, which is not yet well understood (IEA, 2016b). As HELE technologies may be run for an average lifetime of 50 years, there is a serious need to reconsider the economic, environmental and social costs of running a sizeable coal fleet for decades to come (IEA, 2016b).

A greater focus on renewables could achieve the twin aims of increasing energy security and achieving a low-carbon future. One of the principal aims of the PDP is to increase Thailand's energy security by diversifying the energy mix and reducing its dependence on largely imported natural gas. The International Energy Agency's review of Thailand's electricity sector concluded that Thailand could be more ambitious in its adoption of renewables without adversely affecting energy security, identifying untapped potential in the solar photovoltaic sector (IEA, 2016a). Thailand is already making good progress in this direction, introducing feed-in tariffs to incentivise investment and more than tripling solar photovoltaic capacity between 2013 and 2016 (IEA, 2017b). Feed-in tariffs have been introduced for very small power producers and distributed solar systems at the community level, supporting the aims of cleaner energy and energy security, as well as reducing regional inequality.

Climate change adaptation is equally important

Thailand is highly vulnerable to the effects of climate change. Average annual temperatures have been rising faster than the global average, rainfall patterns are shifting and tropical storms are becoming more intense. Sea levels are also rising faster than the global average. Combined with land subsidence, the net sea level has risen by up to 25 mm per year in areas such as the larger Bangkok Metropolitan Area (Naruchaikusol, 2016). Climate projections for Thailand foresee increasing mean temperatures of between 0.4°C and 4°C in the next 100 years – with the central plain and lower Northeast region particularly affected – and an extension of the hot period. Rainfall is set to become more variable with a monsoon period 3-5% more intense by the 2100s. In addition, mean sea level rise could see shoreline shifts of 10-35 metres along the Andaman coast (Naruchaikusol, 2016). These changes pose major challenges to millions of livelihoods, core economic sectors, essential infrastructure, and – due to the potential impact on the agricultural sector – food security in Thailand.

Climate change adaptation features in Thailand's national plans. The 12th Plan includes a goal "to reduce greenhouse gas emissions and enhance the ability to adapt to climate change". The National Climate Change Master Plan 2015-2050 provides more detail and specifies mitigation, adaptation and capacity-building targets. The adaptation plans focus on six sectors: water management, agriculture and food security, tourism management, public health management, natural resources management, and human settlement and security. Short-term actions include the development of the National Adaptation Plan (NAP), while medium-term actions, looking towards the 2020 horizon, foresee the development of forecasting and early warning climate insurance systems and local adaptation action plans.

The project to develop a NAP began in January 2015, and involves the development of a vulnerability database, followed by the creation of a national database of adaptation methodologies. The intention is to establish and incorporate climate resilience into national development by promoting the integration of adaptation measures into all sectors and at all levels. The plan aims to provide government agencies and other related entities at the national and local levels with an implementation framework, good practices, approaches and guidelines to develop their own strategies, management plans and action plans, suitable for individual sectors and areas, and to provide financial agencies with a budget allocation framework. The implementation of the first NAP is foreseen for 2018-21.

This represents a positive move as adaptation is largely neglected in current sectoral plans or plans for major developments such as the Eastern Economic Corridor. The latter, for example, foresees the expansion of logistics and transportation systems to include new high-speed trains, double-track rail lines connecting to key industrial zones, upgrading of ports and a new motorway connecting Bangkok to Rayong. Given the massive investment decisions involved, it is essential to ensure that this infrastructure is resilient to the effects of climate change – for example, that port developments take into account projected sea level rises.

Given the early stage of drafting or implementation, it is too soon to assess the effectiveness of the Climate Change Master Plan and NAP. The true test will be whether the process translates into awareness, mainstreaming and ultimately implementation of adaptation measures across all sectors from national to local levels. Caution should be exercised as previous assessments of Thailand's readiness for climate change adaptation have warned of complacency (SEI, 2016).

Implementing plans will require effective central co-ordination that involves all relevant stakeholders, a strong evidence base (e.g. for climate projections), capacity building (especially at the local levels), sufficient financing, and mechanisms for monitoring, evaluating and adjusting approaches (OECD, 2014). Linking climate change adaptation and disaster risk management could also improve effectiveness. Disaster risk management needs to take into account future climate change, while adaptation can benefit from longer-established disaster risk management institutions, regulations, infrastructure and practices (OECD, 2014).

Environmental governance in Thailand

Environmental governance in Thailand is in the process of being updated with the replacement of the country's framework environmental law, which has been in place since 1992. As in many countries, the policy mix is diversifying to encompass more economic and informational instruments, in addition to regulatory approaches. Environmental protection could be further strengthened through the addition of strategic environmental assessments to the policy mix.

The legal and institutional framework is being modernised

The primary objective of the Enhancement and Conservation of National Environmental Quality Act (1992) was to enhance and conserve natural resources and environmental quality through environmental policies and planning. The Act calls for and regulates Provincial Environmental Management Plans, Environmental Impact Assessments (EIA), Environmental Protected Areas (EPAs) and Pollution Control Zones, and provides a framework for standard setting and monitoring, public participation and environmental education, and an environmental fund for investment.

Among other measures, the new environmental bill due to replace the 1992 Act will create an environmental fund for subsidising operations to clean up the environment, reward agencies with good environmental practices and set up new environmental quality standards. The bill was agreed by the Council of State and the National Legislative Assembly in January 2018, and is to come into force in the following months.

Thailand's environmental strategies and policies are co-ordinated by the Ministry of Natural Resources and Environment, set up in 1992, which oversees 11 ministerial departments as well as several public authorities (e.g. the Wastewater Management Authority) and public companies (e.g. the Forest Industry Organization). Sixteen Regional Environment Offices are responsible for regional environmental planning and reporting as well as monitoring and inspecting environmental quality. Provincial Offices for Natural Resources and Environment are located in each of Thailand's 76 provinces.

The National Environmental Board has powers and duties related to submitting policy and governing related agencies in the area of environmental quality management. For example, they consider and approve the Environmental Quality Management Plan (the major 20-year long term policy on the environment) and other environmental plans at national and sub-national levels, set emission of effluent standards, and specify measures to strengthen co-operation and co-ordination among government agencies and the private sector.

The policy instrument mix is evolving

As in many countries, regulatory approaches remain the dominant environmental policy instrument in Thailand, although economic instruments, information instruments and voluntary approaches form an increasing part of the policy mix.

In terms of economic instruments, feed-in tariffs, tax incentives, and access to investment grants and venture capital have been introduced to promote renewable energy. Various environment-related funds also exist, such as the Energy Conservation Promotion Fund, which was set up in 1993. There are also a number of environmental charges, but these tend to be set too low or are inappropriately designed and, as such, are ineffective (see above).

Environmental taxes efficiently encourage broad-based action in tackling environmental challenges (such as water and air pollution). Moreover they offer a less distortive source of revenue and are transparent in their coverage and impact. In the past Thailand has endeavoured to develop a detailed proposal for comprehensive environmental tax reform (the 2010 Draft Framework Law on Economic Instruments for Environmental Management). While no comprehensive environmental tax reform has been introduced in recent years, Thailand has put in place other instruments. For example, a new system of vehicle registration taxes based on CO_2 emissions was introduced in 2015 and the Ministry of Finance has developed a proposal for a carbon tax on transport fuels (UNESCAP, 2017).

In addition, Thailand is further developing the foundation for a national carbon price through its Voluntary Emissions Trading Scheme (Thailand V-ETS), launched in 2013. The V-ETS is a pilot project for a potential national, mandatory emissions trading system. The pilot scheme is focusing on the measurement, reporting and verification of emissions at company level, and companies are expected to be given tradable certificates by 2018-22.

Thailand still subsidises some fossil fuels, although the country has made substantial progress in reforms. The government has revised liquefied petroleum gas (LPG) subsidies, gradually reducing them for different user categories. In January 2015, it set a uniform LPG wholesale price across all sectors to better reflect international market prices. In 2016, it deregulated prices for compressed natural gas. Energy subsidies were 0.6% of GDP in 2014, but dropped to 0.2% in 2015 (IEA, 2017c). However, Thailand still subsidises petroleum and natural gas through the Oil Stabilization Fund, tax exemptions, and caps on retail prices for certain fuels such as biofuel blends (IEA, 2017d). The government has committed to abolish these subsidies in the future.

Information instruments have also been progressively introduced since the 1990s. For example, the "Thai Green Label" environmental certification was established in 1994 and applies to products and services (excluding foods, drinks and pharmaceuticals) that are shown to have a less detrimental impact on the environment in comparison with other products serving the same function. Thailand has introduced has an energy efficiency labelling scheme (the "No. 5 label") that applies to 19 electrical products and eight heating products, and there are plans to extend the number of products covered under the new Energy Efficiency Plan.

Strategic Environmental Assessments ought to complement environmental impact assessments

EIAs have been required for certain types of projects since 1981 and are regulated under the Enhancement and Conservation of National Environmental Quality Act 1992. Currently, 35 types of projects require an EIA according to the Notification of the Ministry of Natural Resources and Environment. In addition, three factors determine EIA requirements: (i) the size of the project – for instance, an EIA is required for iron and steel industry projects if production exceeds 100 tonnes/day; (ii) its location – for instance, an EIA is required for highways (or roads legally defined as such) passing through the Mangrove Forest Area; and (iii) its type regardless of size or location – for instance, projects related to the petroleum industry, the Central Waste Treatment Plant, the cement industry, the sugar industry and the mining industry as defined by the Mineral Act. EIA reports must be prepared by a consulting firm or an academic institution registered with the Office of Natural Resources and Environmental Policy and Planning (ONEP). EIA reports must be first submitted to ONEP and approved by Expert Review Committees. Then, the project is authorised by the permitting agency. If the project requires further approval by the Cabinet, it must undergo an ultimate revision by the National Environmental Board (NEB) (ONEP, 2012).

Additionally, projects and activities that may severely impact the community with respect to environment quality, natural resources and health are required to submit an Environment and Health Impact Assessment. Currently, 12 types of projects fall into this category, including coke and coal industry projects.

The assessment of certain projects has been decentralised from the central to the provincial level. The Provincial Natural Resources and Environment Office and the Provincial Expert Review Committees are now in charge of reviewing and approving EIA reports related to: (i) building, urban services and housing projects in Environmental Protection Areas (EPAs) or high urbanisation provinces – currently, this regime is in force in 20 provinces and only affects projects for buildings whose height is below 23 metres or whose surface is less than 10 000 square metres; and (ii) industrial projects located in the Border Special Economic Zone – currently, this includes 10 provinces.

The current EIA system faces a number of challenges including: a lack of inter-agency co-ordination that has led in some instances to project permits being issued before final EIA approval, and in some cases even to construction of projects starting before EIA approval; insufficient public participation; non-compliance by project owners with the environmental management and monitoring plan; and poor quality EIA studies (Sano et al., 2016).

In cases of smaller, lower-impact projects where EIAs and/or Environment and Health Impact Assessments are not required, an Initial Environmental Examination (IEE) may be necessary. IEEs studies forecast environmental impacts using primary data or other available information. Perhaps surprisingly, EIAs and IEEs are not always required for projects taking place in EPAs or forest conservation areas. Projects proposed for such areas are instead required to provide an environmental checklist with environmental impact mitigation and preventive measures and environmental impact monitoring measures.

In some instances, there have been failures to follow or exceptions made to prescribed procedures. For example, in 2009 the Administrative Court ruled in favour of local activist organisations who had filed a lawsuit against the National Environmental Board and other ministries focusing on their failure to conduct environmental and health impact assessments before issuing licenses to 76 new industrial expansion projects in the Map Ta Phut zone (Excell and Moses, 2017). In the case of the Eastern Economic Corridor, a PPP process is being fast-tracked over 8-10 months instead of the typical 40 months. While greater efficiency in processes is to be welcomed, authorities will need to ensure that EIAs can be carried out effectively in this shortened timeframe.

More broadly, environmental protection is strongly undermined by the lack of Strategic Environmental Assessments (SEAs) (Sano et al., 2016). Unlike EIAs, which are typically used to assess the implications of specific projects or activities, SEAs comprise a set of analytical tools and participatory approaches to integrate environmental concerns into government plans, policies and programmes. SEAs are commonplace in OECD countries and have been introduced in Southeast Asian countries such as Lao PDR and Viet Nam. In Thailand, SEAs have seldom been used – only for some large-scale state-owned project and on a voluntary basis.

Some encouraging steps towards the implementation of a general SEA have nevertheless been taken. Guidelines were first approved by the NEB in 2009, and then improved in 2014 by ONEP and NESDB. The 12th Plan (2017-2021) envisages the use of SEA in five pilot watersheds. The National Reformation Council, moreover, recently urged the implementation of SEAs, in particular for the following plans: (i) the Transportation and Infrastructure Plan; (ii) the Energy Development Plan (Power Plan and Petroleum Industry); (iii) the Watershed Management Plan; (iv) the Special Area Plan; (v) the City Plan (including the Country Plan, Regional Plan and Provincial Plan); (vi) the Industrial Estate Development Plan; and (vii) Megaprojects. In August 2017, the Sustainable Development Board appointed a Sub-Committee on SEA, consisting of experts and representatives from relevant ministries, which is to lay down the regulatory framework for the implementation of SEAs and determine the type of policies, plans and programmes potentially affected.

References

CBD (2017), "Thailand Country Profile", Convention on Biological Diversity, website, *www.cbd.int/countries/profile/?country=th.*

DLT (2017), "Number of vehicles registered 2000-2016, as of 31 December 2016", Transport Statistics Group, Planning Division, Department of Land Transport, Bangkok.

Excell, C. and E. Moses (2017), *Thirsting for Justice: Transparency and Poor People's Struggle for Clean Water in Indonesia, Mongolia, and Thailand*, World Resources Institute, Washington, DC, *www.wri.org/sites/default/files/17_Report_STRIPE.pdf.*

FAO (2016), AQUASTAT (database). Food and Agriculture Organization of the United Nations, Rome, *www.fao.org/nr/water/aquastat/data/query/index.html?lang=en.*

Fornes, J. and K. Pirarai (2014), "Groundwater in Thailand", *Journal of Environmental Science and Engineering*, B 3, pp. 304-315, doi:10.17265/2162-5263/2014.06.003.

Hockings, M., P. Shadie and S. Suksawang (2012), *Evaluating the Management Effectiveness of Thailand's Marine and Coastal Protected Areas*, IUCN-WCPA, Bangkok.

IEA (2017a), CO_2 *Emissions from Fuel Combustion: 2017 Edition*, International Energy Agency, Paris.

IEA (2017b), *Southeast Asia Energy Outlook 2017*, International Energy Agency, Paris, *www.iea.org/publications/freepublications/publication/WEO2017SpecialReport_SoutheastAsiaEnergyOutlook.pdf*.

IEA (2017c), Energy Subsidies (indicator), *www.iea.org/statistics/resources/energysubsidies*.

IEA (2017d), *Tracking Fossil Fuel Subsidies in APEC Economies: Toward a Sustained Subsidy Reform*, International Energy Agency, Paris, *www.iea.org/publications/insights/insightpublications/TrackingFossilFuelSubsidiesinAPECEconomies.pdf*.

IEA (2016a), *Thailand Electricity Security Assessment*, International Energy Agency, Paris, *http://dx.doi.org/10.1787/9789264255852-en*.

IEA (2016b), "Reducing emissions from fossil-fired generation: Indonesia, Malaysia and Viet Nam", *IEA Insights Series 2016*, International Energy Agency, Paris, *www.iea.org/publications/insights/insightpublications/ReducingEmissionsfromFossilFiredGeneration.pdf*.

Marks, D. and L. Lebel (2016), "Disaster governance and the scalar politics of incomplete decentralization: Fragmented and contested responses to the 2011 floods in Central Thailand", *Habitat International*, 52, pp. 57-66.

MFA Netherlands (2016), *The Water Sector in Thailand*, Netherlands Embassy in Bangkok, Ministry of Foreign Affairs of the Netherlands.

MIE Netherlands (2016), *Netherlands National Water Plan 2016-2021*, Ministry of Infrastructure and the Environment of the Netherlands, The Hague.

MOE (2016), "Thailand Integrated Energy Blueprint", *EPPO Journal Special Issue 2016*, Energy Policy and Planning Office, Ministry of Energy, Bangkok.

MOI (2013), *Disaster Report 2013 (Statistics), 1 January – 31 December 2013*, Department of Disaster Prevention and Mitigation, Ministry of Interior of Thailand, Bangkok.

Naruchaikusol, S. (2016), "Climate Change and its impact in Thailand", *TransRe Factsheet*, Issue No. 2, *www.transre.org/files/3114/6522/5151/Climate_Change_in_Thailand_TransRe_Fact_Sheet_No.2.pdf?utm_content=bufferdd4a5&utm_medium=social&utm_source=twitter.com&utm_campaign=buffer*.

NESDB (2017), *Social and Quality of Life Database System*, National Economic and Social Development Board, Bangkok, *http://social.nesdb.go.th/social/Default.aspx?tabid=40*.

OECD (2017), Municipal Waste (indicator), doi:10.1787/89d5679a-en.

OECD (2015), *Green Growth in Bangkok, Thailand*, OECD Green Growth Studies, OECD Publishing, Paris, *http://dx.doi.org/10.1787/9789264237087-en*.

OECD (2014a), *Climate Resilience in Development Planning: Experiences in Colombia and Ethiopia*, OECD Publishing, Paris, *http://dx.doi.org/10.1787/9789264209503-en*.

OECD (2014b), *Water Governance in the Netherlands, Fit for the Future?* OECD Studies of Water, OECD Publishing, Paris, *http://dx.doi.org/10.1787/9789264102637-en*.

OAE (2017), *Agricultural Statistics of Thailand 2016*, Office of Agricultural Economics, Bangkok.

ONEP (2015), *Thailand's Intended Nationally Determined Contribution (INDC)*, Office of Natural Resources and Environment Policy and Planning, Ministry of Natural Resources and Environment, Bangkok, *www4.unfccc.int/ndcregistry/PublishedDocuments/Thailand%20First/Thailand_INDC.pdf*.

ONEP (2014), *Thailand's 5th National Report on the Implementation of the Convention on Biological Diversity*, Office of Natural Resources and Environment Policy and Planning (ONEP), Ministry of Natural Resources and Environment, Bangkok, *www.cbd.int/doc/world/th/th-nr-05-en.pdf*.

ONEP (2012), *Environmental Impact Assessment in Thailand*, Office of Natural Resources and Environment Policy and Planning (ONEP), Ministry of Natural Resources and Environment, Bangkok, *www.onep.go.th/eia/images/7handbook/Environmental_Impact_Assessment_in_Thailand.pdf*.

PCD (2015), *Thailand State of Pollution Report 2015*, Pollution Control Department (PCD), Ministry of Natural Resources and Environment, Bangkok, *www.pcd.go.th*.

PCD (2010), *Thailand State of Pollution Report 2010*, Pollution Control Department (PCD), Ministry of Natural Resources and Environment, Bangkok, *http://infofile.pcd.go.th/mgt/Report_Eng2553.pdf*.

PCD (2017a), *Data Archives for Air and Noise Pollution* (database), Air Quality and Noise Management Bureau, Pollution Control Department, Ministry of Natural Resources and Environment, Bangkok, *http://aqnis.pcd.go.th/en/node/8182*.

PCD (13 January 2017b), "Thailand State of Pollution 2016", Press Release, Vol. 2/2017, Pollution Control Department, Ministry of Natural Resources and Environment, Bangkok.

PRD (23 February 2015), "Reforming Thailand's irrigation and water management systems", Foreign Office, The Government Public Relations Department, Office of the Prime Minister, Government of Thailand, Bangkok, *http://thailand.prd.go.th/ewt_news.php?nid=59&filename=index*.

RFD (2017), Royal Forest Department (RFD), website, Ministry of Natural Resources and Environment, Bangkok, *http://forestinfo.forest.go.th/55/Content.aspx?id=9*.

Sano, D. et al. (2016), "Strengthening EIA in Asia", Working Paper prepared for the Asia EIA Conference 2016 in Nagoya, Japan, Institute for Global Environmental Strategies, Hayama, *www.env.go.jp/policy/assess/7-1asiaeia2016_pdf/asiaeiaconference2016-11.pdf*.

SEI (2016), "Climate change adaptation readiness in the ASEAN countries", *SEI Discussion Brief*, Stockholm Environment Institute Asia, Bangkok, *www.sei-international.org/mediamanager/documents/Publications/Climate/SEI-DB-2016-Climate-adaptation-readiness-ASEAN.pdf*.

Thaiturapaisan, T. (24 March 2016), "Thailand's drought crisis 2016: Understanding it without the panic", *Note by EIC*, Economic Intelligence Center (EIC) Siam Commercial Bank Public Company Limited EIC, Bangkok, *www.scbeic.com/en/detail/product/2127*.

Thepgumpanat, P. and P. Tanakasempipat (9 March 2016), "Thailand facing worst water shortage in two decades – government", *Reuters*, *http://af.reuters.com/article/commoditiesNews/idAFL4N16H2O6*.

UNESCAP (2017), *Environmental Tax Reform in Asia and the Pacific*, United Nations Economic and Social Commission for Asia and the Pacific (ESCAP), Bangkok, *www.unescap.org/sites/default/files/S2_Environmental-Tax-Reform.pdf*.

VNR Taskforce (2017), *Thailand's Voluntary National Review on the Implementation of the 2030 Agenda for Sustainable Development*, Voluntary National Review Taskforce of Thailand, Bangkok, *https://sustainabledevelopment.un.org/content/documents/16147Thailand.pdf*.

World Bank (2017a), World Development Indicators (database).

World Bank (2017b), "Deforestation and biodiversity", *World Development Indicators*, *http://wdi.worldbank.org/table/3.4#*.

Chapter 5

Peace: Strengthening governance

The Peace pillar of the 2030 Agenda for Sustainable Development encompasses a diverse range of issues including stability and effective governance. Reforming the public sector is high on the government's agenda, but involves a number of challenges: the gap between planning and implementation of policy objectives remains large; insufficient public participation in policy making is undermining the efficient allocation of resources toward public needs and development goals; under-development of evidence-based regulations is hampering the creation of a business-friendly environment essential to high value-added activities; and high levels of perceived corruption are weakening business confidence and public trust in the government.

Thailand's 12th Economic and Social Development Plan emphasises the importance of public sector reform. It sets out measures to strengthen co-ordination across ministries and agencies aimed at improving implementation of policy programmes, boosting public participation in policy making, improving online access to government services and combating corruption by strengthening integrity measures. The upcoming 20-year National Strategy and the accompanying National Reform Plan are expected to pave the way for future development. However, an inclusive and consultative process will be essential to ensure the success of reform efforts.

The Peace pillar of the 2030 Agenda for Sustainable Development encompasses a diverse range of issues including stability and effective governance. According to *Transforming our World*, peace and sustainable development go hand in hand and reinforce each other (United Nations, 2015). Sustainable and inclusive development requires the effective delivery of public services including education, healthcare, social protection and basic infrastructure. At the same time, good governance is essential to enable markets to provide goods and services in an efficient manner, with minimal diversion of resources to less productive uses. Good governance calls for adequate stakeholder consultation, but also needs to be underpinned by strong and well-co-ordinated institutions, working across policy areas and levels of government to ensure coherent strategies and implementation. It is also important to overcome any immediate economic and social pressures that may undermine longer-term strategic policy priorities.

This chapter reviews the progression toward a peaceful society with respect to national harmony and interpersonal trust. It assesses governance and institutional capability with a focus on the implementation of development plans, stakeholder engagement in the policy process, the regulatory environment and efforts to curb corruption.

Thailand is making progress towards a more peaceful society

Thailand ranks 120th (out of 163 countries) on the Global Peace Index 2017, up five places from the previous year (IEP, 2017). However, periods of political uncertainty have been accompanied by lingering problems in the southernmost provinces (Burke et al., 2013). Numerous efforts have been undertaken to address the problem including, notably, the creation of a National Reconciliation Commission in 2005; regional policy reforms on language, culture and education; and efforts to expand educational and employment opportunities in the region over the next five years (NESDB, 2017).

A peaceful society requires the presence of a properly constituted, well-functioning democratic system of governance free of political corruption (Huang and Throsby, 2011). The political structure of Thailand has evolved over time, with 20 different constitutions adopted since the country became a constitutional monarchy in 1932, the most recent of which was approved in April 2017. A newly elected government is expected to be in place after the next general elections which may take place in the near future. This transition will play an important role in assuring the integrity, participatory nature and transparency of law making, and maintaining people's trust in government (OECD, 2017a).

Trust is relatively high in Thailand, but efforts are needed to ensure its preservation

In Thailand, the level of trust in government, as measured by the Gallup World Poll 2017, is comparatively strong, with over 60% of respondents stating that they have confidence in the national government (Figure 5.1A). Even so, on this measure confidence has declined somewhat since the early 2000s (Figure 5.1B). Trust in government is key for governments to successfully carry out public policies, especially with regard to more ambitious reforms (OECD, 2017b).

Competent execution of public mandates, and a transparent and participatory approach to decision-making can help strengthen trust in government (OECD, 2017b).

Interpersonal trust, which is closely linked to social capital, is also key to achieving sustainable development and peace. People need to feel that the members of the community with whom they interact can be trusted. Moreover, a co-operative society is much more likely to be peaceful and inclusive (OECD, 2017c; Scriven and Smith, 2013). All economic interactions involve some degree of trust, which in turn reduces transaction costs and supports national prosperity (Algan and Cahuc, 2013; Temple, 2000).

Figure 5.1. **Thai citizens have confidence in their government, but trust has declined over time**

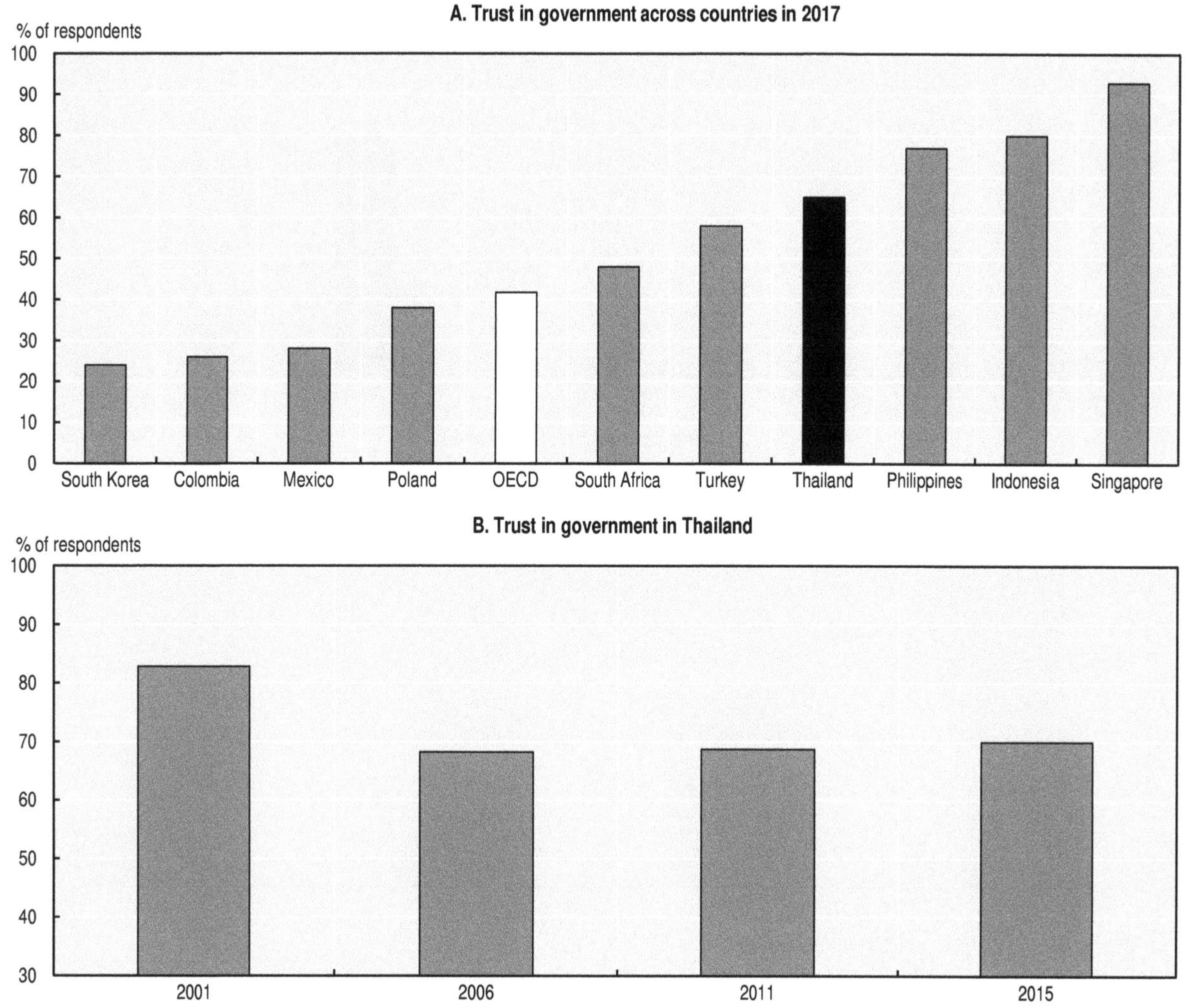

Note: Data refer to the percentage of respondents answering "yes" to the question: "In this country, do you have confidence in the national government?". The Gallup World Poll is an annual international survey that measures attitudes in countries around the world. Like the Asianbarometer and the World Values Survey, it relies on a small sample size of around 1 000 respondents per country.

Source: A: Gallup (2017), Gallup World Poll, *www.gallup.com/services/170945/world-poll.aspx*; B: Asianbarometer (2015), Asianbarometer database, *www.asianbarometer.org/data/data-release*.

StatLink *http://dx.doi.org/10.1787/888933692598*

Interpersonal trust is relatively high in Thailand relative to comparator countries, with a third of the population indicating that other people can be trusted (Figure 5.2A). This social capital represents a key resource for individual well-being and economic growth.

Nevertheless, trust levels have declined over time: in 2001, 82% of the Thai population reported that they trusted other people (Figure 5.2B). Experience from OECD countries suggests that policies that focus on reducing inequality and improving institutional quality can help maintain a society's social capital stock and improve social stability. Good and inclusive governance, as well as a fair, effective justice system, enable individuals to extend trust to strangers without placing themselves at risk (OECD, 2017c).

Figure 5.2. **Interpersonal trust in Thailand is generally strong, but has eroded over time**

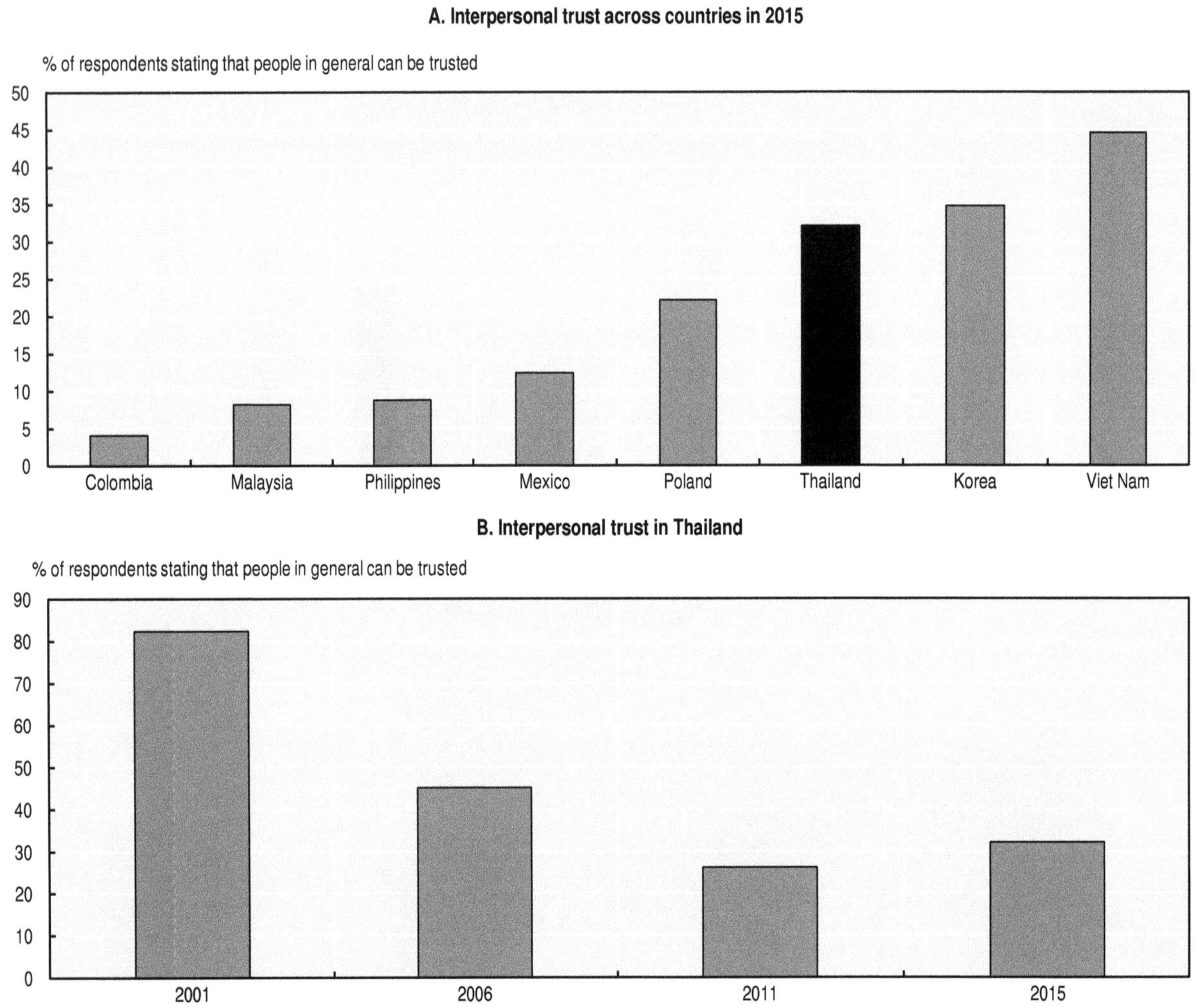

Note: Data for Colombia, Malaysia, Mexico and Poland refer to 2013.

Source: Asianbarometer (2015), *Asianbarometer* database, *www.asianbarometer.org/data/data-release*, and World Values Survey (2013), *World Values Survey* database, *www.worldvaluessurvey.org/WVSContents.jsp*.

StatLink http://dx.doi.org/10.1787/888933692617

While interpersonal trust between Thai people is relatively high (Figure 5.2), trust in people with other nationalities and religions compares less favourably. Trust in these groups is lower relative to comparator countries (Figure 5.3), consistent with findings from a 2010 survey covering Australia, Japan, Korea and Thailand (Ward et al., 2014). Given that international tourism and migration are major contributors to the Thai economy, improvement in this area would strengthen social cohesion and inclusion for all citizens and residents, and make it easier for Thai companies to draw on the best talent available.

Figure 5.3. **Trust in outsiders is low**

Trust across countries, 2013

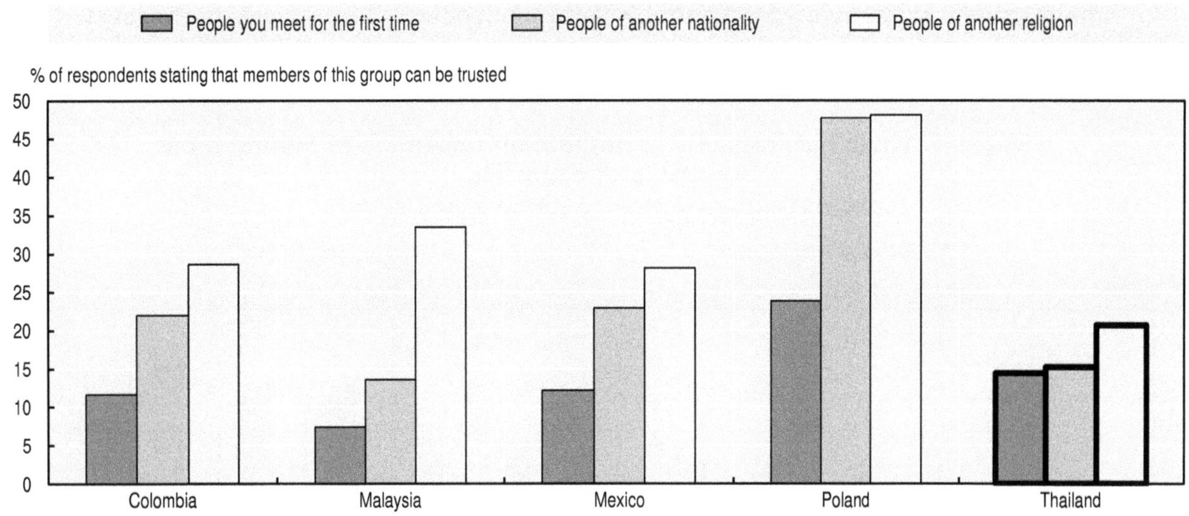

Source: World Values Survey (2013), *World Values Survey database*, *www.worldvaluessurvey.org/WVSContents.jsp*.

StatLink http://dx.doi.org/10.1787/888933692636

The gap between policy planning and implementation needs to be narrowed

Institutional capacity conditions the success of any reform efforts. In Thailand, the existence of several ministries and agencies competing in similar policy spaces often leads to conflicting policy agendas. A case in point is the highly fragmented institutional framework in water management (Chapter 4), which has led to overlapping responsibilities, conflicting interests and lack of co-ordination between the various bodies involved. Indeed, Thailand does not compare favourably with respect to the implementation of reforms (Figure 5.4). For example, this is evidenced by the low disbursement rate of public infrastructure investment (Chapter 2). Co-ordination issues among ministries and agencies, as well as institutional inflexibility in adapting policies to evolving economic and social conditions, represent a challenge (Figure 5.5). Such inefficiencies, together with poorly allocated government spending, can undermine competitiveness (Figure 5. 6). To help address these issues the government established a range of reform committees tasked with building management capacity and fostering collaboration between the planning and implementing agencies.

The authorities recognise the existence of inefficiencies at regional and local level, and have attempted to rationalise the tasks carried out by each layer of government. Since the end of the 1990s, efforts have been underway to downsize the presence of central agencies in regions (Kokpol, 2011). Such decentralisation allows local public administrations to focus on providing basic public services, while broader policies and guidelines are set at the central and regional level. However, in practice, responsibilities over service delivery between central and local administrations remain unclear, with central government officers often maintaining de facto management control (Marks and Lebel, 2016). In pursuing further decentralisation Thailand needs to sufficiently equip local authorities in terms of both technical capacity and resourcing to deliver on their increased responsibility. Failure to do so could result in an increase in regional disparity in terms of outcomes in health, education, infrastructure and corruption as was experienced in Indonesia (Vujanovic, 2017). Subnational governance in Thailand encompasses both a provincial and a local level. Almost all officials in the provincial administration are appointed by central government bodies, while officials in the local administration are elected (see Box 5.1).

Figure 5.4. **Thailand's capacity to implement reforms lags behind most comparator countries**

Reform capacity and long-term strategy score (0-4), 2016

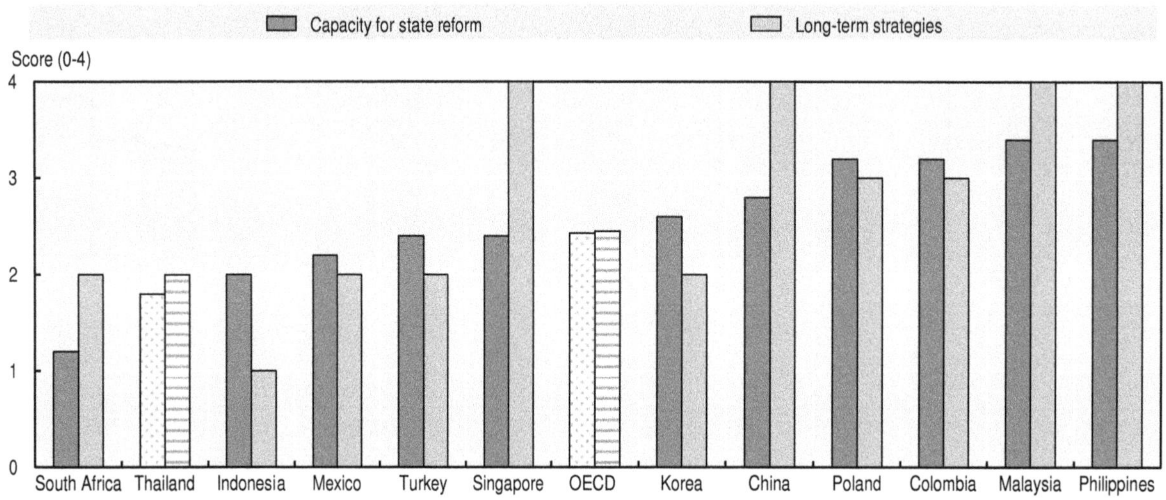

Notes: Capacity for state reform measures the "authorities' ability to decide and actually implement reforms" (scores range from 0 for very low capacity to 4 for strong capacity). Long-term strategies indicate whether "the public authorities have a long-term strategic vision" (scores range from 0 for very weak strategic vision to 4 for strong strategic vision).

Source: CEPII (2016), Institutional Profiles Database.

StatLink http://dx.doi.org/10.1787/888933692655

Figure 5.5. **Thailand can improve cross-agency coordination and its capacity for policy adaptation**

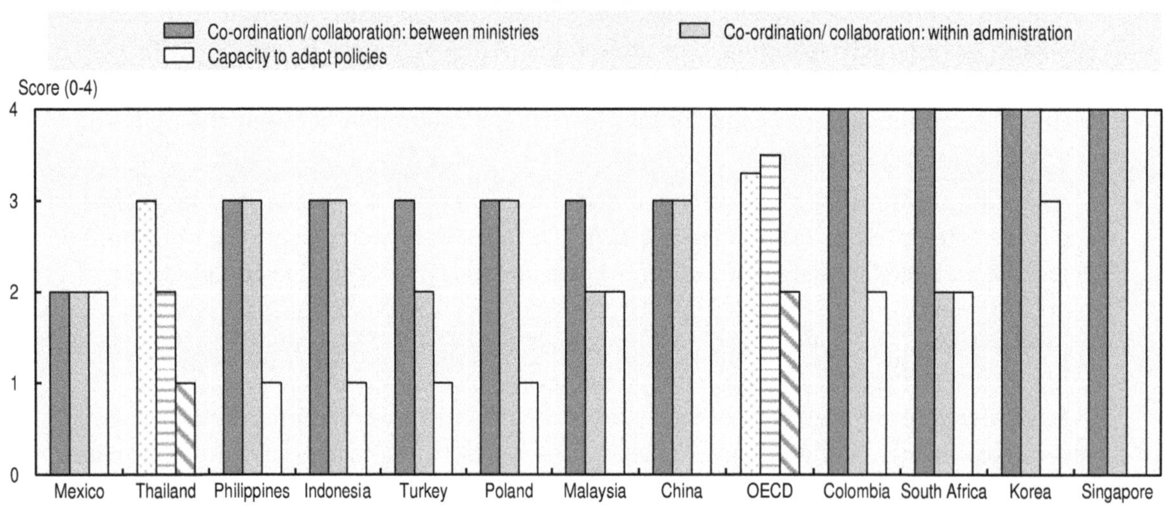

Source: CEPII (2016), Institutional Profiles Database.

StatLink http://dx.doi.org/10.1787/888933692674

Figure 5.6. **Inefficiencies of the government can undermine competitiveness**

Institutions pillar in the Global Competitiveness Index 2017-18, score ranges from 0 (worst) to 7 (best)

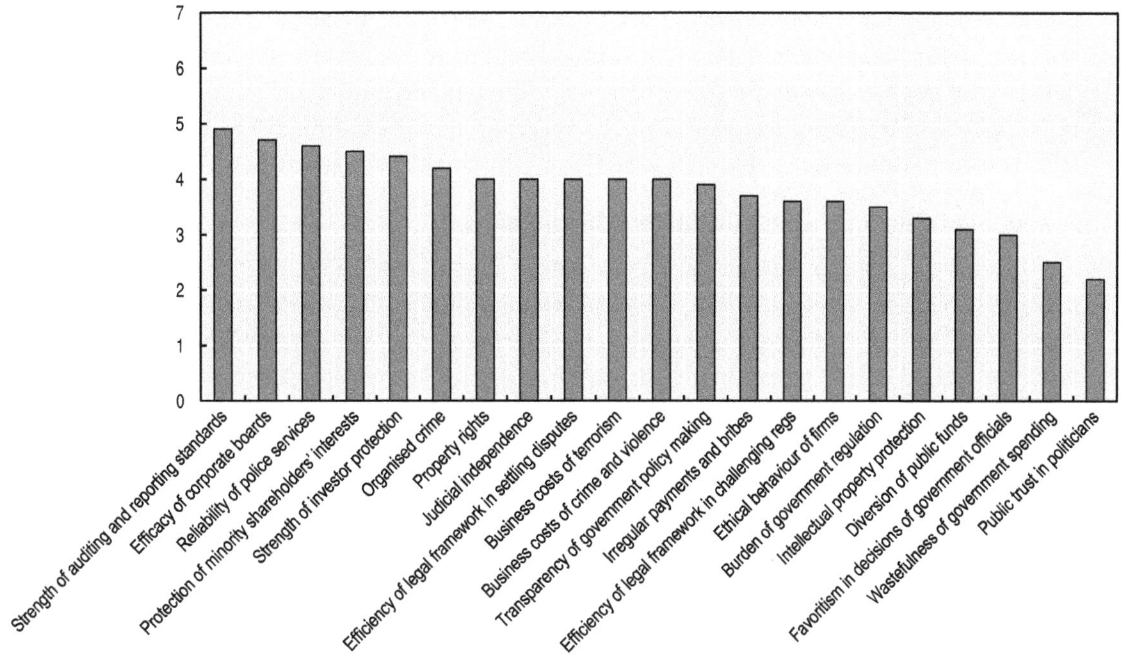

Note: The score for "strength of investor protection" has been normalised to the scale of 7 (original score is 6.3/10).

Source: World Economic Forum (2017), *The Global Competitiveness Report 2017-2018.*

StatLink http://dx.doi.org/10.1787/888933692693

Box 5.1. **Organisation of Thai local governance**

The 1991 State Administration Act sets out three levels of state administration in Thailand: central, provincial and local.

There are 76 provinces nationwide, each supported by a provincial office headed by a provincial governor. The provincial governor is appointed by the central government, except in the Bangkok Metropolitan Administration (BMA), where residents directly elect their governor. Governors are usually officials from the Ministry of Interior and are responsible for implementing central government policies. Provinces are then organised into 928 districts, with 7 416 sub-districts and 61 032 villages. The Ministry of Interior's Department of Provincial Administration appoints the districts' chief officers. Sub-district heads are generally chosen from among the village heads in each sub-district, and village heads are elected by their constituents. Both sub-district and village heads fall under the direct guidance and supervision of provincial governors and chief district officers, who are under central government control.

Thailand's local administration is based on a two-tier system comprising 76 Provincial Administrative Organisations (PAOs), 2 441 municipalities, 5 333 Sub-district Administrative Organisations (SAOs), and two special Local Administrative Organisations (BMA and Pattaya City). PAOs function as the upper tier of the local administration and operate large-scale administrative duties and public services. Municipalities and SAOs constitute the lower tier and are responsible for small-scale duties. Municipalities govern urban areas, while SAOs govern rural areas. There are three types of municipalities: cities (50 000 inhabitants or more), towns (10 000 to 49 999 inhabitants) and townships (7 000 to 9 999 inhabitants).

Provincial governors and chief district officers oversee local administrators to ensure central government policy directives are followed. This leaves limited discretion for PAOs, municipalities and SAOs to determine how funds are spent. However, the Decentralisation Act (1999) aimed to create institutional space for citizens to track and monitor the provision of public services and take part in decision making. In the following years, the direct election of local administrators has been gradually introduced. In 2014, local elections were temporarily suspended in the aftermath of the political crisis.

With a view to offering better value for taxpayer money, the authorities are seeking to reduce the public wage bill and increase public service efficiency (NESDB, 2017). As part of this process, the 12th National Economic and Social Development Plan (2017-2021) (12th Plan) outlines continued decentralisation including through greater fiscal autonomy (Chapter 3). LAOs would be given greater flexibility in terms of finance and human resource management to better respond to local needs and priorities. A key challenge in this regard is to ensure this translates into better public service delivery throughout the country (OECD, 2017d).

A new planning approach that takes a longer view

National Economic and Social Development Plans, or NESDPs, span five years and spell out medium-term economic development ambitions. These overarching plans are supplemented by numerous ministry-level policies and strategies that align in principle with the NESDP. Within government, the National Economic and Social Development Board (NESDB) draft the NESDPs, and incorporates inputs from ministries and agencies.

To increase policy continuity from one administration to the next, the government has recently ratified the National Strategy Preparation Act 2017 (NSPA). All future NESDPs will need to be consistent with the goals set under the NSPA. The National Strategy spans from 2017 to 2036, and aims to make Thailand a high-income economy enjoying "security, prosperity and sustainability" based on the sufficiency-economy philosophy (Vimolsiri, 2017). The NSPA identifies six key National Strategies: (i) safeguard national security, (ii) strengthen national competitiveness, (iii) develop and empower human capital, (iv) broaden opportunity and equality in the society, (v) emphasize environmentally friendly development and growth, and (vi) reform and improve government administration.

The NSPA sets out the entire process of formulating, implementing and monitoring the National Strategies in a legally binding framework. A National Strategy Committee (NSC), led by the Prime Minister, is responsible for drafting each National Strategy (Somwaiya and Saardphak, 2017). Under the NSC, several National Strategy drafting committees formulate the strategies for the respective sectors. Once the sectoral strategy is published, the NSC drafts a Master Plan for each sector. Following Cabinet approval, the Master Plan becomes legally binding for all state agencies. The NESDB will play a major role in consolidating all annual reports on compliance and implementation by the respective state agencies. In the event of non-compliance, the state agency in question will be subject to an investigation by the National Anti-Corruption Commission (NACC), and face the possibility of punitive action.

This new approach is meant to reduce recourse to short-term measures that could have adverse future impacts on the long-term goals identified under the National Strategies. The NSPA does allow for reviews of the strategies every five years; however, this is subject to Parliamentary approval. Given the limited flexibility the NSPA provides in reviewing and changing National Strategies, it is crucial that each strategy and their associated master plan are robust and properly reflect the multifaceted nature of policy objectives. Policy trade-offs should be made explicit at an early stage, so as to reduce frictions when policy corrections are required.

National reform is high on the government's agenda

A National Reform Plan is being prepared in parallel with the above processes. The areas it will cover are: (i) politics, (ii) state administration, (iii) legislation, (iv) the judicial process, (v) education, (vi) the economy, (vii) national resources and the environment, (viii) public health, (ix) mass media and information technology, (x) society, and (xi) other sectors, as determined by the Cabinet. The plan is enshrined in the National Reform Plans and Procedures Act 2017 (NRPA), which mandates a National Reform Plan to ensure 'the country has peace and order ... society has peace and happiness, and the people have ... a good quality [of] life and participation in the country's development and administration under the democratic system with the monarchy as the Head of State' (Somwaiya, 2017). The National Reform Plan is to be formulated and aligned with the National Strategy prepared under the NSPA.

OECD experience suggests that governments undertaking reforms face common challenges, albeit in different contexts, and points to factors that can enhance the likelihood of success (OECD, 2010). In particular, reforms require strong institutions and leadership, with authoritative, non-partisan institutions that command trust across the political spectrum. Consistency of reforms across policy areas is also critical. In addition, engaging with the opponents of reform through an inclusive and consultative policy process usually pays dividends over time, creating greater trust among the parties involved, including those most affected, who then become more willing to accept commitments on steps to mitigate personal costs resulting from the changes.

Thailand is embracing greater stakeholder engagement and digitalisation for better policy making

Governments need to balance expectations for faster and continuous adaptation with calls for more inclusive policy making, offering information and broader access to stakeholders at earlier stages of the decision-making process (OECD, 2017d). In this regard, Thailand ranks behind most comparators in terms of co-operation between local stakeholders and in bureaucratic efficacy in developing and improving public policies (Figure 5.7). Greater stakeholder engagement is needed during policy formulation in addition to the government's efforts to enhance the overall coherence of public policies through the aforementioned plans and strategies.

To help address these issues, Thailand has released Public Consultation Guidelines designed to help government officials carry out public consultations with relevant stakeholders (NESDB, 2016). They outline suggestions on who to consult (e.g. business entities, consumers, general public) depending on the type of regulation to be introduced (economy-wide, industry specific, or generic). The guidelines take into consideration the OECD *Guiding Principles for Public Consultation*, which highlight the need for public consultation and active participation early in the policy process, so as to allow a greater range of policy solutions to emerge (OECD, 2001). While this is welcome, it is vital to ensure that the guidelines are actively followed across ministries and agencies.

Digital government solutions are being rolled out

Digital government can make public administration more responsive and agile in service delivery and administrative procedures, while promoting greater efficiency and transparency, as well as a more competitive environment for economic activity and job creation (OECD, 2017e).

The uptake of digital technologies in the public sector has been slow, which has contributed to administrative inefficiencies and opacity. In 2017, the Global Innovation Index ranked Thailand 77th and 65th in provision of online government services and the e-participation index, respectively, behind most comparators and the OECD average (Figure 5.8).

Figure 5.7. **Stakeholder engagement in public policy can be improved**

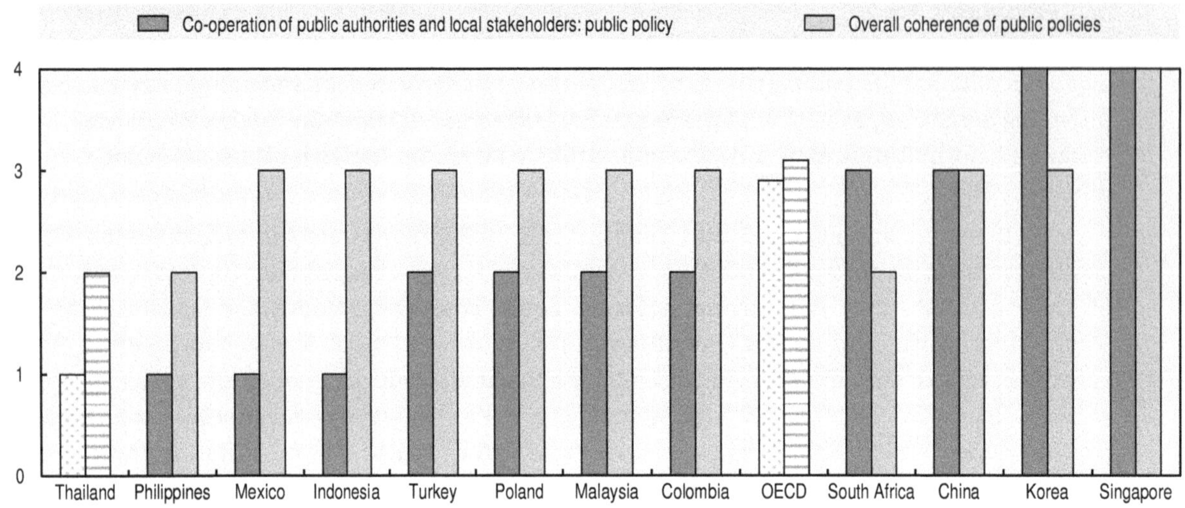

Note: "Cooperation of public authorities and local stakeholders" measures whether "national public authorities and local stakeholders (local authorities, private sector, NGOs, etc.) work together to develop and improve public policy effectiveness" (scores range from 0 for very low cooperation to 4 for strong cooperation). The overall coherence of public policies scores range from 0 for very weak coherence to 4 for strong coherence.

Source: CEPII (2016), Institutional Profiles Database.

StatLink http://dx.doi.org/10.1787/888933692712

Figure 5.8. **Thailand can make greater use of online government services**

Presence and use of government services online, 2017

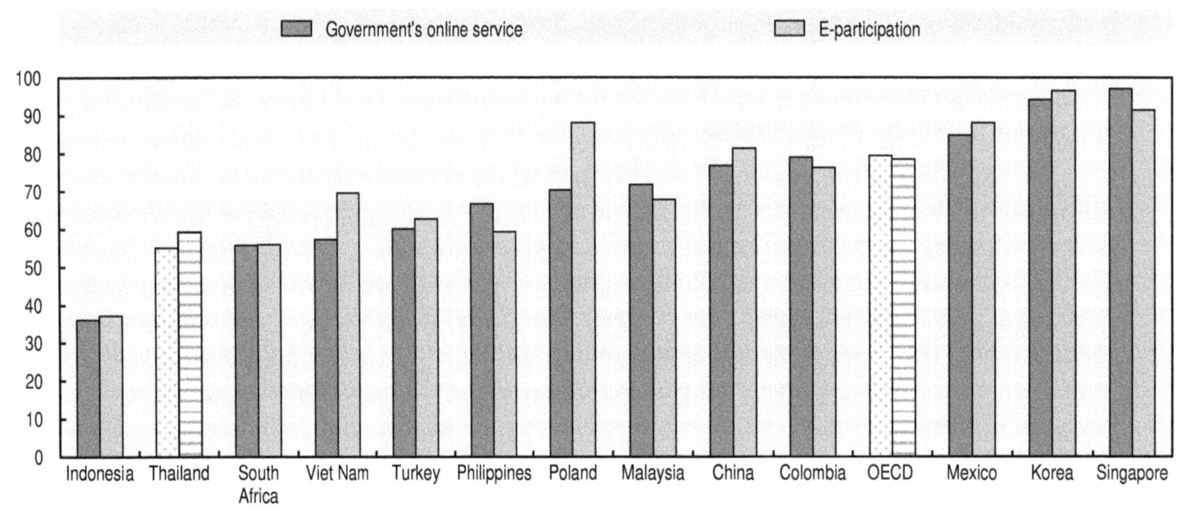

Note: The higher the score, the more aligned with international best practice.

Source: Cornell University, INSEAD and WIPO (2017), *Global Innovation Index.*

StatLink http://dx.doi.org/10.1787/888933692731

Thailand has developed a Digital Government Development Plan (2017-21) as part of a broader digitalisation push (Chapter 2). The plan seeks to improve the convenience, speed and accuracy of government services; provide greater access to government data, fostering transparency and civic participation; and integrate back-office government infrastructure and data. To that effect, the government is prioritising the development of a mobile government communication system, and introducing a range of digital laws to build confidence in online transactions. It is also rolling out a shared ICT platform for government agencies, and building a one-stop portal to access government news and services, which will be available via a website or mobile application. Moreover, the government is piloting a "GovLab" to test technical solutions to public service delivery challenges. The first four pilot projects will seek to address queuing systems at public hospitals, ISO certification processes, registration and approval of new herbal medicine products, and social protection payments to the elderly. Thailand is also promoting the use of big data to enhance the efficiency and effectiveness of policy delivery. For example, the Welfare Registration Programme links individuals' tax, financial and social protection data, helping the government to provide more targeted social protection for low-income households.

Improving evaluations of policy implementation will lead to better allocation of resources

The 12th Plan stresses the importance of monitoring and evaluation of policy programmes to ensure efficient implementation and consistency with socio-economic development goals. In particular, the 12th Plan strengthens the evaluation framework for key performance indicators (KPIs). Since 2003, each ministry needs to submit KPI goals to the Office of the Public Sector Development Commission (OPDC) before the beginning of the fiscal year in October. The OPDC then negotiates with each ministry to ensure the KPIs are robust, measureable and consistent with broader objectives in line with the National Strategy, the 12th Plan, Thailand 4.0 and the SDGs. KPIs often include indicators developed for international benchmarking (Table 5.1). By the end of March the following year, each ministry will conduct an interim self-assessment and submit the results to the OPDC for evaluation at a meeting attended by a Deputy Prime Minister and relevant ministers. The final output is then sent to the Prime Minister. The exercise is repeated again at the end of the fiscal year. With respect to cross-sectional issues across government, joint KPIs are set to evaluate the country's overall development efforts (Table 5.2). Policy evaluations based on KPIs are also carried out at the local government level. The performance evaluation process is open to the public to ensure accountability and disclosure of information. OECD experience recognises that KPIs can improve vertical and horizontal coordination at different levels of government. However, in determining KPIs it is important that authorities consider potential unintended consequences, including the prioritisation (and possible diversion) of resources to what is measured at the expense to what is not, strategic behaviour (gaming) and the political risk of unduly revealing performance results (OECD, 2009).

Table 5.1. **Selected KPIs for the Ministry of Digital Economy and Society, FY 2017**

Strategy/Goal	KPIs
Public access to government information and services through a secure broadband network	Improvement in technological infrastructure as assessed by IMD's World Competitiveness Index Percentage of villages with high-speed internet service
Increased economic value of digital technology in business	Additional digital business operators and an increase in e-commerce sales by SMEs and community enterprises
Government services are easy to use, linked and disclosed to all sectors	Improved ranking in the Global Open Data Index by the Open Knowledge Network Accuracy of public information necessary to the public
Public and private individuals receive meteorological information and disaster alerts quickly and easily	Confidence level of people who have been alerted about weather conditions Increase in the number of stakeholders who receive disaster warnings

Source: Office of the Public Sector Development Commission.

Table 5.2. **Selected joint KPIs related to the government's target for revenue from tourism, 2017**

Outcome KPI	Output KPIs
Number of standardised tourist attractions	Achievements in developing and increasing tourist attractions (Ministry of Tourism and Sports, Ministry of Culture)
Trust in products and services	Achievements in tourism standard certification Tourism human resource development (Ministry of Tourism and Sports)
Rank in Travel and Tourism Competitiveness Index	Achievements in infrastructure development Improvements in signage to meet international standards (Ministry of Tourism and Sports, Ministry of Transport)
Tourist satisfaction and return rate	Number of tourist complaints resolved Share of complaints about tour operators and tour guides that are resolved (Royal Thai Police, Ministry of Tourism and Sports)
Level of achievement in assisting tourists	Share of functional Wi-Fi services in major attractions Achievements in measures of tourists' safety and security (Ministry of Tourism and Sports)

Source: Office of the Public Sector Development Commission.

With regard to the evaluation of policies and programmes, indicators that highlight underlying problems that drive such policies or point to other areas of public concern are an essential aid to policy makers (Coglianese, 2012). As such, good government policies depend on sound statistics as a basis for evidenced-based decision making and accountability (OECD, 2015). In Thailand, the National Statistics Office (NSO) acts as the central authority for developing, collecting and managing statistics, in accordance with Thailand's Statistical Master Plan 2016-2021 (see Box 5.2).

Enhancing competition policy and promoting regulatory reform will foster more efficient markets

One of the fundamental roles of the public sector is to provide an environment for fair and effective competition in the domestic market. Competition enhances productivity, innovation and growth by driving businesses to continuously improve efficiency, products and services. Areas of particular importance in this regard are: (i) the elimination or reform of anti-competitive regulation and the enhancement of regulatory transparency, which fosters competition and reduces opportunities for corruption; (ii) the introduction of a system of effective government procurement that encourages competition and improves public service delivery by reducing costs ultimately borne by the taxpayer; and (iii) a well-functioning competition enforcement regime based on the sound application of economic principles, which provides a stable and predictable regulatory and business environment conducive to investment.

With the adoption of the 1999 Trade Competition Act, Thailand became one of the first ASEAN countries to introduce competition policy. The Act covered both anti-competitive practices (related to agreements, abuse of dominant position, mergers) and some forms of restrictive/unfair trade and commercial practices. However, despite nearly a hundred complaints submitted since its enactment, there have been no findings of infringement. This may be due to the under-development of rules and regulations necessary for enforcement, and to political pressures inhibiting enforcement (Thanitcul, 2015). Indeed, there are indications that the Trade Competition Committee (TCC) is not sufficiently independent from government (OTCC, 2017). International evidence shows that a significant degree of independence from political and business interference is key for the competition regime to be effective (OECD, 2016).

Box 5.2. **Statistical capacity assessment**

Overall, Thailand's national statistical system is well placed to respond to national and international data requirements. Statistical activities are conducted under the Statistics Act of 1965 and are organised in decentralised fashion with clear roles, responsibilities and relations among the relevant agencies:

- The National Statistics Office (NSO) is the central state agency in charge of technical statistical work. It oversees the census and range of surveys including the population and housing census, agricultural census, industrial census, labour force survey, socio-economic survey, establishment survey on the use of ICT and household survey on the use of ICT.
- The Bank of Thailand collects, compiles and disseminates a broad range of economic and financial statistics.
- The National Economic and Social Development Board is responsible for the production of national accounts statistics.
- Other statistical units in line ministries also produce statistics from their administrative records and/or conduct surveys for their own purposes.
- The Central Registration Office is responsible for the registration of births and deaths.

The NSO is an office under the Ministry of Digital Economy and Society that has the mandate to set up and coordinate, with other agencies, a statistical network with the stated objective of building and maintaining a high-quality and timely statistical database for the country. The NSO makes all decisions on data collection and dissemination independent of political influence or pressure. A National Statistical Committee meets annually and advises the NSO on statistical activities.

Thailand's current statistical agenda is guided by the Thailand's Statistical Master Plan (TSMP) 2016-2021, which aligns with the 12th Plan. The objective of the TSMP is to integrate, exchange and link data between agencies, so they can be jointly used for decision and policy making at every level (national, agenda-based, area-based). It also seeks to improve data quality (administrative and survey data) in accordance with international standards. The TSMP is complemented by smaller statistical plans focusing on 21 sectors (e.g. population, transport, etc.), which have their own targets and subcommittees working within relevant line ministries. The NSO coordinates with relevant agencies and prepares the TSMP, ensuring it is consistent with the NESDPs and the international agenda.

Thailand's official statistics can be classified into three areas: (i) economic (11 sectors); (ii) social (9 sectors); and (iii) natural resources and environment (1 sector). The main data collection operations (surveys, censuses, etc.) of the NSO are listed in Table 5.3.

Table 5.3. **NSO main data collecting operations and frequencies**

Economic data		Socio-demographic data	
Industrial census	Every 5 years	Population and housing census	Every 10 years
Business trade and service census	Every 10 years	Labour force survey	Annually
Agricultural census	Every 10 years	Multiple Indicator Cluster Survey (MICS)	Every 3 years
Household socio-economic survey	Annually	Migration and population survey	Annually
Commodity survey	Every 2 years	Skill development survey	Annually
Trade and price survey	Annually	Disability survey	Every 5 years
Hotel and guesthouse survey	Every 2 years	Mental health survey	Annually
Use of ICT in households survey	Annually	Smoking and drinking behaviour survey	Every 3 years
Use of ICT in establishments survey	Annually	Elderly survey	Every 3 years
Non-profit organisation survey	Every 5 years		

Note: The MICS is conducted to fill data gaps during monitoring of the situation of children and women (e.g. child health, maternal and newborn health, nutrition, water and sanitation, etc.).

Box 5.2. **Statistical capacity assessment** *(cont.)*

Regarding data needs for the 2030 Agenda, Thailand plans to integrate the SDG indicators into the Master Plan once a final national list of indicators is agreed upon. For many of the SDG Tier 3 indicators, Thailand plans to select their own data or proxies to monitor and evaluate national plans in line with the global targets of the SDGs.

Thailand has allocated sufficient resources to undertake the statistical activities outlined in the TSMP (including staff, computing facilities, database management systems and financing). The NSO is government funded with around 2 000 employees specialising in census/survey planning, survey design, sampling, field operations, data processing, data analysis evaluation and dissemination. The data compilation processes are highly computerised and efficient.

The methodologies used and the selection of sources and modes of dissemination are broadly consistent with internationally accepted standards, guidelines and best practices. The NSO assesses the quality of official statistics across government to ensure they meet international standards. Thailand is also compliant with the IMF Special Data Dissemination Standard for the provision of economic and financial data to the public. Compliance with these standards is important to ensure the availability of statistics needed for sound macroeconomic policies, international borrowing and access to multilateral funding mechanisms. The methodologies for price indices and monetary statistics broadly follow current international methodological standards. National accounts follow the System of National Accounts 1993 (SNA 1993), with 2012 as the base year, but are transitioning to SNA 2008, with the incorporation of public R&D spending in gross fixed capital formation and the inclusion of indirectly measured financial intermediation services. Thailand uses the fifth edition of the Balance of Payments Manual (BPM5) and the latest Manual on Government Finance Statistics (GFSM 2014).

Access to data and reports has improved across the national statistical system following Thailand's adoption of an Open Data Policy in 2012. Reports and data are now downloadable from the NSO website and are disseminated through social media (Facebook, Twitter, etc.). Microdata are pay-walled but free for researchers and students. The NSO considers user needs when producing data and carries out an annual user satisfaction survey for all statistics. For survey and census projects, the NSO organises meetings focused on user needs before and after conducting projects. Data sharing between various administrative levels has improved following the 2007 amendment to the Statistics Act, which complies with the United Nations Fundamental Principles of Official Statistics. This assists the NSO with its co-ordination role of the national statistical system. The NSO also regularly collects data from other agencies for the Statistical Yearbook, and collaborates with other ministries for official statistics (using publicly available data or issuing requests for specific data).

Despite the strengths of Thailand's Statistical System there is room from improvement, especially with respect to data coverage. National accounts data, based on SNA 1993, cover the whole country and include both the formal and informal sectors, as well as some, though not all, illegal activities. However, certain indicators are not representative of the whole territory. As in many other countries, the consumer price index (CPI), while covering all goods and services purchased by the reference population for the purposes of consumption, only extends to a subset of urban areas (43 provinces including Bangkok, out of 77 provinces) and excludes rural areas. The Bank of Thailand is in talks with the Ministry of Commerce regarding the possible inclusion of the price of goods distributed through e-commerce channels in the inflation basket. Employment data are also incomplete and data from the Labour Force survey are not seasonally adjusted. In addition, there is no replacement for missing households in the household survey.

Source: NSO (2007), *Thailand, The Statistics Act, B.E. 2550*; NSO (2016), *Thailand's Statistical Master Plan (TSMP)*; IMF (2017), *Thailand Special Data Dissemination Standard (SDDS)*; and World Bank (2017a), Thailand, Statistical Capacity Indicator Dashboard.

A revised Trade Competition Act came into force in October 2017, against the backdrop of the ASEAN Economic Community Blueprint 2015, which called for harmonised competition policies. The revised Act strengthens alignment with international best practice, including through the introduction of a prior approval merger control regime. The revised Act also covers the commercial operations of state-owned enterprises to ensure a more level playing field between public and private firms. In addition, some anti-competitive practices are newly designated as subject to administrative penalties rather than criminal ones, which simplifies enforcement procedures.

Efforts have also been made to reform the TCC to a more independent legal institution, with its own budget and staff separate from that of the Ministry of Commerce. In order to benefit from the new legal framework, Thailand should endow the TCC with adequate financial and human resources together with sufficient autonomy to use them to match its ongoing needs. Without sufficient resources, the TCC will struggle to have a meaningful impact on markets and to deliver the potential economic benefits of a strong competition law. Indeed, faulty or inadequate enforcement of competition law can do more harm than good. This will require a selection of qualified and representative commission members to reflect various stakeholder interests (i.e. public, firms and consumers), and dedicated training of all staff, including decision makers and case handlers, especially given that competition law lies at the cross-section of economics and law and requires very specific skills. In order to align further with international best practice, it will also be necessary to improve subordinate regulations and guidelines to ensure transparent, clear and non-discriminatory enforcement. Introducing a leniency programme would also help to gather information for enforcement.

Promoting good regulatory practice by improving regulatory impact analysis

More generally, good regulatory practice helps effective resource allocation, promotes fair and robust competition and minimises the compliance burden on business. The Recommendation of the OECD Council on Regulatory Policy and Governance recognises that a good regulatory management system requires a whole-of-government approach underpinning how it develops, implements and evaluates regulation (OECD, 2012). Thailand's quality of regulation (measured by the perception of the government's ability to formulate and implement sound policies and regulations that permit and promote private sector development) has only marginally improved over the past decade, when measured against regional comparators such as Malaysia (Figure 5.9).

Against this backdrop, the government has stepped up regulatory reform efforts to create a more business-friendly environment, on the basis that cutting red tape and cumbersome administrative procedures can be a much less costly and more effective means to attract foreign investment than conventional tax incentives (Nikomborirak, 2016). The Office of the Council of State conducted a comprehensive review of existing Thai laws and has acted on three fronts.

First, to ensure transparency and accountability, the government enacted the Licensing Facilitation Act 2015, which required all relevant government agencies involved in licenses, registrations and permissions to produce publicly available manuals that cover the procedures, timetable and requirements to acquire licenses. When dealing with applications, government officials must follow the procedures set in the manuals to eliminate discretion, and abide by the stated timeline for licensing decisions. The Act is in the process of being amended to include a more active role for government agencies in facilitating the licensing process. It will also include a requirement that all licenses be issued both in English and Thai to facilitate their use domestically and internationally.

Figure 5.9. **The quality of regulation has only marginally improved**

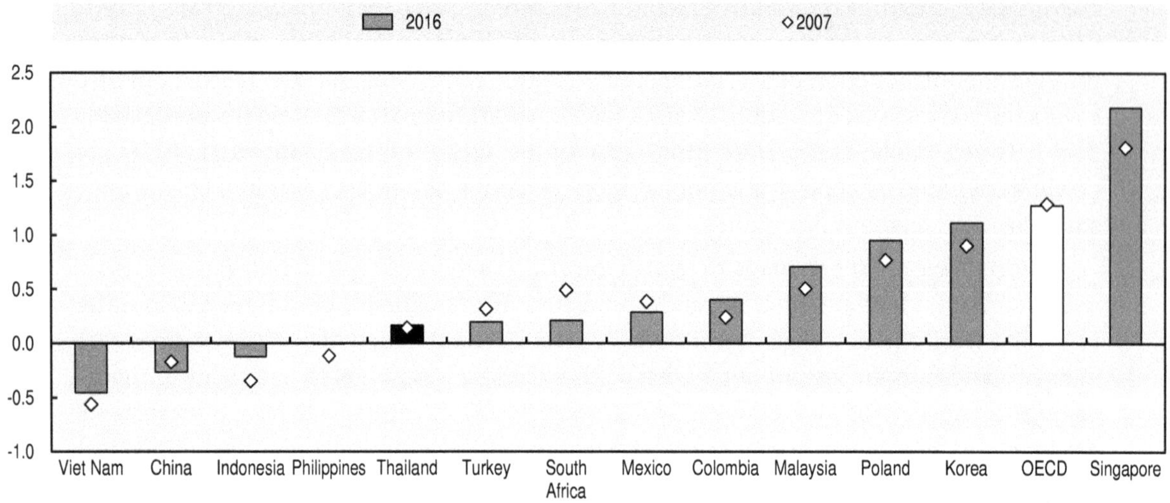

Note: The index ranges from -2.5 (worst) to 2.5 (best).

Source: World Bank (2017c), Worldwide Governance Indicators database.

StatLink http://dx.doi.org/10.1787/888933692750

Second, the government enacted the Royal Decree on Review of Laws and Regulations, generally known as the "Sunset Law", in 2015. This law mandates a review of all acts and regulations every five years to ensure they accommodate changes in business practices. Reviews must be conducted in close consultation with stakeholders, and the corresponding reports should be published and circulated within the Council of Ministers and Parliament for consideration. In addition, English translations of all acts and regulations must be made publicly available online (Ongkittikul and Thongphat, 2016).

Third, Thailand is strengthening its regulatory impact analysis (RIA) laws. Although Thailand introduced RIA procedures in 1998, compliance in the early years was poor. In 2004, in an effort to improve regulatory practice, the Council of Ministers mandated that RIA be conducted in line with the OECD Reference Checklist for Regulatory Decision-Making, prior to the introduction of a legislative bill. However, compliance remained weak owing to the lack of a dedicated agency to scrutinise RIA reports, insufficient RIA coverage (leaving out subordinate laws), underdeveloped RIA guidelines, limited capacity among officials to conduct RIA and insufficient consultation with stakeholders (Nilprapunt, 2015; TDRI, 2014).

Under the new Constitution, RIA and consultation with stakeholders is mandatory before the passing of new regulations, and RIA now covers subordinate laws. The Office of the Council of State and the Secretariat of the Cabinet have been given responsibility for overseeing RIA processes. In collaboration with these institutions, the NESDB published a set of guidelines in 2016 to improve public awareness and the capacity of officials to conduct RIAs. The guidelines include the standard format for RIAs and the procedure for stakeholder consultations. Moving forward, RIAs could be expanded to include ex-post analysis after implementation of the regulations.

The government also launched a "Regulatory Guillotine" project in 2017 to streamline unnecessary regulations that hinder socio-economic development. The first phase aims to improve Thailand's ranking in the World Bank's Ease of Doing Business Index, with the aim of becoming one of the top 20 countries by 2019. Recent progress in streamlining procedures for start-ups, simplifying tax payments and resolving insolvency has helped Thailand advance from 48th to 26th place, and further reform is expected to focus on access to credit, trading across borders and the insolvency regime (World Bank, 2017b). The second phase, from late 2017 onwards, involves a further extensive review of existing regulations and licensing across government, with a view to creating a more business-friendly environment. Preliminary results of the review call for streamlining more than 1 000 licensing procedures.

In this context, the Bank of Thailand has launched several important initiatives. In particular, it has embarked on a change in foreign exchange regulations for greater clarity and transparency, with less redundancy (Bank of Thailand, 2017). This project was conducted as a collaboration between the public sector and the private sector through a taskforce of legal experts, regulators and business representatives. The Bank of Thailand also recently announced an experimental regulatory regime designed around a "sandbox" approach, which allows FinTech firms and financial institutions to test the viability of their products and services in a well-defined space and duration, without being fully subject to all existing regulatory requirements. This approach is expected to help regulators assess risks arising from the proposed products and services, while providing sufficient consumer protection (Santiprabhop, 2017).

Despite efforts, corruption remains a constraint on development

Corruption perpetuates inequality and poverty, hurting the well-being of citizens. It tends to worsen the distribution of income and undermine opportunities for individuals to participate equally in social, economic and political life (OECD, 2017a). Corruption also has a negative impact on investment, competition, human capital formation and government efficiency, and thus hampers a country's economic development (OECD, 2013).

Thailand has long recognised the need to address corruption. The first attempt to combat corruption took the form of the Counter Corruption Act 1975, accompanied by the establishment of the implementing agency, the Office of the Commission of Counter Corruption, later reorganised into the National Anti-Corruption Commission (NAAC). Anti-corruption legislation has expanded over time, improving the independence and effectiveness of the NACC. Several other agencies have been set up that complement and support the efforts of the NACC, including the Constitutional Court, the Administrative Court, the Office of the Auditor-General and the Public Sector Anti-Corruption Commission (PACC). Additionally, in October 2016, Thailand introduced a new anti-corruption court to speed up the prosecution of corruption offenses, including those that involve the private sector. The Thai government has declared corruption an urgent issue and anti-corruption efforts now form a key part of the national agenda.

Despite this commitment, corruption persists in Thailand and its perception remains higher than the average of OECD and most ASEAN countries (Figure 5.10). Over 40% of surveyed citizens reported that they have to pay bribes, offer a gift or perform a favour for somebody when accessing public services (Figure 5.11).

To intensify anti-corruption efforts, the 12th Plan set a target to improve the country's ranking on Transparency International's Corruption Perceptions Index. The third phase of Thailand's National Anti-Corruption Strategy (2017-21) includes bold strategies to fight corruption and to mitigate corruption risks.

Figure 5.10. **Continuing government efforts to reduce corruption are needed**

Corruption Perceptions Index, 2017

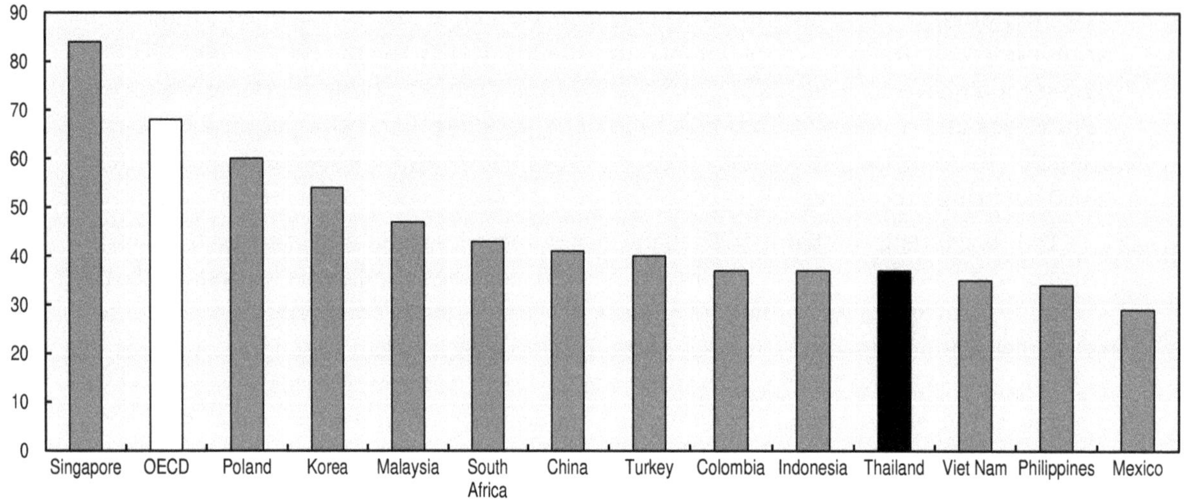

Note: Index ranges from 0 (highly corrupt) to 100 (very clean).

Source: Transparency International Corruption Perceptions Index (2017a), *https://www.transparency.org/news/feature/corruption_perceptions_index_2017*

StatLink *http://dx.doi.org/10.1787/888933692769*

Figure 5.11. **Reported incidence of corruption remains high**

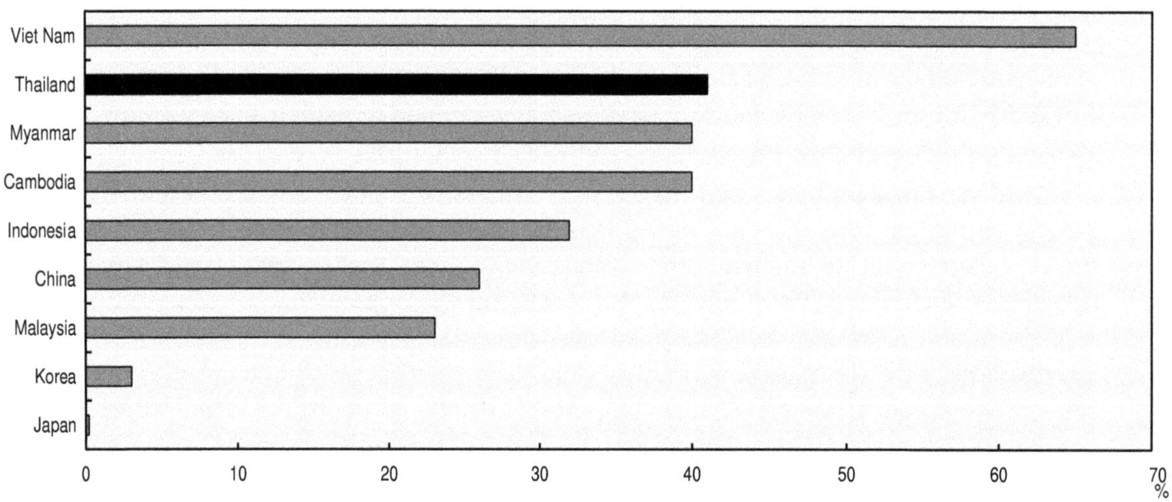

Note: Percentage of respondents reporting to have paid a bribe, offered a gift, or done performed a favour for somebody when accessing public services in selected Asia-Pacific countries.

Source: Transparency International (2017b), *People and Corruption: Asia Pacific – Global Corruption Barometer, www.transparency.org/whatwedo/publication/people_and_corruption_asia_pacific_global_corruption_barometer*

StatLink *http://dx.doi.org/10.1787/888933692788*

In this context, the OECD has undertaken an Integrity Review of Thailand (OECD, 2018), to provide in-depth analysis with reference to the recently-adopted OECD Recommendation on Public Integrity. The Review shows that Thailand could consider streamlining the anti-corruption mandates of various institutions, particularly the NACC and the PACC, in order to enhance the coherence of integrity and anti-corruption policies. In terms of monitoring the National Anti-Corruption Strategy, and in order to move beyond the public perception of corruption, Thailand could strengthen the measurement framework for anti-corruption policies by using policy indicators. Thailand could also benefit from further elaborating civil servants' ethical obligations and ethics training. Setting high ethical standards would help restore trust in the public sector and the proper use of public funds. Expanding the scope of asset disclosure to include senior public officials and other at-risk officials, as well as strengthening the online auditing capacity of the NACC could also strengthen accountability and manage possible conflicts of interest of public officials. Moreover, Thailand could also benefit from developing a dedicated whistle-blower protection law that clearly defining defines the scope of whistle-blowing, wrongdoings and retaliation, and offering protection to whistle-blowers. This would foster an open public organisational culture where integrity concerns can be discussed freely, leading to a more effective detection of ethical violations.

References

Algan, Y. and P. Cahuc (2013), "Trust, growth and well-being: New evidence and policy implications", *IZA Discussion Paper*, No. 7464, *http://ftp.iza.org/dp7464.pdf*.

Asianbarometer (2015), Asianbarometer (database), *www.asianbarometer.org/data/data-release*.

Bank of Thailand (2017), "Foreign exchange regulation reform" (Press Release), Bank of Thailand, Bangkok, *www.bot.or.th/Thai/PressandSpeeches/Press/News2560/n2760e.pdf*.

Burke, A., P. Tweedie and O. Poocharoen (2013), *The Contested Corners of Asia: Subnational Conflict and International Development Assistance: The Case of Southern Thailand*, The Asia Foundation, San Francisco, *https://asiafoundation.org/resources/pdfs/SouthernThailandCaseStudyFullReport.pdf*.

CEPII (2016), *Institutional Profiles Database 2016*, Centre d'Études Prospectives et d'Informations Internationales, AFD and Directorate General of the Treasury (DG Trésor) of the Ministry of Finance, Paris, *www.cepii.fr/institutions/en/ipd.asp*.

Coglianese, C. (2012), *Measuring Regulatory Performance: Evaluating the Impact of Regulation and Regulatory Policy*, OECD Publishing, Paris, *www.oecd.org/gov/regulatory-policy/1_coglianese%20web.pdf*.

Cornell University, INSEAD, and WIPO (2017), *The Global Innovation Index 2017: Innovation Feeding the World*, Cornell University, INSEAD, and WIPO, Ithaca, Fontainebleau, and Geneva, *www.globalinnovationindex.org/gii-2017-report*.

Gallup (2017), "Gallup World Poll" (database), *www.gallup.com/services/170945/world-poll.aspx*.

Huang, S. and D. Thorsby (2011), "Economic, political and social determinants of peace", *Economics of Peace and Security Journal*, Vol. 6/2, *http://dx.doi.org/10.15355/epsj.6.2.5*.

IEP (2017), *Global Peace Index 2017*, Institute for Economics and Peace, Sydney, *http://visionofhumanity.org/app/uploads/2017/06/GPI17-Report.pdf*.

IMF (2017), *Thailand Special Data Dissemination Standard (SDDS)*, International Monetary Fund, Washington, DC, *www.bot.or.th/English/Statistics/Standard/SDDS/Pages/default.aspx*.

Kokpol, O. (2011), "Decentralization Process in 1990-2010: in Case of Thailand", First meeting of the research committee of decentralization in Asian countries, Tokyo, *http://www.kpi.ac.th/media_kpiacth/pdf/M10_141.pdf*.

Marks, D. and L. Lebel (2016), "Disaster governance and the scalar politics of incomplete decentralization: Fragmented and contested responses to the 2011 floods in Central Thailand", *Habitat International*, Vol. 52, pp. 57-66, *https://doi.org/10.1016/j.habitatint.2015.08.024*.

NESDB (2017), *The Twelfth National Economic and Social Development Plan (2017-2021)*, Office of the National Economic and Social Development Board, Bangkok, *www.nesdb.go.th/nesdb_en/ewt_w3c/ewt_dl_link.php?nid=4345*.

NESDB (2016), *Public Consultation Guidelines*, Office of the National Economic and Social Development Board, Bangkok, *www.nesdb.go.th/download/RIA/publicConsultationEN.pdf*.

Nikomborirak, D. (13 January 2016), "Thailand lags with excess laws and red tape", Thailand Development Research Institute, Bangkok, *https://tdri.or.th/2016/01/thailand-lags-with-excess-laws-and-red-tape*.

Nilprapunt, P. (2015), "Thailand's legislative process: Overview", Lawdrafter blog, *http://lawdrafter.blogspot.fr/2015/11/thailands-legislative-process-overview.html*.

NSO (2016), *Thailand's Statistical Master Plan (TSMP) 2016-2021*, National Statistical Office of Thailand, Bangkok.

NSO (2007), *Thailand, The Statistics Act*, B.E. 2550, National Statistical Office of Thailand, Bangkok.

OECD (2018), *OECD Integrity Review of Thailand: Towards Coherent and Effective Integrity Policies*, OECD Publishing, Paris, *http://dx.doi.org/10.1787/9789264291928-en*.

OECD (2017a), *Preventing Policy Capture: Integrity in Public Decision Making*, OECD Public Governance Reviews, OECD Publishing, Paris, *http://dx.doi.org/10.1787/9789264065239-en*.

OECD (2017b), *Trust and Public Policy: How Better Governance Can Help Rebuild Public Trust*, OECD Public Governance Reviews, OECD Publishing, Paris, *http://dx.doi.org/10.1787/9789264268920-en*.

OECD (2017c), *OECD Guidelines on Measuring Trust*, OECD Publishing, Paris, forthcoming, *http://dx.doi.org/10.1787/9789264278219-en*.

OECD (2017d), *Government at a Glance 2017*, OECD Publishing, Paris, *http://dx.doi.org/10.1787/gov_glance-2017-en*.

OECD (2017e), *Benchmarking Digital Government Strategies in MENA Countries*, OECD Publishing, Paris, *http://dx.doi.org/10.1787/9789264268012-en*.

OECD (2016), *Independence of Competition Authorities: From Design to Practices*, Background Paper by the Secretariat, Global Forum on Competition, OECD, Paris, *https://one.oecd.org/document/DAF/COMP/GF(2016)5/en/pdf*.

OECD (2015), *Development Co-operation Report 2015: Making Partnerships Effective Coalitions for Action*, OECD Publishing, Paris, *http://dx.doi.org/10.1787/dcr-2015-en*.

OECD (2013), "Issues Paper on Corruption and Economic Growth", OECD, Paris, *www.oecd.org/g20/topics/anti-corruption/Issue-Paper-Corruption-and-Economic-Growth.pdf*.

OECD (2012), *Recommendation of the Council on Regulatory Policy and Governance*, OECD Publishing, Paris, *www.oecd.org/governance/regulatory-policy/49990817.pdf*.

OECD (2010), *Making Reform Happen: Lessons from OECD Countries*, OECD Publishing, Paris, *http://dx.doi.org/10.1787/9789264086296-en*.

OECD (2009), *Governing Regional Development Policy: The Use of Performance Indicators*, OECD Publishing, Paris, *http://dx.doi.org/10.1787/9789264056299-en*

OECD (2001), *Citizens as Partners: OECD Handbook on Information, Consultation and Public Participation in Policy-Making*, OECD Publishing, Paris, *http://dx.doi.org/10.1787/9789264195578-en*.

Ongkittikul, S. and N. Thongphat (2016), "Regulatory coherence: The case of Thailand", in D. Gill and P. Intal, Jr. (eds.), *The Development of Regulatory Management Systems in East Asia: Country Studies*. ERIA Research Project Report 2015-4, Economic Research Institute for ASEAN and East Asia, Jakarta, *http://www.eria.org/RPR_FY2015_No.4_Chapter_7.pdf*.

OTCC (2017), *Charts on Prohibited Behaviours in the Trade Competition Act 2017* (in Thai), Office of Trade Competition Commission, Bangkok, *http://otcc.dit.go.th/wp-content/uploads/2017/09/broad-otcc19-final.pdf*.

Santiprabhop, V. (2017), "Moving Thailand towards a new business and financial landscape", speech given at the European Association of Business and Commerce, Bank of Thailand, Bangkok, *www.bis.org/review/r170130b.pdf*.

Scrivens, K. and C. Smith (2013), "Four interpretations of social capital: An agenda for measurement", *OECD Statistics Working Papers*, No. 2013/06, OECD Publishing, Paris, *http://dx.doi.org/10.1787/5jzbcx010wmt-en*.

Somwaiya, K. and O. Saardphak (2017), *Thailand National Strategy Preparation Act*, LawPlus Ltd., Bangkok, *https://www.lawplusltd.com/2017/08/thailand-national-strategy-preparation-act*.

Somwaiya, K. (2017), *Thailand National Reform Plans and Procedures Act*, Lawplus Ltd., Bangkok, *www.lawplusltd.com/2017/08/thailand-national-reform-plans-procedures-act*.

Temple, J. (2000), "Growth effects of education and social capital in the OECD countries", *OECD Economic Studies*, Vol. 2001/2, OECD Publishing, Paris, *http://dx.doi.org/10.1787/eco_studies-v2001-art11-en*.

TDRI (2014), *Research Project on Regulatory Impact Analysis* (in Thai with English summary), Thailand Development Research Institute, Bangkok.

Thanitcul, S. (2015), "Competition in Thailand", *CPI Antitrust Chronicle*, August, Competition Policy International, Boston, *www.competitionpolicyinternational.com/assets/Uploads/ThailandAug-151.pdf*.

Transparency International (2017a), Corruption Perceptions Index, *https://www.transparency.org/news/feature/corruption_perceptions_index_2017*.

Transparency International (2017b), *People and Corruption: Asia Pacific – Global Corruption Barometer*, *www.transparency.org/whatwedo/publication/people_and_corruption_asia_pacific_global_corruption_barometer*.

United Nations (2015), *Transforming Our World: The 2030 Agenda for Sustainable Development*, United Nations, New York, *https://sustainabledevelopment.un.org/content/documents/21252030%20Agenda%20for%20Sustainable%20Development%20web.pdf*.

Vimolsiri, P. (2017), "Thailand 20 Year National Strategic Plan and reforms", Presentation at the Thailand Focus 2017 Conference, Stock Exchange of Thailand, Bangkok, *www.set.or.th/thailandfocus/files/20170829_Dr_Porametee.pdf*.

Vujanovic, P. (2017), «Decentralisation to promote Regional Development in Indonesia», *OECD Economics Department Working Papers*, No. 1380, OECD Publishing, Paris, *http://dx.doi.org/10.1787/d9cabd0a-en*

Ward, P., L. Mamerow and S. Meyer (2014), "Interpersonal trust across six Asia-Pacific countries: Testing and extending the 'High Trust Society' and 'Low Trust Society' theory", *PLoS ONE*, Vol. 9/4: e95555, *https://doi.org/10.1371/journal.pone.0095555*.

World Bank (2017a), *Thailand, Statistical Capacity Indicator Dashboard*, World Bank, Washington, DC.

World Bank (2017b), *Doing Business 2018: Reforming to Create Jobs*, World Bank, Washington, DC, *www.doingbusiness.org/~/media/WBG/DoingBusiness/Documents/Annual-Reports/English/DB2018-Full-Report.pdf*.

World Bank (2017c), "Worldwide Governance Indicators" (database), *http://info.worldbank.org/governance/wgi/#home*.

World Economic Forum (2017), *The Global Competitiveness Report 2017-2018*, World Economic Forum, Geneva, *http://reports.weforum.org/global-competitiveness-index-2017-2018*.

World Values Survey (2013), "World Values Survey" (database), *www.worldvaluessurvey.org/WVSContents.jsp*.

ORGANISATION FOR ECONOMIC CO-OPERATION AND DEVELOPMENT

The OECD is a unique forum where governments work together to address the economic, social and environmental challenges of globalisation. The OECD is also at the forefront of efforts to understand and to help governments respond to new developments and concerns, such as corporate governance, the information economy and the challenges of an ageing population. The Organisation provides a setting where governments can compare policy experiences, seek answers to common problems, identify good practice and work to co-ordinate domestic and international policies.

The OECD member countries are: Australia, Austria, Belgium, Canada, Chile, the Czech Republic, Denmark, Estonia, Finland, France, Germany, Greece, Hungary, Iceland, Ireland, Israel, Italy, Japan, Korea, Latvia, Luxembourg, Mexico, the Netherlands, New Zealand, Norway, Poland, Portugal, the Slovak Republic, Slovenia, Spain, Sweden, Switzerland, Turkey, the United Kingdom and the United States. The European Union takes part in the work of the OECD.

OECD Publishing disseminates widely the results of the Organisation's statistics gathering and research on economic, social and environmental issues, as well as the conventions, guidelines and standards agreed by its members.

OECD DEVELOPMENT CENTRE

The OECD Development Centre was established in 1962 as an independent platform for knowledge sharing and policy dialogue between OECD member countries and developing economies, allowing these countries to interact on an equal footing. Today, 27 OECD countries and 25 non-OECD countries are members of the Centre. The Centre draws attention to emerging systemic issues likely to have an impact on global development and more specific development challenges faced by today's developing and emerging economies. It uses evidence-based analysis and strategic partnerships to help countries formulate innovative policy solutions to the global challenges of development.

For more information on the Centre and its members, please see *www.oecd.org/dev*.

OECD PUBLISHING, 2, rue André-Pascal, 75775 PARIS CEDEX 16
(41 2018 14 1 P1) ISBN 978-92-64-29327-4 – 2018

www.ingramcontent.com/pod-product-compliance
Ingram Content Group UK Ltd.
Pitfield, Milton Keynes, MK11 3LW, UK
UKHW051502290926
15471UKWH00008B/1364

9 789264 293274